Time-Out

for the
Spirit

Two-Minute Quiet Times for Times That Aren't Quiet

Guideposts Books
CARMEL, NEW YORK

ACKNOWLEDGMENTS
Every attempt has been made to credit the sources of copyrighted material used in this book. If any such acknowledgment has been inadvertently omitted or miscredited, receipt of such information would be appreciated.

All Scripture quotations, unless otherwise noted, are taken from *The Holy Bible, New King James Version*. Copyright © 1997, 1990, 1985, 1983 by Thomas Nelson, Inc.

Scripture quotations marked (KJV) are taken from *The King James Version of the Bible*.

Scripture quotations marked (NAS) are taken from the *New American Standard Bible*, © The Lockman Foundation, 1960, 1962, 1963, 1968, 1971, 1972, 1973, 1975, 1977. Used by permission.

Scripture quotations marked (NIV) are taken from *The Holy Bible, New International Version*. Copyright © 1973, 1978, 1984 International Bible Society. Used by permission of Zondervan Bible Publishers.

Scripture quotations marked (NLT) are taken from the *Holy Bible*, New Living Translation. Copyright © 1996. Used by permission of Tyndale House Publishers, Inc., Wheaton, Illinois 60189. All rights reserved.

Scripture quotations marked (RSV) are taken from the *Revised Standard Version of the Bible*. Copyright © 1946, 1952, 1971 by Division of Christian Education of the National Council of Churches of Christ in the U.S.A. Used by permission.

Scripture quotations marked (TLB) are taken from *The Living Bible*. Copyright © 1971 by Tyndale House Publishers, Wheaton, IL 60178. All rights reserved.

www.guideposts.org
(800) 431-2344
Guideposts Books & Inspirational Media Division

Compiled by Lucile Allen
Cover photograph by Mel Curtis/Photodisc Green/Getty Images
Design by Cindy LaBreacht
Typeset by Nancy Tardi

Printed and bound in the United States of America

Contents

Introduction...1

When a door closes 3

When a friend disappoints you 4

When a friend is depressed 5

When a friend is feeling overwhelmed...........................6

When a friend is getting on your nerves.......................7

When a friend is going through a difficult time.............8

When a friend is in pain 9

When a friend is in the hospital....................................10

When a friend is struggling spiritually.............................11

When a friend needs comfort 12

When a friend needs encouragement 13

When a friend needs faith 14

When a friend needs help 15

When a friend's marriage has ended...............................16

When a loved one is afraid 17

When a loved one is grieving 18

When a loved one is ill 19, 20, 21

When a loved one is near death......................................22

When a loved one needs to feel loved...........................23

When a loved one needs to hear the truth 24

When a prayer doesn't seem to be answered...............25, 26, 27, 28

When a significant person in your past comes to mind.................29

When a young person you know is struggling with doubts...........30

When an elderly friend is housebound 31

When an old friend comes to mind..32

When back-to-school preparations have you frazzled....................33

When God feels near 34

When God is silent..35

When God seems far away 36

When it "rains on your picnic"..37

When it's hard to find time to pray 38

When it's hard to say, "I love you"..39

When it's time to give rather than receive 40

When life is too hectic 41, 42, 43

When life seems stormy 44

When life's got you down 45

When someone around you is in a bad mood 46

When someone rubs you the wrong way 47

When tragedy strikes...48, 49

When you are (or a friend is) newly alone....................................50

When you can't get through to a struggling friend......................51

When you can't see life's blessings...52

When you can't see the forest for the trees...................................53

When you can't seem to get anything
out of your Bible reading..54

When you can't sleep 55

When you disagree with your child's choices.................................56

When you don't feel able to finish a task 57

When you don't know what to say...58

When you don't like someone 59

When you don't like yourself 60

When you doubt God cares...61

When you doubt God's love 62

When you doubt your abilities 63

When you feel abandoned 64

When you feel an urgent need to pray 65

When you feel helpless 66

When you feel like complaining 67

When you feel like giving up 68

When you feel like quitting your job 69

When you feel that you've failed 70, 71, 72, 73

When you feel you've been attacked 74

When you feel you've disappointed God 75

When you have a case of the "if onlys" 76

When you have a dream 77

When you have a grumpy coworker 78

When you have a negative attitude 79

When you have to learn a new skill 80

When you have to let go 81

When you have to put aside your own preferences 82

When you haven't had time for God 83

When you just don't understand 84

When you lack vision 85

When you need a break 86

When you need a friend 87

When you need a good cry 88, 89

When you need a good laugh 90

When you need a pick-me-up 91

When you need a reminder of God's love 92

When you need a rest 93

When you need a spiritual boost 94

When you need comfort 95, 96

When you need God the Father 97

When you need guidance 98

When you need help 99

When you need help but can't bring yourself to ask for it 100

When you need patience 101

When you need refreshment...102

When you need self-discipline...103

When you need some emotional and spiritual remodeling........104

When you need someone who understands................................105

When you need to feel loved...106

When you need to forgive 107

When you need to forgive . . . or be forgiven 108

When you need to lighten up 109

When you need to pray...110

When you're afraid 111, 112, 113, 114, 115, 116

When you're afraid to admit you need help.......................117, 118

When you're angry...119, 120

When you're angry at a friend 121

When you're angry with someone you love 122

When you're attempting something new 123

When you're battling an addiction 124

When you're blessed with abundance 125

When you're bored 126, 127

When you're carrying a heavy load 128

When you're caught in the middle of a conflict...........................129

When you're concerned about a loved one 130

When you're confused......................................131, 132, 133

When you're dealing with a difficult child...................................134

When you're depressed..135

When you're discouraged about reaching a goal 136

When you're exhausted 137

When you're facing a new commitment..138

When you're facing a serious illness 139

When you're facing an unwelcome change 140

When you're facing challenges 141, 142

When you're facing difficult decisions 143

When you're facing hostility from someone 144

When you're facing temptation 145

When you're feeling betrayed 146

When you're feeling discouraged 147

When you're feeling disorganized 148

When you're feeling down.. 149

When you're feeling empty 150

When you're feeling faith-fatigue... 151

When you're feeling frazzled 152, 153

When you're feeling hemmed in by "Thou shalt not's"..............154

When you're feeling impatient 155, 156

When you're feeling insecure... 157

When you're feeling insignificant.. 158

When you're feeling lonely.. 159

When you're feeling lost...160, 161

When you're feeling off-balance 162

When you're feeling overcommitted 163

When you're feeling overwhelmed...............................164, 165, 166

When you're feeling proud of yourself.. 167

When you're feeling spiritually dry.. 168

When you're feeling stuck in your job 169, 170

When you're feeling that God has let you down 171

When you're feeling that you've let down a loved one 172

When you're feeling threatened 173

When you're feeling unattractive.. 174

When you're feeling unloved...175, 176

When you're feeling uprooted and alone 177

When you're feeling useless 178

When you're feeling vulnerable 179

When you're feeling weary 180

When you're finding it hard to go to church 181, 182

When you're fretful about the future 183

When you're giving up on a dream 184

When you're grieving...185, 186

When you're harboring resentment 187

When you're having a conflict with your children 188

When you're having business problems 189

When you're having doubts...190

When you're having marriage problems........................191

When you're having trouble trusting...........................192

When you're hoping for something 193

When you're ill..194, 195

When you're in pain 196

When you're learning a new skill...................................197

When you're looking for love..198

When you're losing a beloved pet.................................199

When you're losing a loved one....................................200

When you're losing hope...201

When you're making room for a new person in your life...........202

When you're newly retired and don't know
what to do with yourself...203

When you're nursing feelings of rejection 204

When you're overextended 205, 206

When you're praying for a friend 207

When you're procrastinating..................................208, 209

When you're ready to quit...210

When you're regretting the past 211

When you're reluctant to reach out 212

When you're sad...213, 214

When you're searching for the perfect gift
for a loved one...215

When you're seeking direction 216

When you're self-absorbed 217

When you're shy about sharing your faith 218

When you're struggling to reach a goal 219

When you're struggling with a job offer........................220

When you're struggling with a problem........................221

When you're struggling with doubts...............................222

When you're stuck in a project 223

When you're stuck in the darkness.................................224

When you're stuck on "What if?" 225

When you're suffering from a chronic condition......................226

When you're tackling a difficult project...........................227, 228

When you're taking life too seriously 229

When you're tempted to be preachy 230

When you're tempted to get even....................................231

When you're thinking negative thoughts about someone 232

When you're too busy 233

When you're trying to diet......................................234, 235

When you're waiting for guidance..................................236

When you're wondering if God cares..............................237

When you're wondering if God hears you 238

When you're worried 239, 240, 241

When you're worried about aging parents....................242

When you're worried about finances.............................243

When you're worried about your children 244, 245, 246

When you've been asked to serve 247, 248

When you've been disappointed 249

When you've been humbled 250

When you've been hurt 251, 252, 253

When you've been rejected 254

When you've been the victim of gossip 255

When you've disappointed yourself 256

When you've had a falling-out with a friend 257

When you've had a setback 258, 259, 260

When you've hurt someone 261

When you've listened to gossip 262

When you've lost a loved one 263, 264

When you've lost the joy of living 265

When you've made a mistake 266

When you've missed your morning quiet time 267

When you've quarreled with a loved one 268

When you've quarreled with someone 269

When you've received a kindness 270

When you've taken your blessings for granted 271

When your child is facing a challenge 272

When your child's heart is burdened 273

When your children and grandchildren have moved out
on their own 274

When your children are acting up 275

When your children are getting on your nerves 276

When your children are getting ready to leave the nest 277

When your children are growing more independent 278

When your children delight you 279

When your children need attention 280, 281

When your children rebel 282

When your conscience is bothering you...283

When your creative juices seem to have dried up 284

When your dreams have yet to blossom 285

When your faith doesn't seem to make sense..............................286

When your hurts won't heal..287, 288

When your life is changing...289

When your life is in turmoil 290

When your life seems to be going nowhere 291

When your plans have been thwarted 292

When your spirit needs a lift 293

When your struggles seem too much to bear 294

When your teenager is feeling misunderstood 295

Authors and Subjects Index...297

Scripture Index...303

Introduction

◄○►

We all have days when nothing seems to be going right, when the stresses and strains of life are trying our patience and frazzling our spirits. Though we may not realize it when we're in the midst of such troubles, these are the times when what we need most is to say, "Time-out!" and refresh our souls in the presence of the Lord. This book is designed to help you do just that—to give your spirit a quick pick-me-up in the midst of a busy stressful day.

No matter what your need for today is, whether you're angry with a friend—or with God, or you or a loved one is ill, or you're feeling sad or lonely or afraid, or you need extra energy to finish a project or accomplish a task, or if your children need help or just some attention, you'll discover an opportunity to relax, reflect and reconnect with the God Who is the source of hope and healing.

If you're burdened with caregiving or your bills seem overwhelming, if the clutter around you has gotten out of hand or you're having a bad day at work, if you're grieving or having trouble seeing the answers to your prayers, you'll find a helping hand to hold in the presence of the One for Whom all yokes are easy and all burdens light.

Just find your need for today in the alphabetical table of contents or in the index, and then turn to the special "two-minute quiet time." Each of these one-page time-outs features an inspiring Scripture to ground you in God's Word, a brief first-person reflection to lift your spirits, a prayer to lift your mind and heart to God, and a practical tip—something you can do right now or in the days ahead that will help restore your spiritual equilibrium.

As you read, reflect, pray and put the practical "to do" tip into action, you'll find that these brief time-outs will help you find peace and refreshment, whether it's in your morning or evening prayer time or in the tougher moments of any day. At your bedside, on your desk, or in your workplace, it is our prayer that *Time-Out for the Spirit* will help you turn your everyday hassles into moments of grace.

When a door closes

READ: *A great and effective door has opened to me, and there are many adversaries.*

—1 CORINTHIANS 16:9

REFLECT: Sometimes, when things go wrong, I remember Herman Gockel. At thirty-two, his dream of becoming a great preacher shriveled like grapes in the hot sun. He had spent eleven years preparing. Now, suddenly, his voice was gone. Doctors had no remedy. He resigned from his church.

While his wife worked, he took care of their home and four-year-old daughter. Then he wrote rhymed verses for Christmas cards. He pushed a cart in the shipping department of a wholesale bookstore.

Slowly, doors began to open, and eventually he pioneered Christian television as religious director of "This Is the Life." When Dr. Gockel retired after twenty years, the program had received twenty-five awards. Over two thousand letters poured in every week. The man who couldn't speak spoke to millions.

Has God closed a door for you? Let your hands trace the length of the wall until they find another door. It is there. Open it.
—MILDRED TENGBOM

PRAY: *Dear God, I can't deny the disappointment I feel at this lost opportunity. Help me to accept this closed door as being Your will, and give me faith to believe that You shall open an even more perfect door for me.*

DO: Call a friend or loved one. Tell him/her about your disappointment and ask him/her to pray for you to be able to trust in God and wait patiently for the perfect opportunity.

When a friend disappoints you

READ: *The Lord is merciful and gracious, slow to anger, and abounding in mercy.*

—PSALM 103:8

REFLECT: How do you deal with people who disappoint you? One night as I read Psalm 103:8–10, I seemed to hear God say, "This is the way *I* deal with those who let *Me* down."

The Lord is compassionate and gracious.... How often do I show mercy, compassion, clemency—to my children? My spouse? My friends or coworkers?

Slow to anger and abounding in mercy.... "Abounding" means "filled to the very brim with." Can I be filled with enough love to give up my own quick temper and respond to others with steadfast, "never-failing" love?

He will not always accuse.... God is no nag.... *Nor will He harbor His anger forever.* God holds no grudges. Can I give up my own nagging and grudges?

He does not treat us as our sins deserve.... Can I learn to be gentle in dealing with the faults of others? Can I overlook their flaws?

God's way of dealing with people who disappoint Him is not my most natural way. It's harder. But it's also a far better way.

—PATRICIA HOUCK SPRINKLE

PRAY: *Father, please forgive my slowness to forgive, my tendency to think I have a right to hold a grudge because someone deserves it. Thank You for Your abounding love and mercy.*

DO: Memorize Psalm 103:8 and repeat it until you are able to forgive your friend the way God does.

When a friend is depressed

———————◄○►———————

READ: *For You are my lamp, O Lord; the Lord shall enlighten my darkness.*

—2 SAMUEL 22:29

REFLECT: Hustle-Bustle, our turquoise parakeet, would sample breadcrumbs from the table. Nestled on a shoulder or perched in his cage, he'd repeat compliments he'd memorized. "Pretty Hustle-Bustle," he'd croon. "Pretty boy."

Hustle-Bustle disliked darkness. If we turned out the light in one room, he'd head for the light in the next. We used to laugh about it, but there came a time when I could not only sympathize with him but also followed his example.

I was going through a dark time of depression when it seemed someone had turned out the lights in my life. Watching Hustle-Bustle showed me a way to get through my dark times—that is, to follow whatever light I did have. I found that if I looked, those lights were there, maybe in the lyrics of a song or a friend's kind word. By seeking the light, I found my way back into it.

—JOAN RAE MILLS

PRAY: *My friend dislikes darkness, too, Father, but can't seem to find his/her way out of it. Would You turn on a light or two along the way to guide him/her to You?*

DO: Send a little light to your friend in the form of a card, a Scripture or even this little story about Hustle-Bustle.

When a friend is feeling overwhelmed

READ: *Bear one another's burdens, and thereby fulfill the law of Christ.*

—GALATIANS 6:2 (NAS)

REFLECT: One day Mother sent my brother Jim and me to the grocery store. About halfway home, shifting the bag of groceries on his hip, Jim said, "I think you should carry one." He handed me the smallest bag.

After we had walked about a block I got tired of carrying the bag and put it down. "I can't carry it anymore," I said. "It hurts."

"Oh, come on," Jim said. "It can't hurt that much."

"No," I answered stubbornly. And to settle the matter I simply walked away.

Jim sighed and picked it up. I knew he would. I snickered to myself. I had won again.

The next time Mother asked us to go to the grocery store, Jim wouldn't let me go with him. I began to see what I had lost—my brother's friendship, and his respect. Since then I've tried to pick up life's little grocery bags. For part of friendship is carrying each other's burdens.

—PAT EGAN DEXTER

PRAY: *Father, thank You so much for friends who have carried more than their share of my burdens. I'll try to be more like them, Lord.*

DO: Call your friend and offer to help.

When a friend is getting on your nerves

READ: *Therefore let us not judge one another anymore. . . .*

—ROMANS 14:13

REFLECT: My son John and his friend, whom I'll call Brent, have been buddies since they were in elementary school. One day John and I were sitting at the kitchen counter having a snack when Brent's name came up. "He's certainly a loyal friend," I said. Then, after a pause, I added, "But he's so loud and boisterous!"

John considered that for a minute. "I think you've got it backward, Mom. The way I see it is that Brent may be rambunctious, but he is a loyal friend."

Moving Brent's loyalty to the other side of the word *but* helped me focus on what was really important about John's friend. It also made me rethink some of my own relationships.

If there's someone you'd like to have as a friend, but he talks too much or is too gloomy or wears funny-looking clothes, try putting his good qualities on the other side of the word *but*.   —MARILYN MORGAN KING

PRAY: *Father, please forgive my judgmental tendency.*
Help me to accept others in spite of their faults,
just as I'd like to be accepted in spite of mine.

DO: Reach out to a person you could really like . . . if it weren't for that one thing you find so irritating!

When a friend is going through a difficult time

<o>

READ: *They shall bear the burden of the people with you, that you may not bear it yourself alone.*

—NUMBERS 11:17

REFLECT: I once heard the mother of a teenage boy who was paralyzed in an accident explain how she kept from having a breakdown herself.

"Our church friends formed a circle around us so tightly, there was no room to fall."

I love her description. Can't you just picture people holding hands, surrounding that devastated huddle of a family like children playing "Farmer in the Dell"? Of course, they didn't literally encompass them. But they surrounded them with love. They sent cards and letters of encouragement, brought meals, built a wheelchair ramp, chipped in money for expenses, visited with jokes and news and tutoring and prayed, all of which helped pull the family through a difficult time.

—B. J. CONNOR

PRAY: *Thank You, Father, for loving friends who have helped me and for the friends You've allowed me to help. Show me what I can do to help _____ feel loved and supported through this time.*

DO: Get input from someone close to your friend about how you can help.

8

When a friend is in pain

READ: *I cried out to God for help; I cried out to God to hear me.*

— PSALM 77:1 (NIV)

REFLECT: I once underwent surgery that turned out to be more extensive—and painful—than expected. As I lay sleepless in my hospital bed the first night, only one thing comforted me: the knowledge that dozens of friends were part of a "prayer chain" that was holding me before the Lord.

An elderly man in the next room seemed in even worse agony than I. He'd had both legs amputated at the hip. As I listened to his cries, I wondered who was praying for this poor man. Did he have friends who were seeking God's healing touch for him? What if he did not?

The idea nearly broke my heart.

My prayers that night were not eloquent, but they were fervent and frequent. And when the man's cries grew less anguished as dawn approached, I willed myself to focus on him, determined not to stop praying until he was able to sleep. Finally, he was. And so was I. — SUSAN WILLIAMS

PRAY: *Father, for _____ and for all the people in pain today, I ask You to relieve their pain, grant them rest, and bring healing, in Jesus' name.*

DO: Start a prayer chain for your friend. Share the need without the name if that would violate your friend's privacy, but pray with faith that God knows his/her name and can meet his/her every need.

When a friend is in the hospital

—◁◦▷—

READ: *I was sick, and you visited me....*

—MATTHEW 25:36 (NAS)

REFLECT: I was browsing in the "Get Well" section of our local card shop. My neighbor was in the hospital.

"*Hmmm*...flowers and a bluebird," I heard over my shoulder. "A bit run-of-the-mill, wouldn't you say?" I turned and was confronted by the twinkling eyes of my minister.

"I guess so," I said, "but it's for a friend in the hospital. She loves birds, and that little bluebird might cheer her."

"I'll tell you something that would cheer her up more," he said. "Send yourself to the hospital."

"I can't take hospitals," I said.

My minister said, "Do you remember what Jesus said? 'I was sick and ye visited Me.' Jesus never mentioned a cheery card with a bluebird on it. He said, 'visited.' Think about it."

I visited Mary that day.   —FRANCES FOWLER ALLEN

PRAY: *Lord, send comfort and healing to my friend*
            _____ in the hospital today.

DO: Buy a card for a friend in the hospital—and hand-deliver it.

When a friend is struggling spiritually

◄○►

READ: *The Lord is my rock, and my fortress, and my deliverer. . . .*

—PSALM 18:2 (KJV)

REFLECT: A friend always had trouble with the first two words of the Lord's Prayer—*Our Father.* Her own stern father always came to mind, with memories of a harsh upbringing that left her feeling unworthy of love from her earthly or her heavenly Father, even though she knew the Bible taught differently.

As she was searching her Bible for this very love-assurance she craved, the face of her favorite uncle popped into her mind. Gentle, attentive Uncle Jim always made time for her. He'd prompted her patiently through long division, made an embarrassingly wonderful fuss over her first semiformal gown. When a romance fizzled, it was Uncle Jim's concerned face she sought.

Might my friend have been stumbling over the word *Father* when all God wanted was to be more like Uncle Jim in her life? She began praying to "Uncle God," and her feelings began to agree with what she knew to be true from Scripture.

—KATHIE KANIA

PRAY: *Father, draw _____ to Your Word. Show him/her the truth about Your love and concern— the truth that will set him/her free to embrace You.*

DO: Help your friend find three characteristics of God in his/her father.

When a friend needs comfort

READ: *The Lord is with you. . . .*

—JUDGES 6:12 (NIV)

REFLECT: When I was fifteen years old, my parents took me with them to visit an elderly neighbor who lay dying. For an hour we sat with her in a deep silence, although occasionally she and my mother and father exchanged gentle smiles. I squirmed uncomfortably in my chair, wondering why no one spoke.

Several years after that I lost a beloved brother and I was utterly inconsolable. There was absolutely nothing anyone could say to me that eased my heartache. Then one afternoon an old and dear friend came to my home, gave me a warm hug, and sat down with me, saying nothing. Her very presence was a comfort far beyond the power of any words she might have spoken.

Don't ever be afraid to go to someone who is contending with a deep sorrow even though you think you don't know what to say. Just be there. That's all.

—MADGE HARRAH

PRAY: *Dear God, I ask You today to comfort _____.*
Give me the courage to offer him/her my presence,
even when it feels uncomfortable.

DO: Go sit with your grieving friend, and if you're afraid that you won't be able to find the right words to say, take a card to say it for you.

When a friend needs encouragement

READ: *He heals the brokenhearted and binds up their wounds.*

—PSALM 147:3 (NIV)

REFLECT: When I first started teaching college in New York City, I admired a veteran professor named Jim. He was a happy-go-lucky person, until he lost a valued promotion. Then I watched him slide into depression. I wanted to make Jim feel better, but I didn't know what to say. Though I sympathized with his pain, I had never gone through what he had. So I did nothing. Finally, out of cowardice, I wrote Jim a note. I avoided the issue of his promotion and focused on his fine teaching. Then I slipped the note in his mailbox hoping I hadn't done the wrong thing.

The next day, as I was tiptoeing past Jim's office, his door opened. I looked up to find Jim's face beaming at me. "Thanks," he said. "That note was just the comfort I needed. You did exactly the right thing." —LINDA CHING SLEDGE

PRAY: *Even if I've never experienced what my friend is going through, God, I know the deep pain of disappointment. Show me how to best encourage my friend through this difficult time.*

DO: When it comes to showing support for a friend, the only wrong thing to do is nothing. Send a note or call to express your love and concern.

When a friend needs faith

◄○►

READ: *In lowliness of mind let each esteem others better than himself.*

—PHILIPPIANS 2:3

REFLECT: I silently groaned when I realized the caller was Martha. I had figured her problems were insoluble. I felt it was too bad she had not had the religious exposure I had.

I was braced against hearing more about her troubles, when I realized her tone was joyous.

"You sound happier than I've ever heard you," I said tentatively.

"I am," she bubbled. "A woman I met recently gave me a Bible. It has changed my life. You don't go in for reading the Bible and going to church, do you?" she asked gently. "It really helps you see what is wrong in your life and what to do about it."

I was aghast. I had considered myself a good Christian. But I had kept my faith a secret because I felt awkward discussing religion. And now this woman I had judged to be beyond salvation was generously sharing her new faith with me!

—LORENA PEPPER EDLEN

PRAY: *I praise You, Father, for every life changed by Your redeeming love. Give me faith to believe You can do the same for my friend and the courage to tell her/him about You.*

DO: If you can't find the words to share your faith with your friend, buy a Bible and let His Word do the talking.

14

When a friend needs help

◄◦►

READ: *But be doers of the word, and not hearers only, deceiving yourselves.*

—JAMES 1:22

REFLECT: My friend Sharon was struggling in her new business. She was tired and fearful from the stress. I prayed for her daily, but her problems only worsened. So one day I "laid it on the line" with God.

"What are You going to do about this, Lord?" I asked, angry that Sharon was still suffering.

Just that quickly, I heard my question come back. "What are *you* going to do about it?"

Then I remembered the three levels of prayer I'd read about. The first is *Give me.* The second, *Help me.* And the highest level is *Use me.* I was stuck at the first level.

How could God use me to help Sharon? I wrote checks and balanced her checkbook, even shopped and cooked dinner so she could relax at the end of a trying day. It wasn't much, but it meant fewer worries for her and a good feeling for me.

—GINA BRIDGEMAN

PRAY: *Thank You, Father, for answered prayers, answers that change me.*

DO: In addition to your prayers for your friend, call and make yourself available to help relieve his/her stress.

When a friend's marriage has ended

READ: *I will weep for you. . . .*

—JEREMIAH 48:32

REFLECT: I didn't know what to do as I sat across from my friend. Deep, heavy sobs shook her body. Her marriage was in serious trouble. I ached to say something that might take away her pain. I longed for words of wisdom or answers. I felt so helpless to do anything.

Then I remembered a story about a big-eared mouse named Buford whose Uncle Jake died accidentally.

My favorite line is where Buford consoles Uncle Jake's son George: "Buford hugged George and said, 'I'm here and I care. I have come to help you cry.'"

I looked again at my friend. I didn't have any words that would take away her pain. But I was there and I cared. So I did what Buford did—I wrapped my arms around her and helped her cry.

—TERRY HELWIG

PRAY: *Father, I pray for _____ right now.*
Love and comfort him/her by Your Spirit, Lord,
while I wrap my arms around my friend to help
him/her cry.

DO: The only wrong thing to do is stay away and say nothing because you don't know what to say. Any expression of love and support will surely be appreciated.

When a loved one is afraid

READ: *Through patience a ruler can be persuaded, and a gentle tongue can break a bone.*

—PROVERBS 25:15 (NIV)

REFLECT: Years ago, my mother stumbled and nearly fell as she was about to get on an escalator. She vowed that if she made it down, she would never step on an escalator again.

She never did. For thirty years, my mother was afraid to ride an escalator. My sister and I accepted this for what it was—a quirk, a mild hindrance.

Then she married my stepfather Joe. Every time they passed an escalator, he'd say, "Well, Elaine, are you ready to try this today?" My mother would just smile and shake her head.

Then once, when I phoned my mother, she said, "Linda, I have something good to tell you. I rode down an escalator today!"

With gentle coaxing, patience and understanding, we, too, can persuade a reluctant heart or fearful spirit to overcome the odds or make a bold leap of faith—or feet.

—LINDA NEUKRUG

PRAY: *Lord, I can see my friend walking in total victory over this fear. I pray freedom into my friend's life and thank You for it in advance.*

DO: Gently present opportunities for your friend to overcome his/her fear. Picture him/her in your prayers celebrating a victory over that fear until it comes to pass.

When a loved one is grieving

READ: *For I am the Lord, I do not change....*

—MALACHI 3:6

REFLECT: One evening my husband Glenn slipped a paper-back book onto my lap. It was titled *Kicking Your Stress Habits* by Donald A. Tubesing, PhD. "Why don't you take a look at this?" he suggested. "I think it could help you feel better."

We had just moved to a new state and said good-bye to dear family and friends. Our daughter Lauren had moved south for a new career and, worst of all, Glenn had lost his job in a corporate takeover.

I thumbed through the book and stopped, puzzled, at the chapter on grief. That had nothing to do with how I was feeling. Stress, yes. But *grief?* Not me. Then I read that "Grief is the process of healing from the pain of loss. If you've ever had to say good-bye, then you've experienced grief."

Glenn and I talked to each other, cried, lent support and, slowly, we came out of our crisis.

—ELLEN SECREST

PRAY: *Father, it feels so good to grieve a loss, not only deeply and without shame, but with someone who shares the same grief. You understand, Lord; walk through it with him/her.*

DO: Express your sorrow and tell your loved one that you'll be there for him/her, without trying to rush him/her through the grief.

When a loved one is ill (1)

◄◦►

READ: *I will be a Father to you, and you shall be My sons and daughters, says the Lord Almighty.*

—2 CORINTHIANS 6:18

REFLECT: One time when I was little, I was deeply frightened by an event far beyond my comprehension. My father's sister was seriously ill and the family had gathered at her bedside. We children were instructed to remain outdoors.

Not understanding the situation, but sensing its gravity nonetheless, I huddled alone beneath the shade of the big pear tree—until suddenly the quietness seemed overwhelming. Crying out in utter terror, I ran toward the forbidden parlor and its gloom. Immediately a warm, familiar hand closed reassuringly over mine. My father scooped me up into his arms and I knew then that, no matter what, everything was going to be all right—Daddy was with me.

To this day, it is not the grief on the faces of those around me at that time that I best recall. It is the tender memory that my father was with me in my time of deepest need.

—JUNE MASTERS BACHER

PRAY: *I tend to run and hide when I'm scared, Lord. Today, I run to Your outstretched arms instead.*

DO: Make a special effort to make yourself available to the children in a family facing a serious illness.

When a loved one is ill (2)

READ: *Be anxious for nothing, but in everything by prayer and supplication, with thanksgiving, let your requests be made known to God. . . .*

—PHILIPPIANS 4:6

REFLECT: The telephone's shrill ring pierces our sleep. I hear my husband say, "Papa," and know the call is about his elderly father. "Papa is retaining fluids," he says. "It may be heart or kidney failure."

Later, our five-year-old daughter Elizabeth is full of tears and questions. "Will Grandpa die?" "Does he hurt?" "Can we pray for him?"

We pray, asking God to do what is best. During the day, she frequently mentions Grandpa. I struggle to help her. Then I remember a quotation on my refrigerator: "Thanksgiving is the antidote to worry."

Alex and I smile when Elizabeth spontaneously prays. "Thank You, God, for taking care of Grandpa and helping the doctors." After that, when we voiced our anxieties, we remembered Elizabeth and prayed, "It's all in Your hands. Thank You, Lord."

—MARY BROWN

PRAY: *And thank You, Lord, that _____ is in Your hands too.*

DO: Keep your prayers of thanks coming for God's power to heal (whether physical healing comes or not), for His comfort, for the good He's going to bring out of this crisis.

When a loved one is ill (3)

READ: *They shall bear the burden of the people with you, that you may not bear it yourself alone.*

—NUMBERS 11:17

REFLECT: "It could be Hodgkin's disease." Those five words exploded into our lives one gray day. The doctor was speaking to Joy, my love, my wife. She took it calmly, asking questions about tests and treatment. I did what might be expected of a man in that situation—I fell apart.

During church the next Sunday, our pastor noticed something wrong. He called on Monday and I blurted out my fears and asked him how I could be strong when everyone needed me. "You should have told our people," he said. "Burdens are to be shared."

The next Sunday, Joy said, "I think we need to ask people to pray for us, and you must do it." I don't know what I said, but for thirty minutes after the service people came to us. They hugged, squeezed a hand and promised to pray. Our burden was lighter.

Jesus said, "Bear one another's burdens." I understand better what He meant.

—ERIC FELLMAN

PRAY: *Father, I praise and thank You for the many people around us who would be more than delighted to pray for our every need.*

DO: Go ahead and do it—ask your church body, family and friends to pray for you and your loved one.

When a loved one is near death

READ: *But lay up for yourselves treasures in heaven, where neither moth nor rust destroys and where thieves do not break in and steal.*

—MATTHEW 6:20

REFLECT: A beloved grandmother who became ill was taken into the home of her daughter and family. She especially enjoyed bedside visits with her four-year-old great-granddaughter Jill. Jill smoothed the covers, discussed the things she and her doll Moppet had been doing, and often brought Moppet with her to visit too.

One day, the door to the bedroom was softly closed and Jill's mother told her gently, "Grandmother just went to heaven."

"In her nightgown?" Jill exclaimed. "She should have got ready."

Jill didn't understand that grandmother had gotten ready a long time before. For this final journey, Grandma had packed days with prayers for family and friends; she had gathered up knowledge of God's greatness and shared it with many; she had given her love, her time, her tithes.

—ZONA B. DAVIS

PRAY: *Father, whether we're expecting to leave this earth in the next few days, months or who knows when, make us ready daily to die, with debts paid, promises kept and hearts that have forgiven.*

DO: Write down three qualities of your loved one that you want to make your own.

When a loved one needs to feel loved

◄○►

READ: *Love never fails.*

—1 CORINTHIANS 13:8

REFLECT: A large, withering plant stood abandoned in our office. "Sam, why don't you take this one on?" a coworker suggested, poking his head into my office.

"I don't know," I mumbled, looking around at the greenery that already surrounded me. I gave the plant an unsympathetic glance. It looked hopeless.

"Come on, Sam. He'd fit right into that sunny corner."

"Oh, all right," I reluctantly agreed. We tied up its stem with an old brown tie, watered it and dusted off its lackluster leaves. Then we named it. *Leif!*

The plant became a center of attention. People dropped by to give it words of encouragement. "Come on, Leif, you can do it!" "Good morning, Leif, have a good day!" In just two weeks, Leif completely revived and towered proudly over my desk. I was amazed—and elated.

"Plants aren't too different from people," one of the secretaries said. "A little love, and they perk right up."

—SAMANTHA MCGARRITY

PRAY: *Make me more sensitive, Father, to people who are wilting right outside my door due to lack of love and affection. Bring the words of encouragement they need to perk them right up.*

DO: Look a little more carefully at those around you. Who could use a little attention—a smile, a hug, an expression of praise?

When a loved one needs to hear the truth

<hr>

READ: *For whom the Lord loves He corrects, just as a father the son in whom he delights.*

—PROVERBS 3:12

REFLECT: Some years ago my daughter surprised her artist great-grandmother with a fistful of hastily colored pictures. Grandma looked them over carefully, then remarked gently, "You know, these aren't really pictures. They're more like scribbles!"

I had always greeted Rebecca's efforts with a casual, "How pretty, dear," and was afraid her feelings would be hurt by Grandma's bluntness. But Rebecca took the criticism evenly. "I'm not too good at coloring," she admitted.

"You could be," Grandma told her. "Bring me your crayons and lots of paper."

The two, separated by more than eighty years, spent a happy hour exploring the world of color and design. Rebecca learned to color, and I learned a lesson too: Criticism, offered in love and followed by constructive action, is far more valuable than empty praise.

—PENNEY SCHWAB

PRAY: *Lord, help me to gently speak the truth to _____ —truth that will set him/her free.*

DO: Make sure your friend is mature enough to handle the truth, even though he/she may be hurt by it. And make sure your motives are pure before gently speaking the truth in love.

<hr>

When a prayer doesn't seem to be answered (1)

——◄○►——

READ: *And when you pray, do not use vain repetitions as the heathen do. For they think that they will be heard for their many words.*

—MATTHEW 6:7

REFLECT: I started looking for creative ways ten-year-old Andrew and I could pray at bedtime, instead of saying the Lord's Prayer as we had done every night since he was three.

We began simply by making up our own spontaneous prayers. And one night we read Psalm 27. We concentrated on the lines, "Don't be impatient. Wait for the Lord . . ." (verse 14, TLB). Andrew had been talking for days about his lost Cleveland Indians baseball cap, and that night he asked God to help him find it. I knew Andrew had listened to the Psalm, because he stopped talking about the lost cap. And some days later, when he found it, he told me, "Look, I was patient and I waited . . . and found my cap."

Creative prayers. Begin your own search for fresh ways for your family to converse with God, and watch for new opportunities in answered prayers. —PATRICIA LORENZ

PRAY: *Father, if a ten-year-old child can learn to wait patiently for his prayers to be answered, I think I can too. Thank You for showing me how to pray more creatively . . . and to wait more patiently for Your answers.*

DO: Make a list of five of your prayers that have been answered. Put the list in your wallet or purse, and read it whenever you're feeling impatient for God's answer.

When a prayer doesn't seem to be answered (2)

READ: *And you will be changed into a different person.*

—1 SAMUEL 10:6 (NIV)

REFLECT: Once I was given some hand-me-down shoes. The leather was scruffy and a dull olive color. How I hated them! So I prayed, *Please change them, Father. Make them pretty.* But the next morning they were the same old ugly shoes. I was disappointed that God hadn't answered my prayer.

I clomped off to school wondering how I could keep my friends from noticing the hated shoes. For every idle moment I had a diversion. I was relieved that no one mentioned the awful shoes.

One day some of my friends laughed at a little girl who was wearing a patched dress. They weren't going to play with her. In a rush of sympathy, I ran to her and said, "Let's go play!"

Later I helped a girl with a lesson she didn't understand.

"You're nicer than you used to be," she told me. And then I saw that instead of changing the shoes, God had changed *me.*

—LUCILLE CAMPBELL

PRAY: *God, thank You so much for not answering my every prayer in the way I expect!*

DO: Take your mind off the prayer that doesn't seem to have been answered and look for ways God is using it to grow you into the likeness of Christ.

When a prayer doesn't seem to be answered (3)

READ: *If you then, being evil, know how to give good gifts to your children, how much more will your Father who is in heaven give good things to those who ask Him!*

—MATTHEW 7:11

REFLECT: Sometimes when God gives me a "No" answer and I find myself questioning His wisdom, I have only to think of Ann and the red wings.

Although Ann was being raised in a devout Christian family, she arrived at a doubting stage early in life. Was God real? Were prayers heard? To discover the answers, she prayed fervently to God for red wings as proof of His good intentions —and nothing happened! No red wings—ergo, no God.

"Yet, as I grew older," Ann told me, "that was the very fact that brought me to my knees with a hosanna of thanksgiving as I realized how *good* God is. Imagine having to go through life with red wings!"

How we could enrich our faith by looking all the way back through the years and remembering—with gratitude—the times that He said "No."

—ELAINE ST. JOHNS

PRAY: *Lord, it only seems to be years later that we're able to see what Your "No" answers saved us from and be grateful for them. The reality is, "No" doesn't feel good right now. Help me to trust and praise You whether I ever understand "No" or not.*

DO: Look back through the years for "unanswered" prayers for which to be grateful.

When a prayer doesn't seem to be answered (4)

◄◦►

READ: *Father, I thank You that You have heard Me.*

—JOHN 11:41

REFLECT: I walked along the narrow shale beach at the edge of the river. There I watched a giant oil tanker make its way downriver, huge and silent, then growing smaller, leaving the water's broad surface as undisturbed as though no ship had passed. I strolled on downstream.

The noise came from behind me—a roar like an approaching freight train. I whirled around to see two-foot waves rushing across the water that seconds earlier had been so placid. Curling, cresting, crashing in white foam around my feet—where had they come from?

Of course: the tanker, now far away.

Our efforts at prayer are not unavailing. Our pleas are registered in heaven and God's redeeming power is in motion. The effect has just not reached the surface of things where our land-bound eyes are watching.

—ELIZABETH SHERRILL

PRAY: *Lord Jesus, You thanked Your Father for hearing Your prayer even before you prayed it. That's the kind of faith I want, Lord.*

DO: Study Jesus' prayers in the Bible.

When a significant person in your past comes to mind

READ: *I thank my God every time I remember you.*

—PHILIPPIANS 1:3 (NIV)

REFLECT: Everybody has pivotal people in their lives, people they knew in their youth who made a real difference. You can probably name yours, but do you know where they are now?

I'd lost track of all of mine over the years, and I didn't know how sad that was until I found one of them by accident—when my son met his son at a college interview. I wrote to him, and he wrote back, and that's about all that will come of it, but I feel good about being given the chance to say thank you—something we rarely say to these people, being young and callous when they help us.

So I'm saying it here. Thank you, Miss Coons, Miss Roohan, Mrs. Bolton, Dr. Krawiec, Ann Curtiss. I wouldn't be the person I am now without every one of you.

Now *you* try it.

—TONI SORTOR

PRAY: *Father, I didn't—and still don't—say thank you enough to the people in my life. Give me a chance to say it to some of the people from my past and remind me to say it often to those in the present.*

DO: Now *you* try it.

When a young person you know is struggling with doubts

---◀◦▶---

READ: *The testing of your faith produces patience.*

—JAMES 1:3

REFLECT: Doubt. Feeding on hesitation, suspicion and distrust, doubt can destroy.

But doubt can be a healthy thing too. The Spanish novelist Unamuno once wrote that "faith which does not doubt is dead faith." I believe that for I know that open and honest questioning is necessary for anyone who takes his faith seriously. Show me someone who never had a doubt about anything and I will show you someone who is not using the mind that God gave him.

I remember that when I was a theological student I had a professor who said, "I'm going to knock your faith to pieces, boys, and then put it together for you again. If I don't, when you get out into the world, the world will knock it to pieces."

That professor helped me learn that when you struggle through doubt, you toughen your faith.

—NORMAN VINCENT PEALE

PRAY: *God, I pray for all young people whose faith is being challenged, especially _____. Help them to stay faithful to You in their hearts while thinking through the doubts in their minds.*

DO: Send this page to a student you know and love.

When an elderly friend is housebound

———————◄○►———————

READ: *We who are many form one body, and each member belongs to all the others.*

—ROMANS 12:5 (NIV)

REFLECT: In her eighties, too frail to attend church services, Miss Minnie Woods lived alone and "attended services" by radio every week.

"But I miss the people," she told me. "It's not the same when you worship alone."

I thought then of my own church services. How I, too, would miss the warm feelings of support and love that radiate throughout the congregation. While praying alone has its very own special meaning, praying with others provides a oneness with God and community that Jesus spoke of when He said, "For where two or three are gathered together in my name, there am I in the midst of them."

So I joined Miss Minnie every week for her half hour of radio time, and we "attended service" together. We were each other's community. Just the two of us—and Him.

—ZONA B. DAVIS

PRAY: *What a wonderful idea, Lord! I have several housebound elderly friends. Please lead me to the one who needs this support the most.*

DO: When you've arranged your other Sunday morning obligations, call your friend and present your idea.

When an old friend comes to mind

<o>

READ: *Encourage one another daily. . . .*

—HEBREWS 3:13 (NIV)

REFLECT: We were seated around tables in the church Fellowship Hall following a potluck supper. I was the discussion leader and had posed the question, "What is one of the most meaningful gifts you have ever received?" Joe Jack Pearce raised his hand and stood up to speak.

Joe Jack was the International Racquetball Champion in the eighty to eighty-four-year-old bracket. He said, "Several months ago I received a call from some boys I coached on a high school basketball team in 1941. They were having a reunion. They called to tell me how much I had meant to them and that I helped shape their lives."

Joe Jack paused as his voice choked up. Shaking his head, he mumbled, "That just might be the nicest gift I ever received."

The room grew quiet. We were all thinking of phone calls we needed to make.

—SCOTT WALKER

PRAY: *Lord, thank You for the renewed memory of _____. I'm not sure what prompted it, but in case it was a call to prayer, that's what I'll do.*

DO: Do pray for that person and be open to the idea that God could have a renewed relationship in mind. It's so easy these days to track down a name from the past on the Internet; why not give it a try?

When back-to-school preparations have you frazzled

◄○►

READ: *He will yet fill your mouth with laughter. . . .*

—JOB 8:21 (NIV)

REFLECT: I was tired. It was the end of a long school day at the end of June. The kids were eager to begin summer vacation, and it was my job to settle them down. I assigned a composition on "My Pet Peeve."

"My pet peeve," I commented in a serious tone, "is students who don't take their work seriously." I looked pointedly at Cliff, the class "wise guy."

Of course, that night I had thirty-five papers to mark. I groaned, even more so when I discovered Cliff's essay on top. My forehead creased as I read his first line. Then I burst out laughing. "My pet Peeve," he had written, "is a good pet. . . ."

Laughing, I shoved the remainder of the papers back into my briefcase and the next day announced, "As a 'Here Comes Summer' gift, everyone gets an A on that paper!" Then I silently thanked Cliff for teaching me an important lesson: *Lighten up!* —LINDA NEUKRUG

PRAY: *Thank You, God, for teachers with a sense of humor. Let that humor get teachers, students and parents through a long school year in good spirits.*

DO: Send this page to a teacher who could use a good laugh.

When God feels near

READ: *Search me, O God, and know my heart;*
try me, and know my anxieties. . . .

—PSALM 139:23

REFLECT: I especially like to be up and out on Sundays before dawn. There's hardly any traffic and few sounds. Even the rabbits know me and don't bother to scurry into the bushes as I walk. It's a time when I feel closer to God. Yes, I know He's always close to me, but sometimes the busyness of life keeps me from being close to Him.

When I was a little girl, my family spent part of each summer in the mountains. I was amazed by the millions of stars I could see. My parents told me there were just as many stars back home, but we couldn't see them all because too many things got in the way. So I couldn't wait to get back to the mountains and find out that the stars were indeed still there. Close enough, almost, to touch.

That's what I like about early Sunday mornings: getting close enough, almost, to touch God.

—PHYLLIS HOBE

PRAY: *Thank You, God, for being not just near me but, by Your Holy Spirit, living in me. Thank You for these special times when my heart is full to overflowing with Your love.*

DO: Soak quietly in His love as long as you can today.

When God is silent

READ: *Men listened to me and waited, and kept silence for my counsel.*

—JOB 29:21

REFLECT: Sometimes, I get frustrated with those seemingly endless seasons when God is so silent it's easy to doubt that He's ever spoken at all. During those times, I try to reflect on the many ways I've heard God's voice in the past, times when He has:

- directed, corrected, and loved me through the voice of a family member, a friend, a teacher or a preacher;
- guided my steps through changes in circumstances;
- spoken His forgiveness through the timely reading of a perfect passage of Scripture;
- moved me to laughter and tears through the writing of gifted authors;
- and in prayer, stopped my whirling world to sit with me in silence and fill my heart with His perfect peace.

Actually, those silences ... they're the most precious times of all.

—LUCILE ALLEN

PRAY: *Thank You for trusting me with those silent seasons, Father. I'll try to receive those silences as gifts and worship You in them.*

DO: Sit in silence with God until you see Him reflected in the stillness of your heart and mind.

When God seems far away

READ: *And they feared exceedingly, and said to one another, "Who can this be, that even the wind and the sea obey Him!"*

—MARK 4:41

REFLECT: I walked along the path that wove its way toward Lake Michigan. As I got nearer, I faintly heard it; when I topped the last dune, I could hear it clearly: the thunderous crashing of waves. I watched, amazed—as always—at the lake's endless energy.

Finally, I turned for the walk back, the sound of the surf pounding in my ears. I hiked over one dune, then another. When I paused to catch my breath, I was astonished to realize I could no longer hear the water.

Sometimes God's presence seems so real it's almost tangible. At other times He seems so far away—and then it's easy to have doubts. But the lake helps me to remember that God is always there, whether or not I can see Him at work or hear His voice.

—MARY LOU CARNEY

PRAY: *Thank You, Lord, for being near me, even when it feels like You're not.*

DO: Close your eyes and think of a time when you felt very close to God. Perhaps it was in church, walking in the woods, on the beach or when reading the Bible. Use that memory to remind yourself of His presence.

When it "rains on your picnic"

READ: *For whom do I toil and deprive myself of good?*

—ECCLESIASTES 4:8

REFLECT: When I was growing up, I remember looking forward to a Saturday picnic. All week I asked, "How many more days?" "What will we eat?" I even whipped up some envy among my third-grade classmates by bragging about the picnic-to-come.

Well, wouldn't you know it, on Saturday it rained! The sky opened up, just like my own tears. But Mom was unfazed. "We'll just have an indoor picnic!" she announced. And she spread the red-checkered cloth on the living room floor, got out the paper plates, and she and my sister and I ate "oven-barbecued" hot dogs.

Out of that long-ago day came the expression "Let's have an indoor picnic." It became a shorthand way of saying, "Even an unhappy situation has advantages!"

Is there some disappointment in your life today? Ask God to join you in making it into an "indoor picnic."

—LINDA NEUKRUG

PRAY: *I praise You, Father, that You are a redeeming God. You not only redeemed our souls from the wages of sin, You can redeem life's every disappointment.*

DO: Adopt the "Let's have an indoor picnic" phrase—and attitude—as your own.

When it's hard to find time to pray

<o>

READ: *He shall pray to God, and He will delight in him,*
He shall see His face with joy, for He restores to man
His righteousness.

—JOB 33:26

REFLECT: I read about a tribe in Uganda that has the sacred custom of allotting to each adult member a tiny patch of land just outside the village. Each clearing has its own private path and is used as a place of prayer and meditation by its designated owner. Should a tribesman become quarrelsome or overstep himself, he is reminded by others that grass is growing on the unused path to his prayer place.

Suddenly I felt a kinship with those faraway people who not only realize the importance of private contact with God but, by setting aside a special place in their midst, go one step further and prepare the way so that each might pray alone with the Lord.

Whenever you find yourself becoming out of sorts, remember that distant Ugandan tribe and their wise recognition of the soothing power of prayer and meditation. Don't let grass grow on your pathway to prayer!

—DORIS HAASE

PRAY: *Lord Jesus, I need You and I need time in prayer with*
You, not only because it makes me a better person, but
because You enjoy time with me. What an amazing
thought!

DO: Ask a friend to let you know when it becomes obvious, by your disposition, that you've been neglecting time with God—and then thank him/her when he/she does.

When it's hard to say, "I love you"

READER: **READ:** *And surely I am with you always, to the very end of the age.*
—MATTHEW 28:20 (NIV)

REFLECT: I need love, companionship, and reassurance—without having to ask. Perhaps it's a weakness, but it's very real.

Two of our dearest friends visited us from California. Our partings are always a little emotional. "See you guys!" Lucke called a little too gaily to hide her tears as Bob pulled out of the driveway. They didn't look back; and George and I blew our noses.

"Look! I found something in the cookie jar," our son Bryce called as we entered the front door. He held out a folded piece of paper.

"We love you!" It was signed "Lucke and Bob." Immediately there was a warm glow in my heart. Then we began finding little notes everywhere. "Wasn't it wonderful? There's nothing like friends. . . . God bless." Notes beneath our pillows, one in a slipper, and (days later) one in a roll of bathroom tissue!

How rewarding when friends know you hunger for love and give it—spontaneously! —JUNE MASTERS BACHER

PRAY: *Father, I admit that rather than expressing love spontaneously, I tend to wait for expressions of love from others. I want to change that today, starting with, "I love You, Lord!"*

DO: Reach out today with an expression of love for someone you sense needs reassurance.

When it's time to give rather than receive

————————————◄◊►————————————

READ: *Give, and it will be given to you....*

—LUKE 6:38

REFLECT: The good sisters who ran the little Catholic charity in Atlanta, Georgia, were bewildered when George Bessada, an Egyptian foreign student, arranged a fund-raising dinner for them. Yes, they were desperate for money, but how would their friend George be able to help? He had money worries of his own.

Yet there they were, guests of honor at an exotic dinner where some two hundred persons had paid ten dollars apiece for course upon course of North African delicacies.

When George presented the sisters with a check for $1,100, they could barely stammer their thanks. Then one asked what had prompted him to arrange the gala. "Oh," George said, "you Americans are always helping my countrymen. My friends and I thought we'd show you that we can make a contribution too."

George knew that to maintain spiritual health there must be giving as well as getting in every life. And he knew, too, that the giver knows the greater joy.

—ARTHUR GORDON

PRAY: *There's no shortage of need and no shortage of generous hearts, Father. Thank You for Your provision that allows people to help others.*

DO: Make it possible for someone who is normally on the receiving end to be the giver.

When life is too hectic (1)

◄◦►

READ: *Now do not be stiff-necked, as your fathers were, but yield yourselves to the Lord. . . .*

—2 CHRONICLES 30:8

REFLECT: One day I was feeling overwhelmed by the pressures of my job, family, various and sundry commitments—
Time for a flying lesson, I thought.

Flying usually helps me feel refreshed. But on this day the air that had looked so clear from below proved to be turbulent. My heart thudded with fear as the plane bounced around, and I held myself stiffly erect in the seat.

"Just relax and go with it," my instructor advised. "If you'll put your faith in flying this thing to a safe landing, you can sit back and enjoy the view." Soon I accepted the bumps as part of the total experience and was able to give my attention to the beauty of the landscape below.

Maybe that's what we need to do in our lives: relax and give our attention to all the beautiful people around us—in our family, in our job and in our outside commitments.

—MADGE HARRAH

PRAY: *There is so much going on right now, Lord, I feel like I'm about to cave under the pressure. Thank You for this reminder to just relax and enjoy the view.*

DO: Focus your thoughts on those closest to you. Say a special prayer of thanks for God's love and care for each one.

When life is too hectic (2)

READ: *Surely I have calmed and quieted my soul . . . like a weaned child is my soul within me.*

—PSALM 131:2

REFLECT: We had been in Lupton, Arizona, on the edge of the Navajo Reservation when we decided to drive to nearby New Mexico.

As we crossed the state line, there was an elderly Navajo woman tending sheep. She wore a gray sweater over her forest-green velvet blouse and her faded green cotton skirt hung to her ankles. Her face was wrinkled and weathered, but what I have never forgotten was her complete stillness and serenity as she stood there looking down at the sheep. She was still standing there, in almost the same spot, on our return trip three hours later.

Whenever I get the feeling that I have to be in several places at once, I remember the elderly Navajo woman tending her sheep. I see again the acceptance and patience and peace on her face, and I stop and make time for a few quiet moments to sit in the presence of God.

—GEORGIANA SANCHEZ

PRAY: *Lord Jesus, I tend to think of busy as the opposite of peaceful, but that must not be true, because You were busy and peaceful at the same time. Please give me Your Spirit so that I can do that too.*

DO: Most of us can't stay in one spot for hours in quiet acceptance and peace, but we can get away for more than just a few minutes to be with God, the source of peace. Make a commitment to spend some serious time in prayer this week and write it down in your appointment book.

When life is too hectic (3)

READ: *Whoever receives one of these little children
in My name receives Me. . . .*

—MARK 9:37

REFLECT: My wife and I both work, so when we finally pick up six-year-old Timmy from the babysitter, drive home and start dinner, each of us needs to unwind. Sometimes we are talking a mile a minute, trying to solve work-related problems.

One night, as the three of us sat at our small, yellow kitchen counter, Linda and I were rattling on when suddenly we heard a small voice. "Doesn't anybody want to know what happened to me?" Pause. Guilt!

"What happened, son?" Linda asked.

"Nothing, I had a very perfect day. So I guess I don't have anything much to say."

Linda and I exchanged sheepish glances. "Tell us about the good things, Tim," Linda finally said. And he did. And they were very good, because they reminded us how easy it is to let our hectic routine screen out those we love and those who love us.

Even Jesus.

—GARY SLEDGE

PRAY: *Forgive us, Father, when we get so busy we neglect our
sons and daughters, and more importantly, Your Son.*

DO: When you get home from work, tell your children you're going to spend a few minutes together talking about your day—and when you're through, you want to talk to them about theirs. And then do it.

When life seems stormy

READ: *He makes His sun rise on the evil and on the good, and sends rain on the just and on the unjust.*

—MATTHEW 5:45

REFLECT: My mother had many virtues, but she had one persistent if amusing fault. She took the weather personally. A beautiful day, she regarded almost as her individual benediction. She sang and accomplished things and loved the world. On gloomy days, she would stew and fuss.

My grandfather, on the other hand, had two dear homilies that he applied to life's situations, including the weather: "It's all for the best, but we can't see it" and, "No great damage without some small good." When hailstones battered the crops, or droughts parched the fields, or a cyclone took the roof off the barn, "We'll be strengthened by this adversity," he'd solemnly declare. "The barn needs a new roof anyway, and look how many neighbors want to help. Why, except for this, we'd never appreciate how good people are."

Grandpa's philosophy has helped me through many of life's storms.

—MARJORIE HOLMES

PRAY: *Father, I guess I have to admit that I'm more like the mother than the grandfather in this story. Instead of stewing and fussing over some recent gloomy circumstances, help me look for the things to appreciate.*

DO: Do just that. Look past the damage in a recent circumstance for some small good.

When life's got you down

◄○►

READ: *We are hard-pressed on every side, yet not crushed; we are perplexed, but not in despair. . . .*

—2 CORINTHIANS 4:8

REFLECT: Mrs. Scarpa sat in the same spot in the same pew for years. Up until a few years ago, her husband had come with her. Now she came alone, her eyes often swimming in sadness.

This Sunday, as she came up to greet me, I winked at her, grinned and asked, "Where'd you get that pretty red hat?"

She chuckled, patting it fondly. "My husband bought it for me. Told me that in those terrible days of World War II, this red hat was to keep my spirits up.

"A couple of months ago I got it down and dusted it off, and I've decided to wear it again. Every time the world gets me down, I'm putting on this red hat!"

Perhaps you, too, need a "red hat." Find yours, dust it off and get on with life. When you do, you, too, will discover that "we do not lose heart" (2 Corinthians 4:16).

—SCOTT WALKER

PRAY: *Lord, I know that in the grand scheme of things, and compared to a lot of other folks, life's not so bad for me. I've just been a little down. This story was just the attitude-adjuster I needed. Thank You, Lord. I'm ready to get on with life.*

DO: You may have another "red hat" of your own from the past, something that made you smile. Pull it out and dust it off.

When someone around you is in a bad mood

————————————◄◉►————————————

READ: *Do not hasten in your spirit to be angry....*

—ECCLESIASTES 7:9

REFLECT: There once was a TV cartoon about a grouchy wife and her husband. The wife opens her mouth, and in a puff of gray clouds a green dragon comes out, growling and snapping. The man stiffens.

In a few seconds the woman opens her mouth again. Another dragon, larger and nastier, comes from her mouth.

The man takes a deep breath, puffs up his chest, and opens his mouth. Out comes a large bouquet of flowers that floats onto the woman's lap.

The wife then floats up out of her chair, landing gently on the man's lap. She kisses him.

When someone growls dragons at me, my first reaction is to growl back. But now I wonder, wouldn't Jesus want me to reply with a bouquet of flowers?

—PAT EGAN DEXTER

PRAY: *Father, help me to always have Your sweet Spirit, especially when I confront someone in a grouchy mood.*

DO: Apologize to someone you may have hurt with a grouchy response—even if that person was grouchy first.

When someone rubs you the wrong way

◄○►

READ: *Love is patient and kind.*

—1 CORINTHIANS 13:4 (NLT)

REFLECT: A young man complained bitterly to me about his wife's mother who had come to live with them. She came to breakfast in her bathrobe and slippers, which she scuffed at every step. Furthermore, she slurped her coffee. One more scuff or one more slurp would drive the young man insane.

"I can offer you some advice," I said, "but you must agree to follow it."

He swore that he would.

"When you get to your office tomorrow, call and ask your mother-in-law to lunch. Just the two of you."

The young man was aghast. But, with reluctance, he did it. Imagine his astonishment when his mother-in-law appeared—well-dressed, well-groomed, alert and lively, a first-class luncheon companion. Why? She responded to kindness just as she had to hostility.

Is there someone who rubs you the wrong way? Make a special effort to be kind to him or her. It may change his or her attitude a lot. It may also change yours!

—NORMAN VINCENT PEALE

PRAY: *Lord, I don't know why _____ rubs me the wrong way, but would You give me the key to changing my heart toward him/her?*

DO: Your lack of affection is probably no surprise to this person, but a sincere gesture of friendship and acceptance would be. It would be pleasing in God's eyes too.

When tragedy strikes (1)

READ: *And we know that all things work together for good to those who love God, to those who are the called according to His purpose.*

—ROMANS 8:28

REFLECT: On display at the French Academy of Sciences is a shoemaker's awl. It looks ordinary, but behind that awl are both tragedy and victory. It fell from the shoemaker's table and put out the eye of his nine-year-old son. Within weeks the child was blind in both eyes, and had to attend a special school.

At that time the blind read by using large, carved wooden blocks that were clumsy and awkward. When the boy grew up, he devised a new reading system of punched dots on paper. To do it, Louis Braille used the same awl that had blinded him.

Tragedy will come into each of our lives, but we can choose how it affects us. When it strikes, some of us ask, "Why did God allow this to happen?" Others ask, "How will God use it?"

—PATRICIA HOUCK SPRINKLE

PRAY: *Father, You watched Your son being nailed to the cross. It comforts me to know You can understand the pain I'm in right now, and I thank You that You will use the tragedy in my life for good, just as You did Jesus' death on the cross.*

DO: Try to think of three ways God could redeem the tragedy you're facing.

When tragedy strikes (2)

◄○►

READ: *Let not your heart be troubled; you believe in God, believe also in Me.*

—JOHN 14:1

REFLECT: In my vacation Bible school days I memorized a Bible chapter every night. In college, I took an absorbing course in Bible history and looked back in scorn to those childhood exercises. *How utterly dull, all that time just memorizing!* I thought.

Eventually I taught English in a Moravian boarding school, and one Sunday a visiting minister spoke on the church's liturgy. He said that children heard it over and over, perhaps understanding little of it. But later, when they were faced with the great experiences of life, the meanings came clear. And, as a pitcher holds water, so the familiar phrases held the newly perceived truths.

He was right. My fiancé had recently died in an accident. And every night I went to sleep saying the fourteenth chapter of John: "Let not your heart be troubled: ye believe in God, believe also in me . . . ," learned years before in summer Bible school.

—GERTRUDE NAUGLER

PRAY: *Thank You, Father, for the deposit of Your Word within me. Please bring to mind what I need now to get through this painful experience, Lord.*

DO: Get out your Bible and soak yourself in the Word. Use a concordance to find passages that particularly comfort and strengthen you.

When you are (or a friend is) newly alone

─────────────────◄○►─────────────────

READ: *The Lord is near to those who have a broken heart, and saves such as have a contrite spirit.*

—PSALM 34:18

REFLECT: I felt compelled to telephone my friend Nancy. After nineteen years of marriage, her husband had left her.

I stared at the phone. *How could I possibly comfort Nancy? What would I say?* Finally, I dialed her number, hoping that calling would let her know I cared.

Nancy shared her agony: the possibility of losing her house, finding a job, caring for her devastated children. She said, "I begged God to guide me, just as He had led Israel with pillars of cloud and fire. He brought to mind several people from church. 'Let them be pillars to you,' He seemed to say."

Nancy's friends did become her pillars. One took her out to dinner; another slipped a hundred dollars into her purse. Others became pillars of fire, aglow with God's wisdom. Gradually, answers began to unfold.

I hung up, amazed. God had transformed my feeble effort into a pillar of support too—and strengthened my own faith.

—MARY BROWN

PRAY: *I need a pillar or two to lean on, right now, Father, someone aglow with Your wisdom.*

DO: Maybe the best thing to do when you need a pillar is to become one for someone else. Who could you be a pillar to today?

When you can't get through to a struggling friend

——◄◦►——

READ: *To him who is afflicted, kindness should be shown by his friend, even though he forsakes the fear of the Almighty.*

—JOB 6:14

REFLECT: My son and his wife were swimming in the ocean at Daytona Beach, Florida. It seemed to me that they were getting much too far from shore for their own safety, so I stood up and yelled, "Come in closer!" But they couldn't hear me. A lifeguard used his loudspeaker and ordered them to come back to the shallow water.

They hadn't realized how far they had been carried by the waves, and had been frightened when they had some difficulty getting back to shore. And they were thankful for the lifeguard.

Do you know someone who is floundering? No matter how much you try to help them by yourself, they can't hear you.

God can get through to them when no one else can. His whisper is louder than thunder. You can help make it happen —through prayer. You can let them know they have a Lifesaver. His name is Jesus. —PAT SULLIVAN

PRAY: *Precious Savior, I've tried so hard to get through to _____, but he/she can't hear me. Please save him/her, Lord, with Your mighty hand.*

DO: Pray daily for your friend and continue to let him/her know of your love and concern.

When you can't see life's blessings

READ: *Blessed be the God and Father of our Lord Jesus Christ, who has blessed us with every spiritual blessing in the heavenly places in Christ. . . .*

—EPHESIANS 1:3

REFLECT: It is snowing this morning: big, fluffy, lazy flakes floating gently down from the sky. I pull on my coat, gloves, boots, and hat to walk down our long driveway to get the newspaper. I am fascinated by the falling flakes. Left alone in their downward journey, they swirl around and softly land on the ground, where they become lost in the mounds of snow already there. But if I reach out my hand to catch some of them, at least for a fleeting moment, I can appreciate the unique, delicate beauty of each individual flake.

God's blessings come the same way. Unless I pause and reach out my hand to catch them, they fall unnoticed, and too often unappreciated, on a blanket of other blessings down around my feet.

—CAROL KUYKENDALL

PRAY: *Thank you, Father, for every blessing, even those that don't appear to be blessings at first glance.*

DO: Think of a blessing—a person or thing in your life—you've taken for granted lately and imagine what life would be like without that person or thing.

When you can't see the forest for the trees

———◄○►———

READ: *You are the God who does wonders. . . .*

—PSALM 77:14

REFLECT: As I sit at my study window, our front yard is again covered with water overflowing from a nearby creek. This annual flood once bothered me greatly.

Then, a few years ago, I woke one Saturday to find the front yard a virtual lake. Discouragement crept over me. My son Nathan, eight, was sitting beside me as I sipped my morning coffee. Suddenly, Jonathan, six, burst in and shouted, "Dad, God made a lake in our front yard! Hurry, get the canoe!"

As he ran out, Nathan heard my deep sigh. He gave me his wisest look and said, "You've got to understand, Dad, to a third-grader like me it's just a big puddle. But to a first-grader it is a miracle!"

I looked out at the "lake" again. It became a shimmering sea to explore, a raging river to navigate.

Sometimes the "wonders" of the Lord all depend on the eyes we're using.

—ERIC FELLMAN

PRAY: *God, I've most definitely needed new eyes with which to see Your wonders. Thank You for a child's eyes through which to see.*

DO: Try to spend some time with a child today.

When you can't seem to get anything out of your Bible reading

◄○►

READ: *The Son is the radiance of God's glory and the exact representation of His being, sustaining all things by His powerful word.*

—HEBREWS 1:3 (NIV)

REFLECT: Last year I resolved to read the Bible more, but when I read several chapters a day, very little stuck with me. One day I asked the Lord for guidance. It came to me: Read until you reach a special verse that catches your attention. Stop and write it down. Repeat it until it becomes yours.

Now Scripture has become words with living power, helping me in daily trials—and in joys too.

Why not find your own verse as you read the Bible and watch for opportunities each day to exercise its power over any situation?

—SAM JUSTICE

PRAY: *Dear God, I know that Your Word is alive and relevant to any situation we face today. But I have to confess that it seems rather dry and irrelevant lately. Lord, please let Your living Word come alive for me again.*

DO: Do what the author of this reflection suggests—find your verse, write it down, memorize it and put it to work.

When you can't sleep

◄○►

READ: *Therefore I exhort first of all that supplications, prayers, intercessions, and giving of thanks be made for all men. . . .*
—1 TIMOTHY 2:1

REFLECT: I have little trouble falling asleep, but I often wake up in the wee hours. At such times my mind goes on full alert, and I find myself trying to recall things like whether or not I've paid certain bills or how to persuade my grandson to take high school more seriously.

The idea came to me that I could put this time to better use through intercessory prayer. So I made a list of about thirty relatives, friends and even some religious and political leaders to pray for. Then, in the early hours when I woke up, I began going through the list—praying for a healing for this one, a stronger faith for that one, a relief from depression for another.

I soon found that before I could get halfway through the list, I would fall into a sound and peaceful sleep.

—SAM JUSTICE

PRAY: *Tonight, Lord, I pray for all those on my list, especially the ones I won't get to before I drift off again. Until then I pray for _____, and _____ and _____ .*

DO: Make your own intercessory prayer list for those nights when you can't sleep.

When you disagree with your child's choices

◄○►

READ: *Hear my prayer, O Lord; and let my cry for help come to you.*
— PSALM 102:1 (NIV)

REFLECT: Our son John, who planned to be a minister like his father, told me that he wanted to go to a certain seminary. I was very unhappy. All sorts of unorthodox ideas were explored there. I knew our son had a simple, trusting faith that had been taught to him in our home. What if these sophisticated teaching methods destroyed that faith?

So I prayed that John would change his mind. I asked God to change it for him. And what happened? Nothing. God said, "No" to me. John went to the seminary of his choice.

Years later, John told me that he had sensed how I felt. But he had also prayed, and felt that God approved of his decision. "And you know," he said, "the challenge and stimulus of that place woke me up. I came out with my faith deepened and strengthened."

I'm so glad God said, "Yes" to John. And "No" to his apprehensive mother.
— RUTH STAFFORD PEALE

PRAY: *Lord, help me to trust You to guide my children onto Your path for their lives and in their ability to make the right decisions without my input.*

DO: Express your availability to your children, along with your trust in them and God's ability to speak to them. Release them with your blessings to make their own decisions.

When you don't feel able to finish a task

◄◉►

READ: *I have fought the good fight, I have finished the race....*

—2 TIMOTHY 4:7

REFLECT: The church job I'd agreed to do was taking far more time than I'd expected. "If I don't have every book cataloged in the new church library by June first," I told myself grimly, "someone else can finish. I've done my part!" So, on the first day of June, I made that announcement to the church board and went off on vacation to Washington, DC. Frankly, I felt glad to be free of the burden until the last day, when we visited Mount Vernon.

There, in the west parlor over a mantel, the Washington family coat-of-arms caught my eye. The motto was, "The end crowns the work."

I really had not done my part on the church job. Not yet, not until I had finished it.

Two weeks of hard work later, when the last book had been cataloged, I knew the joy that comes from "crowning" the work.

—JEANNE HILL

PRAY: *Thank You, precious Savior, for "crowning" the work You came to accomplish.*

DO: Think of the project that's giving you trouble. Divide it up into doable parts and write them into your calendar. Make a commitment to do a little something each day until it's finished.

When you don't know what to say

---◄◦►---

READ: *The word of our God stands forever.*

—ISAIAH 40:8

REFLECT: My favorite way of speaking my most tender feelings is the one I learned years ago when my friend Patsy returned from the Holy Land bringing me a gift of a Bible.

It was just the right size for my handbag, bound in olive wood with a Crusader's cross on its cover. Patsy handed it to me without saying a word. Opening it, I recognized her handwriting: "For Ellie—(Philippians 1:3, KJV)." I turned the pages to the reference verse and read, "I thank my God upon every remembrance of you".

I'd seldom been so moved. Patsy had let the Bible speak for her. And now I do the same when I want to say, "I hope to offer you some comfort in your grief," or "Don't give up," and don't know how to express it. I send a note with a verse like, "1 Thessalonians 4:13–18," or "Psalm 55:22," or "Hebrews 11:8." Who could say it better than that!

—ELEANOR SASS

PRAY: *God, Your Word is so relevant to our every need today. Give me just the right Scripture at just the right time to bring comfort, encourage or express my love.*

DO: Use this reflection or a concordance to help find just the right Scripture to express your feelings to a friend or loved one.

When you don't like someone

READ: *Love your enemies and pray for those who persecute you. . . .*
—MATTHEW 5:44 (NIV)

REFLECT: A woman in our town seemed to take joy in criticizing people behind their backs, including members of my family. At first I let her wagging tongue really disturb me.

One day I complained bitterly about it to a friend, who gently urged me: "Don't criticize. Pray."

Reluctant to pray for this bothersome woman, I decided to take my friend's advice anyway. *It won't hurt to try*, I told myself. But what happened next took me by surprise. No, my prayers didn't cause the woman to change. They changed me! I simply couldn't bring myself to hate someone for whom I was praying. And at last I felt peace because I was no longer having to deal with all those bad feelings.

Try praying for someone who has used you poorly—not for the other person to change, but for God to bless that person, always remembering that the other is one of His children too.
—SAMANTHA MCGARRITY

PRAY: *Father, I pray for _____. Bless him/her in all he/she does today and especially his/her relationships with others.*

DO: Try to imagine the person you dislike as God sees him/her, with grace and understanding.

When you don't like yourself

READ: *I will praise You, for I am fearfully and wonderfully made; marvelous are Your works....*

—PSALM 139:14

REFLECT: One evening when shepherd's pie, our children's favorite, was on the table, six-year-old Ian enthusiastically volunteered to say the blessing. After he had duly thanked God for the food and the highlights of his day, he paused— and then added, "And thank You, God, for the nice little boy You gave this family!"

"Nice little boy!" I gasped. "Where?"

"Right here," he grinned, pointing to himself. "I was thanking God for me!"

Doing the dishes later that night, I thought. *The boy has a point.* We all come tagged with the designer label: "Individually Crafted with the Compliments of Your Creator."

Suddenly, I was overwhelmed. Hands dripping wet with suds, eyes spilling tears of wonder, there and then I quietly said, "Thank You, God, for all the workmanship You put into making me!"

—FAY ANGUS

PRAY: *Father, I have to confess that I'm more often aware of who I'm not and wish I was than I am grateful for who You made me to be. Forgive me. And, Lord, thank You for me.*

DO: Read the book *Fearfully and Wonderfully Made* by Philip Yancey and Paul Brand. Praise the God Who made us all in such intimate detail.

When you doubt God cares

READ: *Now hope does not disappoint....*

—ROMANS 5:5

REFLECT: While I was in college there was a Chicago Bears football game that I was dying to see. A friend had promised that he could get the tickets, but delayed doing it. One day he called me. "There aren't any tickets left for the game, but—"

I cut him off in midsentence—"But, nothing," I sputtered. I was angry that he had misled me, and I sure let him know about it.

"Jeff," he replied calmly, "I was going to say that we can work for NBC television, in the broadcast booth, and we'll get paid to see it."

I was embarrassed, and apologized profusely.

I often put myself in the same position with God. Frustrated that a prayer has seemingly gone unanswered, I've worried or worse, accused Him of not caring. But soon I often find my answer has come. At last I think I've learned to control my impatience with God, as well as with people.

—JEFF JAPINGA

PRAY: *Forgive me, Lord, for accusing You of not caring just because You haven't given me what I want when I wanted it. And thank You for giving me something even better.*

DO: Think of a time when God withheld something but then gave you something better. Remember that thing the next time you doubt God's love and concern.

When you doubt God's love

READ: *Therefore My Father loves Me. . . .*

—JOHN 10:17

REFLECT: It was a beautiful day. As I headed home at the end of it, I heard two young girls giggling. They were sprawled on the lawn, pulling petals out of a daisy and chanting. *He loves me . . . he loves me not . . . he loves me . . .*

Silly game, I said to myself. *Someday they'll know that true love isn't ruled by chance.*

But you know, old as I am, I'm often just as foolish when it comes to God's love for me. I get a raise at work; God loves me. My hours get cut back; He loves me not. I get a good grade on my test; God loves me. I can't get into a class I want; He loves me not.

How silly of me! Why don't I remember that God loves me all the time, that even my disappointments are part of the love? I don't need a daisy to tell me that!

—JANICE L. HANSEN

PRAY: *It's true, Father, that my understanding of Your love is sometimes that silly. Thank You for Your Word that assures me of Your love in all circumstances.*

DO: Pull the petals off a flower and with each one declare, "He loves me, He loves me, He loves me . . ."

When you doubt your abilities

━━━━━━━━━━━━━━◄○►━━━━━━━━━━━━━━

READ: *You hear, O Lord, the desire of the afflicted; you encourage them, and you listen to their cry. . . .*

—PSALM 10:17 (NIV)

REFLECT: I came to New York to pursue a career as an actor. After several months, the many "No, thank yous" began to take their toll on me. *What am I doing here?* I wondered. *Are my dreams just too big?* My self-esteem sank to an all-time low.

About that time my father visited the city for business. He took me out to dinner and asked me how I was doing. I tried to respond positively, but Dad read right through my façade. At a pause in the conversation, he looked at me and said, "Do you know why I am here?"

I shook my head. "No."

"To remind you, son, that your mother and I . . . we believe in you."

For the first time in months my tension broke. Tears sprang to my eyes as I relaxed in Dad's acceptance of me. That was all I needed—not advice, just words of love and unconditional support.

—RICK HAMLIN

PRAY: *Father, thank You for parents who have modeled Your unconditional love for me for so long. Thank You for teaching me through them that I don't have to perform to win Your approval.*

DO: Write a note or make a phone call to thank your parents for their unconditional love. If your parents are no longer living, send a word of encouragement to someone you know who is struggling with self-doubt.

When you feel abandoned

READ: *And after the fire came a gentle whisper.*

— 1 KINGS 19:12 (NIV)

REFLECT: One afternoon, my husband and I headed to the basement to make some sense out of the maze of items deposited there. I left Mandy, our four-year-old, sleeping in her bed, and soon the dust was flying as we made steady progress.

"Mom!" a voice came from upstairs.

"Down here, Mandy," I began.

"Mommy!" Her voice came a little more frantically this time.

I tried again, "We are downst. . . ."

"Mommee!!" She cried out with real panic.

I raced up the stairs. Mandy had tears streaming down her cheeks.

"I thought you had left me here all alone!" she sobbed into my shoulder.

"Honey, I tried to answer, but you kept calling so you couldn't hear my voice."

Sometimes I wonder if God has the same problem with me.

— KRISTEN ELLIS

PRAY: *This is exactly what I've been doing, Father. Calling so loudly for You, I can't hear You answering me. I'm sorry, Lord, for momentarily forgetting that You promised to never leave me.*

DO: Sit quietly, remind yourself that you're in the presence of God, and listen to the words of comfort He speaks to Your heart and mind. Write them down for the next time you panic.

When you feel an urgent need to pray

<o>

READ: *Though an army may encamp against me, my heart shall not fear. . . .*

—PSALM 27:3

REFLECT: Paul Kopjoe was a gunner in the U.S. Marines Light Armored Infantry Division. My husband David and I had taught Paul in Sunday school. We loved him.

Before we went to sleep one night, David and I said a long prayer for him. Around midnight, I awoke with a sense of foreboding. Paul was in danger. Could he be wounded? Dead? *Pray, keep praying,* some outside force was urging me on. I formed a picture of Paul protected by an impenetrable shield. Throughout the night, I asked God to hold the shield in place.

Later, Paul wrote, "The night the ground war started, the strangest thing happened. With shrapnel flying all around us, suddenly, I felt that God had placed a shield around the men in my division. I looked around and told them, 'Don't worry, we're all going to be all right.' And we were. I could feel the shield in place all night long."

—PAM KIDD

PRAY: *Lord, thank You for this prompting to pray. Thank You for leading me by Your Spirit as I pray now.*

DO: Stop and pray further right now—and any time you feel that urgent prompting to pray.

When you feel helpless

◄○►

READ: *If God is for us, who can be against us?*

—ROMANS 8:31

REFLECT: One summer day our friends Ked and Diane Scheming invited us for halibut fishing aboard their boat *Morning Glory* in Alaska's Katchemak Bay. After several hours, I had caught one small halibut. But I remained undeterred.

When the big one struck, my rod bent clear to the water and I panicked. As I instinctively fought the halibut, Ked hollered, "No! Let him take the hook!" He then instructed me in a cardinal rule of fishing: *Let the pole do the work.* For twenty minutes I kept a rhythm going, drawing the tip of the rod slowly upward, keeping the line taut, and then cranking in the slack as the pole dipped back to the water. When I finally pulled my fish alongside the boat, I'd caught a fifty-five pounder!

Whatever your personal leviathan, try doing less resisting and allow God to do more assisting. In rhythm with Him, "let the Spirit do the work."

—CAROL KNAPP

PRAY: *Powerful God, thank You for my weakness. Help me to let go and let You do Your work in me.*

DO: Make a list of several areas where you've been giving God a hand and picture yourself putting the list in God's outstretched arms.

When you feel like complaining

―◦―

READ: *Oh, give thanks to the Lord, for He is good! For His mercy endures forever.*

―1 CHRONICLES 16:34

REFLECT: One day my pastor asked me to pick up an eighty-eight-year-old member who needed a ride to church from her nursing home. I dreaded the assignment because most of the elderly I knew were complainers.

But Ellen was different. As we drove to church, she told me how thankful she felt that she could walk with a cane. On our next trip, I discovered she played the piano for eight religious services at the home. She confided she was blind in one eye, but praised God for excellent vision in the other.

I introduced Ellen to some church shut-ins; her attitude was contagious. "Be thankful for what you have," she would say, "and what you don't have won't bother you so much."

Soon it was clear to me: complaining has less to do with age than with attitude.

―SAM JUSTICE

PRAY: *All too often, my focus is on what I don't have, Lord. Please forgive me and help me to focus on and be grateful for what I do have.*

DO: Ask your spouse or a friend if he/she sees you as a "half-full" or "half-empty" person. Give him/her permission to point out times when you're focusing on what you don't have instead of the good things in your life.

When you feel like giving up

◄○►

READ: *. . . Strengthened with all might, according to His glorious power, for all patience and longsuffering with joy. . . .*
—COLOSSIANS 1:11

REFLECT: When I was a college student I needed to catch the only train that would take me to Chicago. My sister's new baby was going to be christened the next day, and I was to be the godmother. I had made arrangements for a friend to drive me to the station, but I was running late! When we arrived, there was no train. "You missed it by about two minutes," the station mistress said. "But you could try to catch the train at the next stop."

"We'll never make it!" I said, frowning. "Let's try it," Ken said, heaving my bag up on his shoulder.

"Oh, Ken," I said, "it's hopeless. Why bother?" "Come on, Robin! I think we can do it." We arrived at the next station just as the train was pulling in! Before boarding, I turned to Ken. "Thanks for not giving up."

That lesson comes back to me often: Always try.

—ROBIN WHITE GOODE

PRAY: *I was about to give up, God, but now I'm going to persevere. Please remind me of those two words—* Always try—*the next time, and every time, I'm on the verge of giving up.*

DO: Share this reflection with a family member or friend and ask him/her to remind you of it when you're about to make the mistake of giving up.

When you feel like quitting your job

***

READ: *May the God of all grace, who called us to His eternal glory by Christ Jesus, after you have suffered a while, perfect, establish, strengthen, and settle you.*

—1 PETER 5:10

REFLECT: Mother always seemed to be able to bring out the best in me. For instance, there was my new job with the local newspaper. I loved the work, but one day I hit a snag. In tears, I went home and told Mother I was quitting. A competitive paper had scooped us on a fast-breaking story, and my superior blamed me, the cub reporter, when I had had nothing to do with it.

"All right," Mother said, "leave if you like. But why not wait awhile? If you hang on and make yourself really valuable, they'll be sorry to lose you."

This "make 'em sorry" idea appealed to me mightily, and I returned grimly to my job.

Months later I realized what Mother had been up to. She knew I'd be making a mistake to quit. So, instead of arguing, she had employed a little stratagem to keep a stubborn daughter on the right path. —MAY SHERIDAN GOLD

PRAY: *Father, I'm so hurt and frustrated that I want more than anything to quit. But I don't want to make a mistake. Please help me to do what's right and to leave my job for only the right reasons.*

DO: Write out this reflection and put it in an envelope dated six months from now. Open it when that day comes around, and if you still want to quit your job, maybe it's time.

***

When you feel that you've failed (1)

————◄○►————

READ: *For there is a time there for every purpose and for
every work.*
—ECCLESIASTES 3:17

REFLECT: One day I was deploring some of my missed opportunities, mistakes and blunders to my husband George—and
wondering why God would *let* me fail after I prayed and tried
so hard.

It was comforting to have George remind me, "Nobody's
perfect all the time, honey. Everybody misses. Babe Ruth
struck out more times than he hit. Yet he became world-
famous because he made so many home runs! In baseball,
you're considered good if you get three hits out of ten.

"Three prayers out of ten is a good average, and you've
had a lot more than that. Our failures sometimes actually
are opening the door for something a lot more important
later on."

George was right. And so was God. The things I was blaming myself for proved to be a blessing; God had something
better waiting for me when I was ready to receive.

—MARJORIE HOLMES

PRAY: *Thank You for the failures, Father, that keep me on
Your track for my life as much as the successes.*

DO: Meditate on the Cross for a few minutes—an apparent
failure that proved to be the greatest success story in history.

When you feel that you've failed (2)

◀◉▶

READ: *Our help is in the name of the Lord. . . .*

—PSALM 124:8

REFLECT: Someone said that maybe God engineers our failures because when we are defeated, we may be more receptive to Him and His plans for our lives. Frances J. Roberts writes in his book, *Make Haste My Beloved*, that God uses many vessels while they are still struggling with their failures.

Fascinated, I began to think of some of the people in the Bible who must have felt like failures: Joseph in that deep well; Daniel in the lion's den; Moses, who stuttered and yet was called upon to make speeches.

I looked up "failure" in my thesaurus: "unsuccessful, unfulfillment, forlorn hope, collapse, dud . . ." Not much to cheer about. I don't like the idea of being a failure—who does? And yet there is a magnificent opportunity in failure: it is simply our Lord's way of teaching us to listen to Him, to open ourselves to His help, to do things His way.

—MARION BOND WEST

PRAY: *God, I'm so glad that my feelings are not the defining factor in Your kingdom and that You specialize in turning what feels like failure into victory.*

DO: Make your own list of synonyms for failure, such as *opportunity, growth. . . .*

When you feel that you've failed (3)

◄○►

READ: *Each one has his own gift from God, one in this manner and another in that.*

—1 CORINTHIANS 7:7

REFLECT: Winston Churchill flunked qualifying exams three consecutive years when trying to enter Sandhurst, the military institution. In particular, he could not seem to grasp Latin, which is astonishing when one reads the books of this masterly practitioner of the English language. But then, Thomas Edison was once at the bottom of his class, Albert Einstein flunked math and was called "mentally slow," and Henry Ford was written off by one teacher as "a student who shows no promise."

Each of us has special God-given gifts, but sometimes we speak disparagingly of our gifts, viewing them as inferior to others' gifts.

Using the gift God has given you may be the portal through which you must pass before new opportunities are revealed. Performing your present duties well could be the key to finding an exciting new spiritual dimension in your life.

—FRED BAUER

PRAY: *Father, I've been guilty of coveting the gifts You've given others while disparaging the ones You've given me. Help me know what You've created me to do and give me opportunities to do it.*

DO: Pick a talent you haven't developed or have left behind. Look for a class to take or a group to join that will help you renew that interest and develop that skill.

When you feel that you've failed (4)

◄○►

READ: *Let us examine our ways and test them, and let us return to the Lord.*

—LAMENTATIONS 3:40 (NIV)

REFLECT: The first performance of Rossini's opera *The Barber of Seville* was a fiasco. Boos and hisses rose from the audience on the final curtain, and there was almost a riot. Backstage, the cast was terror-stricken.

Suddenly someone noticed that Rossini was missing. They rushed to his house and discovered that he was already in bed, sound asleep, and they woke him and gave him the dreadful news.

Rossini said: "Well, evidently *The Barber* isn't very good. I will have to do better next time. Now, if you don't mind, I'd like to go back to sleep." And he did.

"*The Barber*" came to be recognized as an operatic masterpiece and has remained so for nearly two hundred years —and Rossini never changed a note.

A failure of any kind can be a severe jolt, but the real setback in a failure is letting ourselves feel that we can't do anything else or anything better. —GLENN KITTLER

PRAY: *Dear Father, I want my definition of success or failure to come from You, not others' responses to my efforts.*

DO: Make up your mind to put this experience behind you, except to use it to advise someone else.

When you feel you've been attacked

READ: *I will give you a new heart and put a new spirit within you....*
—EZEKIEL 36:26

REFLECT: My husband's parents live in a lovely woodland where squirrels and rabbits scamper through their yard. You know what we have? *Lizards—dozens of them.* They scramble beneath our bushes and skitter across our fence, stopping to sun themselves on the warm concrete. They're not beautiful or cuddly-looking, but they are fun to watch. And they've taught me something.

When these resourceful little creatures are attacked, their tails actually break off, allowing them to escape. Some even have striped or brightly colored tails that entice their predators to attack this less vulnerable spot. Then the lizard immediately begins to grow a new tail, and can go through this routine an unlimited number of times.

I wish I could go as easily when I feel under attack.

I've learned a simple lesson from the lizard. *Let it go.* Let go of things and words that can hurt, and let God's love heal the broken places like new.

—GINA BRIDGEMAN

PRAY: *Father, I've been wounded many times before and thought my heart would never heal. But every time, it has—through Your forgiveness, Lord.*

DO: Wear or carry something with a heart on it today to remind you of God's healing touch.

When you feel you've disappointed God

———◀◉▶———

READ: *And the grace of our Lord was exceedingly abundant, with faith and love which are in Christ Jesus.*

—1 TIMOTHY 1:14

REFLECT: One Sunday I sat near a young mother and her three-year-old daughter Cindy, at church. As the service progressed, Cindy grew more and more restless. Finally, she pulled a hymnal from the rack and it slipped to the floor with a resounding thud. Immediately, Cindy received a slap on the hand from her embarrassed mother.

A long pause followed, then Cindy whispered in a choked voice, "M-Mommy, do you l-love me?"

The mother slipped her arm around Cindy and replied softly, "Of course I do. I just don't love what you're doing."

That's the same relationship I have with God, I thought. No matter how undeserving I am, He continues to pour His love and blessings upon me. I glanced at little Cindy's face, and the joy I saw there was reflected in my heart.

—RUTH HEANEY

PRAY: *Loving Father, I'm so grateful that You can love me even while not loving everything I do. Please make me able to extend that grace to others, especially my children.*

DO: Receive God's love as you work to correct the thing you feel is disappointing to Him. Express to your own children your love and acceptance of them, especially during their worst moments.

When you have a case of the "if onlys"

◄○►

READ: *I have learned to be content whatever the circumstances.*

—PHILIPPIANS 4:11 (NIV)

REFLECT: When I was young a carload of us traveled one night to hear a colorful preacher, Gypsy Smith, who was holding evangelistic meetings in a nearby town. That night he told of a woman who came up to him after one of his services and said, "Gypsy, I feel the Lord is calling me to preach—if only I didn't have these ten children!"

"Why, that's wonderful, sister," Gypsy replied, "the Lord is calling you to preach, and He's given you your own congregation. Now go home and preach to them!"

That story has served as a little warning signal for me. Whenever I get an attack of the "if onlys"—if only I weren't tied down to the house; if only I had more talent—then I'm reminded to get on with the business of the Lord. He's given me my own "congregation" that nobody else could serve as well.

—THELMA BRISBINE

PRAY: *Lord, I choose today to be content with what You've given me to do and the skills You've given me to do it.*

DO: Thank a friend or coworker for the way he/she has touched your life by using what he/she may consider to be insignificant gifts or talents.

When you have a dream

◄○►

READ: *So also is the resurrection of the dead. The body is sown in corruption, it is raised in incorruption. It is sown in dishonor, it is raised in glory.*

—1 CORINTHIANS 15:42–43

REFLECT: When I was growing up, my mother always gave each of us six children a present on Easter Sunday.

One year she gave me a set of children's garden tools—a miniature rake, a pint-sized hoe, and a small shovel. From my first chop of the hoe, I was hooked on gardening. With every seed I sow, my hope grows richer and my spirits brighter. The flowers and vegetables that burst forth from the earth are a kind of spiritual lesson in my own backyard.

Perhaps you have some unfulfilled dreams that sit in the back of your mind. Today may be the time to "plant the seeds" so that God can help you realize your dreams. Write down one or two things that you would like to accomplish. Just the act of writing them down is like sowing a seed. Watch carefully to see what opportunities God brings into your life.

—DANIEL SCHANTZ

PRAY: *I'm waiting for You, Lord, to show me which dream to pursue.*

DO: Do just what this reflection suggests: write down one of your dreams and watch for opportunities to begin fulfilling it.

When you have a grumpy coworker

READ: *Be tenderhearted, be courteous; not returning evil for evil or reviling for reviling, but on the contrary blessing, knowing that you were called to this, that you may inherit a blessing.*

—1 PETER 3:8, 9

REFLECT: She works in an office down the hall from mine. She ignores my "good mornings" and stares coldly at my smiles.

"I have spoken to her for the last time," I declared to my friend Ethel. "I will ignore her the same way she does me."

"You're foolish if you do that," Ethel said. "The woman may have all sorts of things on her mind, troubles you never dreamed of."

"No," I was adamant. "I think she's just hateful."

"Then she has a real problem. Why develop one of your own over it? Don't you think it would be better for you to pray about it rather than pout?" Ethel was right, of course, and I started including the woman in my prayers.

Things seem a little better; I think she almost smiled today. The big improvement, though, has been in me.

—DRUE DUKE

PRAY: *Lord, I pray for _____. Forgive me for judging him/her. Only You know what may be causing her to be so unhappy. If there's only one ray of sunshine in her life, Lord, let it be Your light shining through me.*

DO: Look for an appropriate moment to express your concern and acceptance of your coworker just the way he/she is—not when or if he/she becomes a beacon of sunshine herself.

When you have a negative attitude

◄◦►

READ: *Her ways are ways of pleasantness, and all her paths are peace.*

—PROVERBS 3:17

REFLECT: I used to always expect the worst. If I took a test, I'd say, "I'm sure I failed," If I misplaced my keys, I said, "I'll bet they're gone forever." But one day, a friend startled me by saying, "Stop it! You're such a pessimist!"

My feelings were hurt, I'll admit, but I shot back, "I don't consider myself a pessimist. I consider myself a realist."

She looked me in the eye and said, "Linda, that's what an optimist considers herself too!" She then reminded me of Pollyanna, who found something to smile about in even the most harrowing of circumstances. "Just try it," my friend coaxed.

I couldn't resist the challenge. "I'll bet I did well on that test!" I felt like I was boasting. But I had made that promise. "I'm sure I'll like this movie." To my surprise, two friends soon said, "You're so much more pleasant to be around."

I smiled, "Just call me Pollylinda."   —LINDA NEUKRUG

PRAY: *Father, I'm sorry that I am so guilty of this. I'd really like to be different, but the negative just seems to come out of my mouth first. Help my words leave people with a positive feeling instead of a negative one.*

DO: Make renewing your mind, not willpower, the first approach to a more positive outlook. Pick several Scriptures on renewing the mind to memorize until they become truth for you.

When you have to learn a new skill

READ: *I applied my heart to what I observed and learned a lesson from what I saw. . . .*

—PROVERBS 24:32 (NIV)

REFLECT: I knew I should be ready to make my first solo flight. I had all the maneuvers; all I had to do was follow Gary's instructions. He gave me step-by-step directions all the way to a good landing and then said, "Give it the power." And we were off again for another circuit.

However, with each circuit, Gary's instructions became less frequent. When finally 1 looked at him inquiringly, he burst out, "Why don't you fly like you know how to? Do I have to tell you everything over and over again?"

I was shocked. I had felt so comfortable just following his instructions. But he was right. The next three touch-and-gos I did without a word from Gary. And I did the following three without Gary in the plane. It was a simple lesson, but learning to take responsibility to do the things I know how to do is a lesson that never goes out of date.

—BRIAN MILLER

PRAY: *Father, I'm guilty of having to be told again and again about spiritual lessons I learned years ago. I want to grow up, Lord, to take responsibility for the things I know how to do without having to be repeatedly told. Thank You for this great lesson that will help as I learn this new skill too.*

DO: Look for ways to incorporate this principle into other areas of your life and the lives of your children.

When you have to let go

---◀◦▶---

READ: *No one sews a piece of unshrunk cloth on an old garment; or else the new piece pulls away from the old, and the tear is made worse.*

—MARK 2:21

REFLECT: Each of us looked forward to my Irish grandmother Clara's annual weekend rite of spring-cleaning. The first time I helped, I found it unsettling—I'd never encountered anyone with so much to give or throw away.

"But that's perfectly good!" I would protest. When Grandmother realized I was in real distress, she called a story break.

"There was this thriving little town in Ireland that the local folk wanted to see grow, so they decided to build a new town hall. But the town fathers decreed that it had to be built on the same site and of the same material as the old town hall. And the old town hall had to be kept in use until the new one was completed. And so," she said sadly, "the little town never grew.

"What I'm doing today, Elaine, is making way for the new. New growth starts when you let go of the old."

—ELAINE ST. JOHNS

PRAY: *God, there's an awful lot of "old" stuff in my heart— old hurts, old thoughts, old dreams. I give them to You now, Lord, and trust You to replace them with new healing, new thoughts, new dreams.*

DO: Take a mental inventory and toss out things from the past that are getting in the way of new things God may have in store for you.

When you have to put aside your own preferences

---<o>---

READ: *Love . . . does not seek its own. . . .*

—1 CORINTHIANS 13:4–5

REFLECT: All week long, my husband and I had been like ships passing in the night. Saturday afternoon, we helped friends move, arriving home hot and grimy. We put the kids to bed. Then Mike, turning the TV on to a movie, asked, "Mind if I watch this?" in a voice that implied wistfully, "Care to join me?"

"It doesn't matter to me," I said, ignoring the unspoken invitation. "I'm going to take a shower."

After my shower, I luxuriated in the thought of stretching out with a book I was eager to finish. But I couldn't shake the image I'd seen at a marriage retreat, a banner stressing commitment over personal preferences. The words read, "Love is a decision."

I padded back downstairs and squeezed beside Michael in our oversized "big for one, cramped for two" chair. He gave me a surprised smile. And we watched the movie together, two ships anchored contentedly side by side.

—B. J. CONNOR

PRAY: *I only have to open my Bible to find an example of the ultimate laying down of one's own desire. Let me be motivated by Your example, Lord Jesus, every day.*

DO: When you have to make a choice between your preference and a loved one's, do what Jesus did—He thought of the joy set before Him. Think of the joy you'll bring to someone you love.

When you haven't had time for God

◄○►

READ: *Jesus went out to a mountainside to pray, and spent the night praying to God.*

—LUKE 6:12 (NIV)

REFLECT: My friend Martha was telling me why her six-year-old son wanted to give up piano lessons so soon after he'd started. "He said he just doesn't have time to practice every day."

"How long did his teacher ask him to practice?" I asked.

"Fifteen minutes!"

We laughed at the idea of a little boy too busy to practice the piano a mere fifteen minutes a day. What on earth could he have to do that was so important?

But later I began to wonder. Does God also laugh—but sadly—at me when I think I don't have fifteen minutes to give to Him every day? What else do I have to do that is so important?

—PATRICIA HOUCK SPRINKLE

PRAY: *Father, nothing I need to do is more important than spending time with You. Please make it something in my heart that I want to do more than anything else, not something I have to do.*

DO: Lay this book aside and pick up your Bible. Use your concordance to find a passage that expresses your love for God in a meaningful way.

When you just
don't understand

READ: *"The wind blows where it wishes, and you hear the sound of it, but cannot tell where it comes from and where it goes. So is everyone who is born of the Spirit."*

—JOHN 3:8

REFLECT: The letter was addressed to the General Electric Company from a little girl in third grade who had chosen to investigate electricity for her class project. "I'm trying to get all the information I can," her letter ran, "so please send me any booklets and papers you have. Also, would it be asking too much for you to send me a little sample of electricity?"

When I heard about her innocent letter I laughed. Yet, maybe I was laughing at myself as well. For how many times have I wanted concrete examples of the great mysteries? How many times have I asked God to give me tangible proof that He is there?

I think that what that young girl and I need to learn is that there are some mysteries in this life that we must accept—it is the mystery that is their glory.

—JAMES MCDERMOTT

PRAY: *Of all life's mysteries that I'll never fully understand, God, You are at the top of the list. Instead of trying to understand, let me just enjoy the wonder of You.*

DO: Take a walk and look at the stars in the night sky; examine the intricacies of a flower; marvel at a newborn baby . . . and worship the God you can't begin to understand.

When you lack vision

READ: *We do not know what we ought to pray for. . . .*
—ROMANS 8:26 (NIV)

REFLECT: My grandma would take me down to Manhasset Bay on Long Island's North Shore to admire the sleek sailboats moored there. She could tell me where the more distinctive ones had been built, who owned them and which races they had won.

"Grandma," I would say, "do you think I might get a boat like one of these some day?"

"Which one?" she would ask.

"Oh, something like that." I would point to a modest sixteen-footer.

"Your boat will be much nicer than that!" she would say. "Let's pick out a more exciting one for you."

So we would, and had a wonderful time planning how we'd fit it out, where we'd sail it, whom we'd invite aboard.

Whenever I set my sights a bit higher, I've found that I reach goals that once seemed beyond me. Grandma knew that God builds into each of us greater capacities than most of us ever dare to use.

—JAMES MCDERMOTT

PRAY: *I know I've lacked vision, Father, and have failed to instill it in my child/children. Is it too late to start now, Lord? Would You help me be a person who believes You for the unbelievable?*

DO: Ask your child what he/she dreams about, something short-term he/she would like to accomplish. Set some goals and work together to get there.

When you need a break

READ: *In His great mercy He has given us new birth into a living hope....*

—1 PETER 1:3 (NIV)

REFLECT: After fifteen years as a college teacher, I was burned out and decided to take a year off.

I slept the summer away, but I was forced to wake up by fall. My six-year-old was starting first grade, the Sunday school superintendent roped me into leading the high school discussion group, and my thirteen-year-old began a big project on the Revolutionary War....

All of a sudden, my mind was afire! I was making up rhyming games, I dreamed up an Old Testament board game for the teenagers at church and I was haunting hobby shops for a miniature cannon for a model of the Surrender of Yorktown.

Renewal can come in small ways: Change your routine, claim solid resting time, get up a half hour early to look at the sun.

And you will feel the energy flow back in.

—LINDA CHING SLEDGE

PRAY: *I'm sure there are many like me, Lord, who just need a break from the everyday pressures of life. I pray that You will provide refreshment for each one—and for me.*

DO: Call a few friends who need a break and suggest a get-together soon, just to relax and visit.

When you need a friend

READ: *Let everyone call urgently on God.*

—JONAH 3:8 (NIV)

REFLECT: Hurriedly I opened the desk drawer where I keep my address book. And then I remembered—I had loaned it to a friend who wanted to update her phone list.

I felt a sense of panic. The little book contained my list of prayer warriors, and I urgently needed to talk with someone who understood and loved me.

I must talk to someone, I thought, near tears.

As I stared at the telephone, my eyes fell on my Bible on the table. Very gently the suggestion came: *Why not talk to Me about the problem? I understand you. I love you. I really care.*

I picked up God's Word and we had a long conversation. He gave me His undivided attention and the answer I so sorely needed. Later, I was glad that my address book had been out on loan—for I learned that I need never again wonder Whom to call in my need. —MARION BOND WEST

PRAY: *Father, when I need comfort, remind me that I can always turn to You.*

DO: Go ahead and call a friend—*after* you've talked to God about your problem.

When you need a good cry (1)

READ: ... *A time to heal.* ...

—ECCLESIASTES 3:3

REFLECT: After eight hours in the emergency room with a broken hand, my fifteen-year-old son was at the end of his rope. At home, as I slowly tried to elevate his arm with pillows, Phillip was holding his breath, squeezing his eyes shut. "Do you need to cry?" I asked.

A long breath escaped, full of tears.

"Oh, Phillip! Cry! Tears bring healing. It's the body's way of working through the pain!"

I was thinking of all the tears I'd shed over the trials of being a single mother—as if I'd somehow failed *because* I'd cried.

An hour later Phillip was asleep, arm at last propped up, pain under control. As I climbed into bed that night, I promised myself that never again would I pinch my eyes shut and hold my breath in pain. I'd let the tears fall freely and then thank God for His intervening touch—and healing tears.

—BRENDA WILBEE

PRAY: *I need a good cry right now, Jesus. I'm glad that's okay with You and that You can even use my tears to heal the hurt.*

DO: Don't hide your tears from your loved ones. Maybe it will give them permission to let the tears flow when they are hurting.

When you need a good cry (2)

READ: *You number my wanderings; put my tears into Your bottle; are they not in Your book?*

—PSALM 56:8

REFLECT: Emily was a pretty little seven-year-old girl when I first met her. Her parents had moved halfway across the country, and Emily was missing her hometown. I saw her standing in the hallway of our church one day, looking very sad.

"Emily," I asked, "where did you move from?"

"From Missouri," she replied with a shy smile.

"Well, where in Missouri?" I persisted.

For a moment Emily stared at the floor. Then, looking at me with twinkling eyes, she said, "I know exactly where. I found it on my map last night. I can always find it easy 'cause I stained a tear on it."

Now, her words still ring in my head. All things we hold dear in this life—friendship, family, places we love—are marked at one time or another by our tears. The map of our lives without their stains would be devoid of richness and meaning.

—SCOTT WALKER

PRAY: *Thank You, Father, for helping me see that tears are not a weakness, but a marker of the meaningful things in our lives.*

DO: Go somewhere where you can be alone and cry until you have no more tears to cry.

When you need a good laugh

READ: *A merry heart makes a cheerful countenance....*

—PROVERBS 15:13

REFLECT: "Knock-knock." "Who's there?" "Wanda." "Wanda who?"

"Wanda who thinks up these dumb jokes?"

The girls broke into giggles, doubling up on their bunks and kicking their bare feet in glee. It was "laugh night" in my cabin. We had progressed (regressed?) from riddles to nonsense rhymes to knock-knocks.

Long after the girls were asleep, I lay awake, remembering the laughter-lit eyes of those children. What a catharsis it had been. Homesickness vanished, hurt feelings healed, tired spirits rallied. And I realized how seldom I applied this "medicine" to my own life.

I'm going to laugh more. At silly movies. With old friends. With people who jostle me on the way to work. Why, I'll even laugh at myself.

"Knock-knock." "Who's there?" "Noah." "Noah who?"

Noah lot of reasons to laugh!
—MARY LOU CARNEY

PRAY: *Father, I guess I'm too serious sometimes. Give me a happy heart, please Lord, and help me pass on a little happiness.*

DO: Give yourself a good dose of laughter medicine. Watch your favorite funny movie or read a good joke book. Share the laughter by reading a few jokes to your family or coworkers.

When you need
a pick-me-up

READ: *A merry heart does good, like medicine. . . .*

—PROVERBS 17:22

REFLECT: When I'm feeling a little depressed, I get out my "Special Feel Good File." It contains a number of items almost guaranteed to raise my spirits. Here are a few of them:

Several cartoons—some I've cut out and some I've created.

Two laugh-out-loud articles.

Bible verses that attest to God's love: 1 John 4, Psalm 103, John 14.

Three letters from friends that make me feel worthwhile.

Valentines from my husband.

There's more, but you get the picture.

My special file contains anything that forces me to smile or that reminds me I am appreciated. But when I'm really down, I get the most lasting benefit from reading again that God loves me, no matter what, and that nothing can separate me from His love (Romans 8:38–39).

—KATHIE KANIA

PRAY: *For myself and others who are feeling down, Father, I ask for a little humor in our lives today. Anything to cause a smile or a big belly laugh would be so good. And make it something contagious that our loved ones can catch.*

DO: Make a "Feel Good File" of your own.

When you need a reminder of God's love

────────◄○►────────

READ: *Yes, I have loved you with an everlasting love....*

—JEREMIAH 31:3

REFLECT: Whenever I back out of my driveway, the words *I LOVE YOU* appear in the rear window of my car in bold, white letters. Actually, the words are chalked on the back of our neighbor's brick garage. A teenaged girl put them there, hoping her boyfriend would see them.

Most of the time I don't even notice the words, but sometimes they seem to glow like a message from God, written with an angel's hand.

When I am angry, the message reads, "I LOVE YOU." When I am torn with guilt, the words are, "I LOVE YOU." When I am terrified of the future, He whispers, "I LOVE YOU."

Those three words have taught me a lesson about the unconditional love of God. No, God does not love all the things I do, and He would like me to change. But *always He loves me*, no matter what.

—DANIEL SCHANTZ

PRAY: *I know You love me, Father. Thank You for telling me every day in so many ways.*

DO: Even though your friends and family know you love them, it always feels good to be reminded. Say it often.

When you need a rest

◄○►

READ: *He rested on the seventh day from all His work which He had done.*

—GENESIS 2:2

REFLECT: Exercise . . . how I hated it! You see, when I first began my daily exercise routine, I knew nothing about pacing myself. I'd dive right into my hour-long aerobic routine, painfully moving through each exercise without even pausing to catch my breath.

One day, as I relentlessly jogged and jumped, I was reminded of an exercise we'd done in my freshman psychology course. We found that those who provided themselves with rest periods during a learning experience achieved higher levels of success in the end. And so I began to rest at intervals in my aerobic routine and, indeed, enjoyed better results in the end. I was less exhausted and enjoyed myself more!

God rested on the seventh day. As for me, I'm looking for more areas in my life where I could "use a little rest."

—TAMMY RIDER

PRAY: *Father, my need for rest goes way beyond a leisurely evening or a day off. I need rest from myself, from the drivenness that won't let me say no. Would You help me with it, Lord?*

DO: Give yourself permission to rest, to say no to a few things that you really don't want to do and maybe even to some that you'd love to do.

When you need
a spiritual boost

$\longleftarrow\mathbf{\blacktriangleleft\diamond\blacktriangleright}\longrightarrow$

READ: *"Thus says the Lord: 'Set your house in order....'"*

—ISAIAH 38:1

REFLECT: I heard a story about a youth who was hired as a farmhand. He gave as one of his qualifications, "I can sleep when the wind blows."

The farmer wasn't sure what that meant, but he liked the boy and hired him. One night a dreadful storm arose and the farmer and his wife ran around frantically checking on everything, only to find that the shutters and doors were all fastened, the animals calm and secure.

Then the farmer knew what the boy meant. He had done his work faithfully. He had no need to worry when the storm came. He was *prepared.*

I have to apply this principle to my spiritual life too. To be able to face each day serenely, I find I must pray, read and commit Scripture to memory, and help others. These are the things that help me sleep when the wind blows.

—RUTH DINKINS ROWAN

PRAY: *Lord, I'm concerned about being prepared for the spiritual winds that blow. But even a bad day at the office or a day with fussy kids can throw me off kilter. If I'm prepared with Your Presence within, the storms can pass without damage.*

DO: Memorize three Scriptures this week to prepare yourself for the winds that blow.

When you need comfort (1)

READ: *God is our refuge and strength, a very present help in trouble.*

—PSALM 46:1

REFLECT: My daughter was visiting me when her three-month-old baby developed a case of colic. Nothing gave the infant relief until I walked the floor with her, back and forth, holding her paining little tummy close against me. Far into the night she and I kept our tryst, until the hurting was over and she slept quietly in my arms.

For several days following the attack, she clung to me, spurning the efforts of anyone else to hold her. She had found relief from her suffering, had known peace and security in my arms. And she meant to stay with the source of those good feelings.

I know that I, too, have such a refuge. So do you. I can take my pains and problems to the bosom of Jesus to find relief. You can too. I can cling to Him after the hurting is over. So can you.

—DRUE DUKE

PRAY: *Lord, I feel like a bundle of pain right now. Hold me, Lord, when it hurts. And hold me, Lord, when it stops hurting.*

DO: Call a new mother you know and offer to keep the baby for the evening.

When you need comfort (2)

READ: *Rest in the Lord, and wait patiently for Him. . . .*

—PSALM 37:7

REFLECT: My husband John once "heard" a message for our friend Jim: *Do not condemn yourself. Rest in the love of your heavenly Father.*

We stared at each other. What could that possibly mean to Jim? As far as we knew he was still happily married, still doing well at work. Nevertheless, John wrote the words down in our prayer log. And there they remained, month after month. "Call him. Tell him," I'd urge. "If it doesn't make sense, no harm done."

It was three full years before John announced, "I wrote Jim today. Passed on that message."

Jim phoned three days later to tell us he'd been in a near-suicidal depression following the death of his father, from whom he'd become estranged. And what meant the most in John's letter? The fact that "God knew three years ago what I'd be going through today." That "so long ago He was setting His help in motion."

—ELIZABETH SHERRILL

PRAY: *Lord, You knew long ago that I would need comfort today. Thank You for reminding me, when I need You most, of Your involvement in my life and of Your perfect timing.*

DO: Write a note of encouragement to someone you know is discouraged today.

When you need God the Father

◄○►

READ: *And by Him we cry, "Abba, Father." The Spirit himself testifies with our spirit that we are God's children.*

—ROMANS 8:15-16 (NIV)

REFLECT: I discovered that *abba* is one of the few Aramaic words known to have been actually spoken by Jesus Christ. That Jesus addressed God directly at all must have been shocking to His Jewish contemporaries, who held the name of the Lord so sacred and awesome as to be unspeakable. To use the word *abba* in speaking to God, as Jesus did, was unthinkable.

Abba is the familiar term used by Jewish sons and daughters in addressing their father, corresponding more to "daddy" than to the more formal "father." In addressing God as Abba, therefore, Jesus not only claimed His Sonship with God, but also did so in the most intimate way! As children in Christ, it is our wonderful privilege—and obligation—to follow His example. —KATHRYN BRINCKERHOFF

PRAY: *Abba! Abba! What an awesome thing it is that the sound of that delights You!*

DO: Find a Bible dictionary or concordance and look up *abba.* Meditate on what a privilege it is to call God *Abba.*

When you need guidance

READ: *For we walk by faith, not by sight.*

—2 CORINTHIANS 5:7

REFLECT: A man went on a safari in Africa. Naturally, he hired a guide, and for a while he followed the native without question. But when the guide tried to lead the stranger into the vine-thick jungle he balked. "There is no path, no road, no way," the man protested. The guide replied, "There is no road. I am the way!"

As long as we can see our path ahead clearly, faith, for many, is a spare tire. While it's nice to know it's there, we don't really think much about it. But when we come to a place in our lives where we can't see our way—and make no mistake about it, all of us sooner or later will reach such a crossroad of confusion—we will need a trustworthy guide. For Christians, Jesus Christ is not only the Way-shower, but the Way—the Way, the Truth and the Life.   —FRED BAUER

PRAY: *Okay, Lord Jesus, I understand. I don't need to know the road. I just need to follow You each day.*

DO: Talk to an older, respected friend who shares your faith. Ask him/her how Jesus can be your Way, your Truth, your Life every day.

When you need help

---◆◇◆---

READ: *Ask and you will receive, that your joy may be full.*

—JOHN 16:24

REFLECT: For twelve years I was in charge of our yearly Trash and Treasure sale. All year I stored donations in my basement. I would sort, organize, and clean them, and then get them to the church. Every year our Trash and Treasure was a big success, and I was very proud of being in charge of it.

Then, I lifted a heavy box and my back caved in. In the hospital, the surgeon said, "Your box-lifting days are over, my friend!"

Reluctantly, hating to give up my pet project, I asked the congregation for assistance and got an overwhelming response.

People delivered their possessions to the church instead of my basement. Others washed, cleaned and arranged the items. My wife Ruby priced each one.

Accepting help was new to me; but on the proud faces of the helpers, I saw the joy it brought to them too. Asking for help opened doors—a new exchange of gifts.

—OSCAR GREENE

PRAY: *Father, I confess my pride in wanting to do it all myself. Thank You for showing me the joy in a project shared.*

DO: Do yourself—and a friend—a favor. Call and ask for help.

When you need help but can't bring yourself to ask for it

◄○►

READ: *And in the church God has appointed . . . those able to help others. . . .*

—1 CORINTHIANS 12:28 (NIV)

REFLECT: One of my babies had colic for three months. Since she cried most of the time for those weeks, I could get no rest. I dragged myself through long days and nights. Finally, I scarcely knew what I was doing. Then two friends came to me, beaming with happiness at their planned surprise.

They proposed to take care of the baby at night for a while so that I could get some sleep.

"Oh, I couldn't let you do that!" I protested. "It's so much work!" I saw all the glad light die in their eyes. They looked so dejected, so disappointed.

"I really do need your help so much!" I confessed, relenting. "Please do help me." And they did. They really enjoyed those long, dark hours they had the baby, and cared for her with love and tenderness. Their joy was beautiful to see—the joy my pride had nearly robbed them of.

—LUCILLE CAMPBELL

PRAY: *Father, thank You for the friends You've given me who would find great joy in helping me through this time. Please give me the courage to accept their help gratefully.*

DO: Resolve that the next time a friend asks, "Is there something I can do to help you?" you'll say, "Sure!"

When you need patience

❮o❯

READ: *For you have need of endurance, so that after you have done the will of God, you may receive the promise. . . .*
—HEBREWS 10:36

REFLECT: Our refrigerator serves as the family communications center, a huge magnetic bulletin board for vital messages and schedules. That's where I tape cards with inspirational quotes or Scripture aimed at changing my life, or the life of another family member.

I once added a card with only four large letters: "W-A-I-T." A simple word, but a powerful reminder that I need to work on my patience. Often, I am like the impulsive, overzealous Peter who jumped up and sliced the ear off an unsuspecting guard on the night Jesus was arrested at Gethsemane.

I, too, overreact. I am defensive. I get angry. I snap or say something sarcastic. These immediate responses are my instinctive human reactions. Yet, if I remember to W-A-I-T a few seconds or maybe even a few hours, I give the Holy Spirit a chance to work inside me, aligning my self-will with His will. If I W-A-I-T, I am less impulsive and more obedient.

—CAROL KUYKENDALL

PRAY: *Holy Spirit, as hard as it is, I will W-A-I-T, and as I do, will You align my self-will with Your will? Quickly, please, Lord!*

DO: Tape a card with the big letters W-A-I-T on your refrigerator or mirror.

When you need refreshment

READ: *He restores my soul. . . .*

—PSALM 23:3

REFLECT: Years ago my husband Ken and I started going to the country on his day off. Since he had a busy schedule, I knew that he needed a place and time to get away. But I had not realized how much I needed it too.

Waking up to the quail's "bobwhite" calls, sitting on the porch swing, watching the sunset or listening to the rain on the tin roof was restorative. There's something in the rhythm of nature that's healing. We'd return to the city refreshed and better able to do our work.

Taking time apart helps my mind, body and soul to get back into harmony. I find renewed energy for hosting dinners, for being more patient with loved ones and in working on church responsibilities. It puts a song in my heart and on my lips: "God is so good. He's so good to me."

What restores your soul?

—BARBARA CHAFIN

PRAY: *Nothing restores my soul like You, Lord. But certain places help me enter into Your presence. I need Your help to get to one of those places soon, Lord!*

DO: Find a quiet place—a special room, a backyard garden or a favorite chair—that restores your soul. God is waiting for you there.

When you need self-discipline

◄○►

READ: *"Please inquire for the word of the Lord today."*

—1 KINGS 22:5

REFLECT: Our Community Adult Education program was offering a class in self-improvement. Well, I decided, after giving thought to my haphazard and undisciplined ways, I certainly can stand a bit of that. And so I enrolled, hoping for some bit of modern-day magic, some simple method of self-programming, to help me shape up.

And you know what I read in my notebook after I came home from the first class? "For as a man thinketh in his heart so is he" (Proverbs 23:7). "As ye sow, so shall ye reap" (Galatians 6:7). "Love your neighbor as yourself" (Matthew 19:19). All of this "new" miraculous advice I received was right there in my own Bible!

No wonder that Book, written so long ago, is still the world's bestseller. If I want to shape up, I don't need a fancy class or program—I can just open my Bible.

—ALETHA JANE LINDSTROM

PRAY: *I've been trying to work up the willpower to get into shape, Lord, but it's not happening. If You'll be my Coach, I'll follow Your instructions, starting with what I already know Your Word says to do.*

DO: Remember that you can't—and don't need to—change everything at once. Read your Bible. Let the light of God's Word direct your self-improvement path.

When you need some emotional and spiritual remodeling

---◄○►---

READ: *"For I am the Lord who heals you."*

—EXODUS 15:26

REFLECT: "Ugh!"

That was all I could say when the real estate agent led me into the cottage. Paint had peeled from the walls, the floors were water-stained, the woodwork was nicked and scarred.

"Of course, the owner will fix it up," the agent assured me. "He really loves this place."

Well, I needed a house in a hurry and I agreed to rent it. But I had my doubts.

When I returned a month later, ready to move in, I was astonished. The owner had gone over it from top to bottom, sanding the floors, scraping the walls before he painted them, filling in all the scars in the woodwork. His loving care was evident in every room.

As I stood there marveling, I realized how much damage a loving person can undo. This is how our Heavenly Father works. With great care, He repairs the neglect and hurt we may have suffered . . . and makes us whole again.

—PHYLLIS HOBE

PRAY: *Thank You so much, God, for cleaning me up, inside and out, with Your power and loving care.*

DO: Think of someone you can take to the Master Builder/ Remodeler. Invest some time and love in this person and watch what God can do.

When you need someone who understands

————◄○►————

READ: *We took sweet counsel together. . . .*

—PSALM 55:14

REFLECT: The wounds my friend Don received in Vietnam went deep. Physically, he recovered a few months after he returned home. But spiritually, the pain got worse.

"People expected me to get on with my life and forget what I had seen," Don said. He did the best he could. But his memories seemed more real than his everyday life, and no one wanted to hear about them.

Don's life changed when he began to meet with other Vietnam veterans. He was able to open up and let out his bitterness. They responded with equal honesty. As these men and women realized that someone else felt the same kind of pain, the wounds of the past began to heal.

"Everyone has a Vietnam," Don said. "Everyone knows what it is to suffer. The important thing is to realize that someone understands you."

It isn't easy to share each other's pain. But it's strong medicine—and it works.

—PHYLLIS HOBE

PRAY: *Father, I feel like I'm alone in a spiritual battle. Would You send someone my way who understands? Until that help comes, rather than seeking to be understood, Lord, help me be someone who seeks to understand.*

DO: Find several Scriptures to remind you that God understands your situation.

When you need to feel loved

READ: *Satisfy us in the morning with your unfailing love, that we may sing for joy and be glad all our days.*

—PSALM 90:14 (NIV)

REFLECT: One Sunday morning, as I checked out library books in the hallway of our Sunday-school building, I felt an arm encircle me from behind. I turned and looked into the kind eyes of Mrs. Havener, an elderly member of our church. "I just love you," she said, pressing her cheek to mine. Then she was gone, down the hall to her class.

A warm glow enveloped me from my head to my toes, even as I stared after her, puzzled by her action. I'd done nothing to solicit her love, nor had she asked anything of me in return. I had only to accept her free gift. It made my whole day. And then I could not rest until I'd given it away to someone else.

Christ's love is like that—unsolicited and freely given. He loved you and me enough to die for us. He asked only that we accept His love to have eternal life.

—BETTY RUTH GRAHAM

PRAY: *Thank You so much, Father, for people who can express love so freely. Make me one of them, please, Lord.*

DO: Be daring and look for a chance to express your love to an unsuspecting friend!

When you need to forgive

READ: *"For I will forgive their iniquity, and their sin I will remember no more."*

—JEREMIAH 31:34

REFLECT: Cindy and I were strolling in the botanical gardens with her small daughter. "Mommy, look! There's Marie!" her daughter said, running ahead to meet another friend of ours who happened to be in the gardens too.

I knew Marie had said some hurtful things about Cindy in the past. But as the two of them exchanged hellos, there seemed to be no animosity. Later I remarked to Cindy, "You were so pleasant. I was surprised."

Cindy said, "Long ago I realized that I had two choices when someone says something that hurts me." She stooped down and picked up a rock from the garden. "I can pick up a rock and carry it with me for the rest of my days—but I've discovered it will get heavier and heavier as time goes on. Or," she said, picking up a pebble from the gravel path, "I can do this." And she tossed it back onto the path.

—LINDA NEUKRUG

PRAY: *Father, I have more than one rock that's become heavier and heavier through the years. I'll just get rid of all of them right now. Here, Lord, would You take them, please?*

DO: Go outside, pick up a couple of good-sized rocks and throw them—hard.

When you need to forgive...
or be forgiven

◄○►

READ: *"I beg you, please forgive the trespass of your brothers and their sin. . . ."*

—GENESIS 50:17

REFLECT: A truck driver had caused a serious accident in Louisville, Kentucky. The driver not only pleaded guilty, but also told the judge, "I'm truly sorry for what happened."

In court were the parents of two girls killed in the crash. They told of months of agony, grief and anger. Then Walter Queen, the girls' father, spoke directly to the driver. "Today," he said, "I want to express publicly that we forgive you. My wife and I are not angry at you. We do not hate you. I encourage you to seek God's forgiveness and make a new life for yourself." The driver responded with tears, as did many of the spectators in the courtroom.

I have never been called on to forgive in such tragic circumstances. But I pray that whatever situations arise in my life, great or small, God's grace will be the key to my response.

—BARBARA CHAFIN

PRAY: *I pray that any occasion I may have to forgive or be forgiven will be from much less painful circumstances than those in this story, Lord. But when I do need to forgive—or be forgiven—it will require no less measure of Your grace. Thank You for it in advance.*

DO: Use this reflection as a first step toward reconciliation by sharing it with the person you need to forgive or who needs to forgive you.

When you need to lighten up

◀◎▶

READ: *He will yet fill your mouth with laughing, and your lips with rejoicing.*

—JOB 8:21

REFLECT: When I first began teaching high school, I was terrified I'd do a poor job. I feared that the kids would hate me and my principal would be disappointed in me. "Don't smile until Thanksgiving," one education professor had said. So I didn't. Or at least I tried not to. I pretended to be severe and all-knowing—and all of my worst fears began coming true. The kids did hate me.

One day in class, as I reached for a stack of tests, I thought I saw something moving in the papers. Carefully, I lifted the top sheets to reveal a hermit crab wriggling its way across the page. Instantly, I laughed. And everyone else did too. It was the beginning of much shared laughter—and knowledge—in my classroom.

Laughing at myself often helps me keep other people's foibles in perspective. And that's a lesson everyone needs to learn!

—MARY LOU CARNEY

PRAY: *I realize I've been taking myself, and life, way too seriously, Lord. Help me lighten up, starting today.*

DO: Stop at a local video store and rent a good comedy. Invite a friend who could use a good laugh to join you.

When you need to pray

◄○►

READ: *But we all, with unveiled face, beholding as in a mirror the glory of the Lord, are being transformed into the same image from glory to glory....*

—2 CORINTHIANS 3:18

REFLECT: My wife Carol and I were hiking in the High Sierras on a crystal clear day along a trail bordering a fast-rushing stream lined with ferns, rust-colored Indian paintbrush, purple lupine. At the top, we reached a clearing and a glacier-fed lake that was smooth as glass.

The lake showed the image of the blue sky, the treeless mountains, the meadow and the vibrant wildflowers. The water was so placid, not a breath of wind rippling its surface, you could see all of nature reflected there.

I could almost hear what a minister had once told me about prayer: "Find a place where there are few distractions. Let your body be still and your mind uncluttered with thoughts."

Now I understood. A mind unruffled, like a lake undisturbed, can more perfectly reflect the glory of God

—RICK HAMLIN

PRAY: *Father, I need to pray, but not the kind of prayer that keeps the waters ruffled with continuous requests and repetitive chatter. I need to see Your glory reflected in the stillness of my own heart.*

DO: Be still until the thoughts quit coming and that perfect peace reflects Jesus.

When you're afraid (1)

◄○►

READ: *The Lord is my light and my salvation; whom shall I fear?*

—PSALM 27:1

REFLECT: I have a phobia about mice. The disorder ought to be spelled *foe-bia*, for these illogical fears are a very real enemy to those of us who suffer from them. Once, when we discovered a family of mice colonizing our basement, I did my wash at the neighbor's rather than use my own machine. I confess my overreaction to show how desperately a phobic person can behave.

We learn in 2 Timothy 1:7 (NIV), "For God did not give us a spirit of timidity, but a spirit of power, of love and of self-discipline." I am not one hundred percent cured of my phobia, but through prayer, claiming a sound mind, and by trusting God's unlimited power over my weakness, I am making progress.

Whatever fear, real or imagined, is making you panicky today, turn to God in prayer. Remember, His perfect love casts out all fear.

—CAROL KNAPP

PRAY: *Father, I'm afraid, but I know my fear doesn't come from You. Help me to let it go and, by the power of Your Spirit, walk free from fear.*

DO: Try to imagine Jesus confronting the thing you fear most. Think about what He would do with that fear.

When you're afraid (2)

READ: *Who satisfies your mouth with good things,*
so that your youth is renewed like the eagle's.

—PSALM 103:5

REFLECT: One month after I graduated from college I was seriously hurt in an industrial accident. I awoke in a hospital bed to find my lifeless right arm suspended above my head in traction and the prognosis listed as "probable amputation." My mind instantly translated that into surgery performed. Furthermore, I figured no one would want a one-armed journalist, so I gave up my career hopes in despair.

I should have waited on the Lord.

First of all, with Jesus, the "probable" became "unnecessary." My right arm is still quite crooked, but I can punch out fifty-five words per minute. Secondly, before I learned that things might work out okay, I finally did give my fear over to Jesus and accepted the possibilities.

Are you facing some fearful problem? Hang on and give the Lord a little more time. He will restore your strength and give you eagle's wings to soar above any trouble.

—ERIC FELLMAN

PRAY: *When I think of the possibilities in this situation,*
Lord, I am afraid. Help me think of the possibilities
less and Your powerful Word more.

DO: Try to imagine the best-case scenario—the opposite of your fears. Thank God for His perfect resolution to this situation.

When you're afraid (3)

READ: *Do not judge according to appearance, but judge with righteous judgment.*

—JOHN 7:24

REFLECT: A young man had bedded down on a moonless night when he heard loud crashing sounds at the edge of his isolated camp. Slowly the sounds circled, unknown, menacing. Instantly he had visions of TV news clips showing mangled hikers attacked by hungry bears.

"I didn't pause to think, evaluate, pray," he said. "I went on automatic fear. After an hour of shaking terror, the sounds receded and I half-slept through the rest of the night."

At daybreak he examined the area. He was on his hands and knees looking for tracks. Turning slowly, he found himself face-to-face with a mother deer and two lovely spotted fawns. As they saw him the fawns began to make a familiar loud crashing sound as they bounded around their mother. These were the young man's ferocious midnight visitors.

Now I always take a second and ask, "Lord, is it a bear? Or a fawn?"

—ELAINE ST. JOHNS

PRAY: *My fear isn't of the immediate-threat variety, Father, but, still, can You tell me: "Is it a bear, or a fawn?"*

DO: Take a few minutes to think, evaluate, pray.

When you're afraid (4)

READ: *"Do not be afraid. Stand still, and see the salvation of the Lord, which He will accomplish for you today."*

—EXODUS 14:13

REFLECT: "Did you hear about Michael?" my sister Cheryl asked, and went on to tell me about her six-year-old son. "He had to get a shot, and he was so afraid, the nurse, his father and his sister had to hold him down! After all that," she continued, "he said it didn't really hurt!"

I chuckled, but I couldn't help remembering the many times I'd feared something, only to find out that it wasn't so bad after all. Like the time at work when I gave a presentation in front of thirty people. Inside, I was squirming worse than Michael. Afterward, when my boss said I'd done well, I was glad I'd focused on what I needed to say and not on my fears.

That seems to be the key: simply focusing on what it is I'm trying to do and letting go of frantic thoughts.

—ROBIN WHITE GOODE

PRAY: *The anticipation of certain things causes unmanageable fear in me, Lord. One of those is coming up soon. I praise You, the God Who is greater than all my fears, for helping me through it.*

DO: Find a Scripture to hold on to as this task or event approaches. Use it as a lifeline when the fear begins to rise.

When you're afraid (5)

READ: *Let us hold fast the confession of our hope without wavering, for He who promised is faithful.*

—HEBREWS 10:23

REFLECT: Often the vacuum and I would surprise my cat Jessica by entering a room where she was sleeping. Instantly her eyes would flash open, her ears flattened in fear, and she would dart out of the room in panic.

One day as I took out the vacuum, I spoke to her in my most reassuring voice: "It's all right, Jess. Trust me. You're okay." The usual terror filled her eyes, and her ears flattened back, but she remained curled up on the bed as I vacuumed around it. This happened again and again. Finally the day came when she would open one sleepy eye, glance at the vacuum in a ho-hum fashion and continue her nap.

Like Jessica, I'm learning to heed that Voice that comes to reassure me when something frightening looms on the horizon. Standing fast is difficult at times, but when the victory comes—as it surely will—what joy and peace we have won!

—MARION BOND WEST

PRAY: *I'm so familiar with that wide-eyed terror, Father, but I'm learning to heed Your comforting Voice. Even though I'm feeling afraid, I can choose to stand fast in Your comfort until the victory comes. I praise You for peace and joy—the real victory.*

DO: Find a picture of a sleeping cat to remind you that you can be free from fear.

When you're afraid (6)

◀◯▶

READ: *So Abram departed as the Lord had spoken to him. . . .*

—GENESIS 12:4

REFLECT: Years ago in the Jackson, Mississippi zoo there was an elephant named Margaret who had been kept on concrete for such a long time that she was afraid to risk her weight on the ground. When her pen was enlarged so that she could have more living room, she was afraid to walk where she could not feel the familiar concrete beneath her.

I remember seeing that big gray elephant sway back and forth on the edge of the concrete slab, her weight on three of her massive legs. She would swing one front foot forward, touch the ground tentatively, then bring it back to the concrete. Her fear kept her from taking the step she wanted to take.

Sometimes when I have a problem, I think of Margaret. Then I turn to the Lord and rest the whole weight of my difficulty on Him.

—LORENA PEPPER EDLEN

PRAY: *Father, I prefer the security of the familiar, too, and I'm afraid of the unknown. But I do want to change, Lord. Please help me take that first step in obedience to You.*

DO: Find an elephant—a figurine, a necklace, a picture—to remind you of Margaret the fearful elephant and your goal of freedom.

When you're afraid to admit you need help (1)

◄○►

READ: *Pride goes before destruction, a haughty spirit before a fall.*

—PROVERBS 16:18

REFLECT: When my father was a little boy, he became the proud owner of a battered red bicycle. *Proud is* the right word, for he was too proud to ask his big sisters to teach him how to ride. He mounted the bike from the doorstep, and could keep it fairly steady as he steered down the driveway. But he didn't know how to stop!

He could easily have asked for help, but his pride kept him from that. Instead, when he wanted to stop the bike, he would steer down behind the farmhouse where he'd "bump" into the woodpile to bring his bicycle to a halt. One day he was gone for so long that people started looking for him. They found him down by the woodpile just beginning to regain consciousness!

What woodpiles have you been crashing into lately? Isn't it time to admit you need help? God's just waiting for you to ask.

—VICKI SCHAD

PRAY: *Father, I'm struggling under the weight of this problem and getting nowhere. I need help, Lord. Would You show me whom to call, or bring the right person my way, to help me complete this task?*

DO: Look for a professional in the field in which you need help. Ask God for the humility to ask for help and then make that call.

When you're afraid to admit you need help (2)

◄○►

READ: *Now we exhort you, brethren, warn those who are unruly, comfort the fainthearted, uphold the weak, be patient with all.*

—1 THESSALONIANS 5:14

REFLECT: For years, some friends of mine have had a wonderful Labrador retriever named Midge. One evening I was in their home for dinner and found that they had added a young toy poodle to their household. I was surprised to find how affectionate the relationship between the old dog and the new one was. Wherever they went, Midge was following the younger Monsieur. They almost seemed to be touching, they stayed so close to each other.

Then I looked at Midge's venerable old eyes. They were clouded with cataracts. She was blind, and Monsieur was her Seeing Eye dog!

The image of those two dogs has never left my heart. We were put in the world to share our gifts, to know when to give and when to receive. And I need to remember to be able to be both—giver and receiver. —DIANE KOMP

PRAY: *You didn't just accept emotional and spiritual support in Your moment of greatest need, Jesus, You asked for it. That helps me see that giving and receiving are in Your divine plan.*

DO: The next time someone offers help, accept it. Better yet, call a friend and ask for it.

When you're angry (1)

◄◯►

READ: *A friend loves at all times, and a brother is born for adversity.*

—PROVERBS 17:17

REFLECT: Mr. Witchel was eighty and, because of his experience, charged a high fee to tune our piano. We would have paid it gladly, but the upper octaves of our piano still sounded like sour lemons.

We complained and Mr. Witchel reworked it. It wasn't any better, but he denied that anything was wrong. To placate us, he brought another tuner, a man of fifty, who agreed with Mr. Witchel. Suspecting collaboration, we angrily ordered them out of the house.

Half an hour later, the second tuner returned.

"You're right about those high notes," he admitted. "But, Elmer's hearing is going. He taught me how to tune pianos, and for sixty years he has lived for tuning. I just can't tell my friend that his life is over." He corrected the tuning for free, asking us to keep it a secret.

This is the kind of love Jesus wants me to show—a love that preserves the dignity of a friend. —DEE ANN PALMER

PRAY: *Lord Jesus, forgive me when my anger overrules my care and concern for another.*

DO: If you've lost your temper at the expense of another's dignity, it's never too late to apologize.

When you're angry (2)

READ: *Do not hasten in your spirit to be angry, for anger rests in the bosom of fools.*

—ECCLESIASTES 7:9

REFLECT: I called the doctor's office to confirm an appointment. "Hold please," the receptionist commanded, plugging me into the annoying sound of canned music before I could say anything. As the minutes ticked by, *I* got ticked. Later, in a hurry to get downtown, I let a car squeeze in front of me and the driver didn't even wave a "thank-you." Inside, my anger was building. Suddenly, the light in front of me turned red and I stopped abruptly.

I wonder if the feeling of anger isn't like a red light signal in our lives, telling us to *Stop . . . Look . . .* and *Listen. Stop* at the feeling of anger. *Look* for the reason and name it. *Listen* to what God has to say about that reason and then take action. All too often, my reasons are impatience . . . pride . . . envy . . . and I know what God says about that kind of self-centeredness.

—CAROL KUYKENDALL

PRAY: *I've been doing a bunch of stopping and looking, Lord—at the thing that made me angry—but not a lot of listening to what You have to say about it. But I'm here now, Lord. I'm listening.*

DO: Look at where anger got some of the men in the Bible, especially the godly ones.

When you're angry
at a friend

◄○►

READ: *"Be angry, and do not sin": do not let the sun go down on your wrath. . . .*

—EPHESIANS 4:26

REFLECT: Full of anger, I slumped into my favorite reading chair. A friend had betrayed me. I needed to talk with her about it, but my feelings were so intense I knew they would get in the way of what I wanted to say. Then I remembered what Paul wrote to the Colossians:

"Put to death, therefore, whatever belongs to your earthly nature . . . Get rid of such things as anger" (Colossians 3:5, 8, RSV). Put anger to death? I was mad enough to kill something, but I hadn't thought of killing anger itself.

Closing my eyes, I pictured a little round green monster named Anger hovering before me. Beside it stood Resentment, Self-Pity and Malice. I reached for them between my palms—and squeezed. Hard. Then, for good measure, I stood up and stomped them!

Then I asked God to fill me with love, joy and peace. He did—I was full to overflowing. Now I could call my friend!

—PATRICIA HOUCK SPRINKLE

PRAY: *Help me get past wanting to be angry, Lord. Maybe then I'll be able to kill some mental monsters and make that call.*

DO: Give yourself time to cool down and time to get hold of God's grace before talking to your friend.

When you're angry with someone you love

READ: *Love . . . is not easily angered, it keeps no record of wrongs.*

—1 CORINTHIANS 13:4–5 (NIV)

REFLECT: John and I were married only a short time before I discovered his habit of rolling up his sleeves when he went to work. He also wore two pairs of socks inside his construction boots. The trouble was he tossed them into the clothes hamper this way.

For years, every time I folded our laundry I seethed. Things went on like this until my new Bible arrived. The first section I turned to was my favorite, 1 Corinthians 13. "Love is patient . . . it is not self-seeking, it is not easily angered, it keeps no record of wrongs." *Keeps no record of wrongs!*

I went in and stood by the washing machine, bowed my head, and asked for forgiveness.

After that I was able to approach the task of rolling down John's sleeves and pulling his socks apart as I would any normal household chore. It became an act of love.

—ISABEL WOLSELEY

PRAY: *God, I'm so mad at _____ for _____. Help me to realize what a petty, insignificant thing I've been holding on to. I choose to let my irritation go, Lord, willingly and joyfully.*

DO: Think of something especially endearing about the person you've been angry with.

When you're attempting something new

—<o>—

READ: *"Do not look behind you. . . . !"*

—GENESIS 19:17

REFLECT: We floated there, half a mile from shore, two insignificant human specks in the mighty Pacific. It was to be my first attempt to surf at Waikiki. I had expected it to be exciting. Actually, I was scared stiff.

From the trough, enormous mounds of water looked like onrushing mountains. From the crest, they looked like green avalanches. I wished I had stayed home.

But the time had come to try it. I paddled over to the brown-skinned beach boy who had come as guide and protector. "What's the most important thing to remember?" I quavered.

He gave me three words: "Don't look back!"

Well, I survived that day, but I never forgot that advice. Why focus on things that frighten or overwhelm you? Why glance over your shoulder at past regrets or mistakes? Christ Himself, on His way to Jerusalem where He knew death awaited Him, "steadfastly set His face to go to Jerusalem."

—ARTHUR GORDON

PRAY: *Lord, please never let fear hold me back. Give me the courage to try new things, even the scary things, without looking back.*

DO: Find a friend who might like to try this new endeavor with you.

When you're battling
an addiction

◄O►

READ: *Therefore if the Son makes you free, you shall be free indeed.*

—JOHN 8:36

REFLECT: One evening shortly after recommitting my life to Christ, and after months of begging Him to deliver me from my smoking addiction, I was reading a book about spiritual growth. Suddenly, I was overwhelmed with my absolute inability to quit smoking or do anything else Christians are supposed to do . . . or not do.

I can't do this, I thought, in utter defeat. Suddenly, time stopped and I experienced Jesus in crystal clear purity. He said, in my thoughts, *I know you can't do it, but I can, if you want me to.*

Yes, please, I returned.

The next two times I craved a cigarette, I instantly recognized the truth: I *didn't* want to smoke. I was furious and told my addiction, in the name of Jesus, to go away and leave me alone. It had lost the battle because I never smoked a cigarette again—or wanted to.

—LUCILE ALLEN

PRAY: *Lord, Jesus, I want to be free indeed! I've tried so many ways to beat this addiction, Lord, that I have to confess my lack of faith that even You can do it. I want to believe. Would You help my unbelief!*

DO: If you're going to be "free indeed," it's going to be because Jesus sets you free, not because you overcome an addiction with your own willpower. Continue to pray in faith until you are, indeed, free!

When you're blessed with abundance

<o>

READ: *You will be made rich in every way so that you can be generous on every occasion....*

—2 CORINTHIANS 9:11 (NIV)

REFLECT: At a hospital in eastern Zaire, we stopped beside the bed of a small child. "This is Uwonde," the doctor said. "Two months ago his broken leg was set improperly, leaving one leg shorter than the other. We corrected it, but Uwonde must stay here for another month."

The steel pins in the boy's leg were attached to a traction system of bricks, a few boards and a length of rope. He held a blue plastic fish. "He's proud of that fish," the doctor said. "And I'm proud of one of our missionary kids who gave it to him. That fish may be the only toy Uwonde has ever owned."

The next morning another young boy had been installed in the bed next to Uwonde—and was holding the blue plastic fish.

"A gift from Uwonde," the nurse told me. "He felt the new boy needed cheering up." —MARY JANE CLARK

PRAY: *Lord, it's so easy to be generous with an abundance of possessions. Bless those whose compassion moves them to give their only treasure, just as You gave Your only Son.*

DO: Share out of your abundance with someone who has little.

When you're bored (1)

READ: *The flowers appear on the earth; the time of singing has come, and the voice of the turtledove is heard in our land.*

—SONG OF SOLOMON 2:12

REFLECT: When our community hosted the fifth World Hot-Air Balloon Championship, we were wakened at dawn by the roar and hiss of the balloons' burners. My family rushed outside and what a sight greeted us! Over one hundred balloons filled the blue sky. They floated low over our farm, countless colors shimmering in the June sun.

Then we went in for breakfast. Over the radio an excited announcer said, "They are so beautiful! A once-in-a-lifetime spectacle. Probably few of us will ever see such a sight again!"

My thoughts still on the balloons, I sat at the kitchen table, sipping coffee. Outside the window, a stalk of sky-blue delphinium reached high above the garden fence, its lovely petals translucent in the early morning light. How lovely, I thought. Not as spectacular as the balloons, but truly more beautiful, more miraculous. And God's beauty is not once in a lifetime. He gives it to us to enjoy every day.

—ALETHA JANE LINDSTROM

PRAY: *Father, I admit I tend to always be looking for the spectacular. Open my eyes to the beauty in my own front yard every day.*

DO: To get a fresh perspective on the world around you, closely examine a flower, read about the underwater world or consider the intricacies of your own hand.

When you're bored (2)

—◦—

READ: *Therefore you also be ready, for the Son of Man is coming at an hour you do not expect.*

—MATTHEW 24:44

REFLECT: Once, a friend said about faith, "I read a lot about getting through tough times or times of joy, but what about when you go to work and come home, over and over, waiting for something to happen?"

I thought of that the next Saturday, when my son Barnabas played his first soccer game. A brand-new player, he was assigned to the goal to keep the other team from scoring. The ball came his way only twice during the entire game.

I was prepared to console him afterward for missing the action. Instead, he ran up with shining eyes. "Did you see that, Mama? I was ready for them all the time!"

I can still see the way he stood during the game—alert, watching what others were doing, sometimes jumping up and down in his excitement. And I wonder, can I approach my own routine tasks with that same kind of anticipation and readiness?

—PATRICIA HOUCK SPRINKLE

PRAY: *Father, would You give me that childlike enthusiasm and energy in waiting? I want to be ready when the ball comes my way.*

DO: Make something happen in your free time—take a class, join a Bible study, take up a hobby and join a group of others with the same interests.

When you're carrying a heavy load

◀◦▶

READ: *"Ask, and it will be given to you. . . ."*

—MATTHEW 7:7

REFLECT: The mail carrier brought me the college graduation announcement of my friend Sue's eldest boy. A note tucked in with the announcement expressed a mother's pride: "Jimmy graduated *cum laude!*"

My mind flashed back to scenes of a three-year-old confidently declaring, "I can do that!" No matter what the chore, the toddler would give it a try. Most of the time he seemed to succeed.

Where did he get this marvelous assurance? Once, watching him, I had a clue. He was struggling to lift a box of heavy tools that his father had just finished using. I had expected him to cry in frustration when the box wouldn't budge. But not Jim! He looked up at me, a big grin on his freckled face. "Daddy'll help," he said confidently. *"We* can do that!" And they did.

Now *there's* a lesson to live by. When the load is too heavy, get help from your Father. Together you can do anything!

—BETTY RUTH GRAHAM

PRAY: *Yes, Father, without You the load is too heavy every day. Please walk with me and carry the burden with me, Lord. Together we can do anything.*

DO: God may help carry your load today by sending someone in His place. Accept that help with gratitude. Even ask for it, if necessary.

When you're caught in the middle of a conflict

READ: *The tongue of the wise uses knowledge rightly,*
but the mouth of fools pours forth foolishness.

—PROVERBS 15:2

REFLECT: Years ago, as a very young minister, my husband Norman was assigned to a church where a bitter controversy was going on between two factions in the congregation. Each was led by a strong-minded woman; neither would speak to the other. Norman waited until he heard one of the adversaries admit grudgingly that her rival was a fairly good cook. When he repeated this to the other lady, and revealed the source, she was startled into finally saying something conciliatory about her opponent.

Back went Norman with this little fragment of kindness, and gradually the walls that separated the two warring groups came tumbling down. Why not listen for these casual compliments and pass them on? You'll please a lot of people if you do, and you'll have a lot of fun yourself!"

—RUTH STAFFORD PEALE

PRAY: *Father, would You bring reconciliation in this conflict between my friends _____ and _____? Would You help me not to say too much, or too little, and let me know if I should stay out of it altogether?*

DO: Find something positive in either of the two parties and watch for opportunities to use it for good.

When you're concerned about a loved one

—◇—

READ: *Sing to God . . . who rides the ancient skies above, who thunders with mighty voice.*

—PSALM 68: 32-33 (NIV)

REFLECT: I have always loved thunderstorms. My sister Libby has always hated them. When we were children, claps of thunder would send her running to the basement and me scurrying to the window to take in the full show of lightning. I always wondered why the sound of thunder didn't happen at the same time as the lightning. Of course, it *does* happen simultaneously. It's just that sound doesn't travel as fast as light.

Answered prayer is sometimes like the thunder, often arriving so much later than the initial petition that I think it won't come. For years we uttered prayers for my unbelieving father: *Please, God, let Daddy come to know You.* By my adult years, we'd just about given up. Then, on his deathbed, my father prayed his own prayer—a prayer that was the answer to all those I had lifted in his behalf.

I know now that just because the answer isn't immediate doesn't mean it's not in progress.

—MARY LOU CARNEY

PRAY: *Loving Father, I can't possibly be more concerned about _____ than You are. Give me faith to believe that the answer to all the prayers prayed on his/her behalf is already on the way.*

DO: Share this lightning illustration with the person you're concerned about.

When you're confused (1)

READ: *O Lord God . . . fix their heart toward You.*

—1 CHRONICLES 29:18

REFLECT: Have you ever wondered about those highway signs that read, "Look Out for Falling Rocks"? Whenever I see one I'm filled with ambivalent feelings. Should I watch the road and the other cars or should I watch the hillside for descending boulders? What if I hear a rumble, should I drive off the road? Which side? It parallels the dilemma of baseball player Yogi Berra who after striking out was scolded by his manager Casey Stengel for not thinking more while he was at bat. "How can I think and hit at the same time?" Yogi asked.

Life has a way of overwhelming us sometimes. There are so many responsibilities, so many people to please. Fortunately, we have an Advisor Who understands the forces that seek to pull us first one way, then the other. He understands and will help us deal with conflicting loyalties. He does make one demand—that our first loyalty be to Him.

—FRED BAUER

PRAY: *Lord, too often I have so many things on my plate that I don't know what to do first. But I do know that nothing—and no one—is as important as You in my life. Thank You for helping me sort out the rest.*

DO: Take a few minutes to ask God to prioritize your responsibilities for you. Make a list of the top three or four things you need to accomplish today and concentrate on getting those things done.

When you're confused (2)

◄○►

READ: *And where I go you know, and the way you know.*

—JOHN 14:4

REFLECT: A man told me about a drive he and his son had taken from Long Island to Connecticut. They took the ferry across Long Island Sound and, when they debarked, evidently took the wrong road. They drove for a long, long time—too long—without reaching their destination. Finally, totally confused, they pulled up at a garage for directions. "We're lost," they announced to the mechanic.

"Nope," he said, "you're not lost. You're *here*." Then he told them how to find the road they wanted.

Now, whenever I feel really confused and bewildered by the burdens of everyday life, when I feel that perhaps God has forgotten me and my problems as I grope for guidance, I find myself remembering that little story. And then I can hear my Lord saying, like the kindly garagekeeper, *"No, you're not lost, Jeff. You're* here."

Hasn't He told us over and over again that He is with us always?

—JEFF JAPINGA

PRAY: *Thank You, Father, that no matter how lost and confused I feel, You always know where I am, and that You'll get me where You want me to go.*

DO: Sit quietly. Slow your thoughts until you can focus on God and then ask him for direction.

When you're confused (3)

‹o›

READ: *He guards the paths of justice, and preserves the way of His saints.*

—PROVERBS 2:8

REFLECT: "I never saw you do anything that cruel before! Those poor little birds have worked so hard, building that nest," my daughter protested.

I hit the mud shell with my broom again. The last bit of it fell, shattering on the porch.

"Those robins can't raise their babies here," I reminded her. "Five cats live on this porch most of the summer. They'd be sure to eat the nestlings. I want to make the parents build a nest in a safe place. I'm trying to do them a favor, ruining this nest before it has eggs. I'm protecting them."

The birds didn't understand at all. They fluttered about, crying and scolding most of that day. *Is it possible*, I wondered, *that I could be like those birds and misunderstand God's care when sometimes He seems to steer me in directions I don't want to go?*

Yes, it's all too possible!

—LUCILLE CAMPBELL

PRAY: *Yes, Father, I can raise a fuss when I'm confused about my life's circumstances. But I should be wiser than the birds, Lord. Help me to trust You, especially when I don't understand.*

DO: Allow yourself time to relax physically each day—in your favorite chair, by a stream, taking a stroll. And rest spiritually, in prayer.

When you're dealing with a difficult child

━━━━━━━━━━━━━━◄◊►━━━━━━━━━━━━━━

READ: *O Lord, open my lips, and my mouth will declare your praise.*

               —PSALM 51:15 (NIV)

REFLECT: During my first year of teaching, two boys, each named Ted, were in my class. One was a happy child, an excellent student, and a fine school citizen. The second Ted spent much of his time making a nuisance of himself.

Then the PTA held its first meeting, and a mother came up to me and asked, "How is my son Ted getting along?"

I assumed she was the "good Ted's" mother and exclaimed, "I can't tell you how much I enjoy him. I'm so glad he's in my class!"

The following morning, Ted, my problem child, came up to me. "Mom told me what you said last night. I don't think any teacher has ever wanted me before."

That day Ted's work was done neatly and correctly. I had several opportunities to offer him sincere praise, and each time he glowed with pride.

Before long my problem child became one of my best students.

           —ALETHA JANE LINDSTROM

PRAY: *I pray for all "difficult" children today, God. Show those who work with them how to bring out the best in even the most difficult of the difficult.*

DO: Think of something you really like about your "difficult child" and leave a note in his/her room telling him/her about it.

━━━━━━━━━━━━━━━━━━━━━━━━━━━━━━

When you're depressed

—◁◦▷—

READ: *For it is God who works in you both to will and to do for His good pleasure.*

—PHILIPPIANS 2:13

REFLECT: Following a bout of flu, I found myself in a depression I couldn't seem to snap out of. Then one morning I watched a kindergarten teacher distract a weeping child by saying, "Let me help you find something to do."

She led the boy to an easel and set him to work with brushes and jars of paint. As the bright colors flowed onto the paper the child began to smile, his tears forgotten.

I decided I needed to try something like that on myself. I went to my own Teacher in prayer, saying, "Lord, help me find something to do." Soon afterward a friend phoned to ask if I'd help an older woman who'd had surgery and would be unable to drive for several weeks. I said yes, and sure enough, I chauffeured that woman around town (and in the process made a new friend). My spirits lifted and my energy returned.

—MADGE HARRAH

PRAY: *Father, I need Your help even wanting to want something to do. Give me the will—and the energy—to do, Lord.*

DO: Try to keep a healthy balance between rest and productivity as you ask the Lord to show you the root of your depression and the key to restored joy within. If you've been depressed awhile, let your doctor or pastor know that you need some help.

When you're discouraged about reaching a goal

———————————◄○►———————————

READ: *Now faith is the substance of things hoped for, the evidence of things not seen.*

—HEBREWS 11:1

REFLECT: In 1951, Florence Chadwick became the first woman to swim the English Channel in both directions. The following year she attempted to swim the twenty-one-mile channel between Catalina Island and Los Angeles. After fifteen hours in icy water and a thick fog, Chadwick told her trainer that she couldn't continue, even though she was only a half-mile from her goal! Afterward, she told reporters, "If I could have seen land, I might have made it."

Two months later, on another foggy day, she became the first woman to swim the Catalina Channel. That day she kept faith that the coast was there, even though she couldn't see it.

I often stop short of trusting God completely. *If I could have seen . . .* I say. But God wants me to trust without seeing. So the next time I'm struggling through a spiritual fog, I will keep moving toward the land I cannot see. Faith will get me there.

—BONNIE LUKES

PRAY: *God, I feel like I'm swimming through a spiritual fog. I don't have to see the land, Lord, but a little encouragement that You're with me would help me keep moving.*

DO: It wouldn't be a lack of faith to hang a picture of your goal in a strategic location to help you see through the fog until you reach it.

———————————————————————————

When you're exhausted

────────◄◊►────────

READ: ...*Grace, mercy and peace from God the Father and Christ Jesus our Lord.*

—1 TIMOTHY 1:2 (NIV)

REFLECT: I woke up tired after a restless night, and instead of taking it easy I proceeded with my usual crowded schedule. By midday I was impatient with my loved ones and felt like a total failure because I couldn't give more time to my family as well as to my work.

Finally I realized it was time to ask God for help, even if I didn't know what kind of help I needed.

I closed my office door and just sat silently in my chair. I could sense something in me reaching out to God and almost immediately I felt His presence. I began to relax as He offered me a different view of my life.

I wasn't overworked; I was involved. I didn't have too many responsibilities; I had many loved ones. When it came to schedules, however, I was a bit too rigid. If I am tired, then I should rest. And what better way to rest than to let God refresh my point of view?

—PHYLLIS HOBE

PRAY: *Dear Father, thank You for refreshing my point of view just by reading this reflection. And thank You, Lord, for permission to rest.*

DO: Be grateful for all your responsibilities because it really does mean that you are well-involved and have many loved ones. But if you need to, set aside a weekend to rest.

When you're facing
a new commitment

◄○►

READ: *Choose for yourselves this day whom you will serve. . . .*

—JOSHUA 24:15

REFLECT: After attending a time-management seminar, my friend Charles shared this maxim: "Every time you say yes to one thing, you say no to another." It helped me tremendously.

Yesterday, for instance, I received an invitation to speak to a civic club. I was honored by the invitation and wanted to say, "Yes, I'd love to." But the invitation was for Friday, my day off. Normally, I would have accepted. This time, though, I asked myself, *By saying yes, to what am I saying no?*

I would be saying no to my wife and to my hobbies and leisure. I would also be saying no to my church and its members, who expect me to be rested and vital for their ministry. I politely declined the invitation.

Charles's saying has helped me put all my decisions to a spiritual test: *How can I spend my time most wisely in God's service?*

—SCOTT WALKER

PRAY: *God, how can I spend my time most wisely in Your service?*

DO: Make a list of the things you'll be saying no to if you accept the commitment you're considering.

When you're facing
a serious illness

READ: *Weeping may endure for a night, but joy comes in the morning.*

— PSALM 30:5

REFLECT: Years ago a routine mammogram brought a dreaded diagnosis—breast cancer. Fortunately, I came through the surgery well and needed no further treatment. To the outside world I put on an Academy Award-winning act. No wallowing in self-pity for me.

But I was tormented by fear and an unquenchable sense of grief. One day, I heard a familiar voice say, "Hi, Steph. How was your summer?" It was Betty, a friend who had been away.

"I had a mastectomy in June," I blurted.

Betty's face turned ashen, and with tears brimming in her eyes, she put her arms around me and said softly, "I'm so sorry." For the first time since learning about my cancer, I began to cry. As those hot, cleansing tears streamed down my cheeks onto Betty's sweater, the anguish began to lift.

I no longer see tears as a sign of weakness; they're a special gift from God that cleanses our spiritual wounds.

— STEPHANIE ODA

PRAY: *Thank You, Father, for friends who bring out the tears in us. What a wonderful gift of healing those tears are!*

DO: Give this day, this moment, to God. Try to keep positive thoughts and images in your mind as you trust Him to see you through.

When you're facing an unwelcome change

<o>

READ: *God does not judge by external appearance.*

—GALATIANS 2:6 (NIV)

REFLECT: My wife and I put up a fence as we closed in a pasture beside our house and turned two baby lambs loose in their new home. I had strongly resisted Mairi's idea to go into sheep farming.

"I'll do most of the daily care," Mairi answered. "I just want your help with some of the heavy tasks. Besides, the sheep will keep the grass and weeds down."

"They'll also get sick," I countered. Mairi persisted, however, and I finally gave in—expecting the worst.

As we nurtured the tiny lambs I found our effort extremely rewarding. Despite the feeding, watering, deworming and daily checking for injuries, I looked forward to caring for them. I especially enjoyed feeding time, and even coaxed them to eat out of my hand.

Beyond the unexpected joy of shepherding, I learned not to be so quick to negate a new experience.

—JOHN BRAMBLETT

PRAY: *Father, I admit I tend to see the work element in a new idea rather than the pleasure. But for the sake of pleasing You, Lord, I'm willing to change.*

DO: How often has the worst you expected from a new adventure come to pass? Make a "good" and "bad" list from one or two changes you resisted at first.

When you're facing challenges (1)

◄◊►

READ: *Now no chastening seems to be joyful for the present. . . .*

—HEBREWS 12:11

REFLECT: I once saw a mother raccoon lead her three babies out of the tall grass on the far side of a creek and onto a fallen tree that stretched out to deep water. She dove in gracefully and coaxed the little ones to join her. They looked dismayed; obviously they had never tried to swim.

The mother climbed back up on the tree, took one baby in her mouth, and swam across the creek with it. She did the same with the second. The third waited expectantly for his free ride, but nothing happened. He cried piteously and dipped one timid paw into the tide. The mother's answering calls became fainter. She was leaving him—or so she seemed to want him to think.

Finally, the baby threw himself into the creek and floundered frantically to shore.

That raccoon mother chose the toughest of her babies for her little lesson in loving. She knew he could respond.

—ARTHUR GORDON

PRAY: *Lord, let me be a baby in Your nest as you prepare me for whatever tests You think I'm ready to take. Give me the courage to follow when You call and the skills to perform any task You ask of me.*

DO: Make a list of three challenges you've already overcome and the ways God has enabled you to face them.

When you're facing
challenges (2)

◄○►

READ: *The Lord is the strength of my life. . . .*

—PSALM 27:1

REFLECT: I began taking aerobic exercises at the public gym
near my office. One evening, as we were doing a type of side
leg lift that seemed relatively simple, I wondered why everyone else was groaning so much.

Our instructor walked over to me and said, "No, no, your
heel is supposed to be turned up toward the ceiling and your
toes should be turned down!"

So I tried it that way. "Now, what do you feel?" she wanted
to know.

"A horrible pull in my thigh," I groaned.

"You've got it right," she said with satisfaction.

Maybe it's the same with those other kinds of pain—failure
and rejection and disappointment—that I'd felt not too
long ago.

Perhaps I'd been stretching and strengthening spiritually
too. Perhaps I would become more durable, more able to
withstand the stresses and strains of life.

—SAMANTHA MCGARRITY

PRAY: *Lord, I don't like disappointment and failure and
other things that hurt. But I do want to be a stronger
person, Lord. So instead of complaining, I thank You
for the tough times.*

DO: Start back up with those spiritual exercises—try starting
a Bible study on some painful test you've recently been
through.

When you're facing difficult decisions

◄○►

READ: *The Lord also will be a refuge for the oppressed,
a refuge in times of trouble.*

—PSALM 9:9

REFLECT: One summer, some friends and I rented a house at Mombassa Beach on Africa's east coast. It should have been an ideal vacation, but I was troubled by some difficult decisions.

Every day we found shells that would have been lovely had they been intact, but almost always they were broken. One afternoon an African peddler approached, carrying baskets filled with exquisite, perfectly formed shells.

I asked where he found them. "My son and I, we go way out where shells lie still on the bottom. Very peaceful down there. It's when shells are tossed roughly about on shore that they break."

Just like me, I thought. When I rely on myself to deal with the rolling turmoil of life, my spirit breaks. To find peace, I need to immerse myself in the deep stillness of God.

—ELEANOR SASS

PRAY: *Lord, I feel like I'm being tossed and broken like shells in the sea by uncertainty. I'm so glad that You understand how I feel. Thank You for helping me through this season of decision-making.*

DO: Find a place to sit in stillness with Jesus until you find some measure of clarity about the decisions you're trying to make. If clarity doesn't come today, try again tomorrow.

When you're facing hostility from someone

◄◦►

READ: *"And whoever gives one of these little ones only a cup of cold water in the name of a disciple, assuredly, I say to you, he shall by no means lose his reward."*

—MATTHEW 10:42

REFLECT: Richard Kirkland, a sergeant in the Second South Carolina regiment, could no longer endure the cries of "water" coming from the wounded on the battlefield. He hoisted several canteens over the shoulder of his Confederate uniform and scurried from behind a protective wall.

The muskets fell silent as Kirkland knelt beside a wounded soldier—an enemy soldier. He lifted the soldier's head and tilted the canteen toward his lips. Kirkland then removed his own coat and laid it across the soldier's body.

Cheers rang out from the Northern side. The South joined in. For an hour and a half, Kirkland carried water to the dying and wounded.

Kirkland's compassion ran deeper than patriotic loyalty or the fear of losing his life.

—TERRY HELWIG

PRAY: *Lord, I pray Your compassion runs deep in me and all of Your children.*

DO: Think of something you can do today for the person who's antagonistic to you.

When you're facing temptation

<hr>

READ: *Then Jesus said to him, "Away with you, Satan! For it is written, 'You shall worship the Lord your God, and Him only you shall serve.'" Then the devil left Him. . . .*

—MATTHEW 4:10–11

REFLECT: As a lonely teenager I used to seek advice from a sprightly octogenarian named Mother Gibson. Barely five feet tall, with snow-white hair, she was always full of sunshine.

One day I asked Mother Gibson how to handle a thorny problem of temptation I faced.

"Temptation!" she cried, "Why, honey girl, that's just another name for the devil. When he comes around I just read the Bible to him."

I stared at her. "You what?"

Mother Gibson picked up her Bible and held it high. "I tell him, 'Temptation, you old devil, all the promises in this Book are mine. See that? Read it.' Then I read it to him, and say, 'You just skedaddle on out of here.' Try this. It works!"

—ANNAMAE CHENEY

PRAY: *Thank You, mighty God, that Your Truth is more powerful than any lie of the devil!*

DO: Find a passage of Scripture relating to your temptation. Read it, speak it, memorize it and tell that temptation to be gone!

When you're feeling betrayed

READ: *The same Lord over all is rich to all who call upon Him.*

—ROMANS 10:12

REFLECT: It was my sixteenth birthday and I returned from visiting my cousin's only to discover that my best friend and my boyfriend had fallen hopelessly in love.

Dad's imagination swung into action. "Imagine your body's an empty vessel, Mary Jane, the top of your head a golden lid. And God, high above, silver chalice tilted . . ."

"I can't play games right now, Daddy," I interrupted him.

"Sure you can, honey. Besides, this is no game. God is there, waiting to fill your emptiness with the love of forgiveness and understanding. All you have to do is open yourself to Him."

Everett and Jewelle have long since married and raised a family, and I have long since discovered the true magic of Dad's imagination. Because Dad was right. God is always there, waiting to drain the anger, envy or just plain weariness away, and fill me with the balm of His healing love.

—MARY JANE MEYER

PRAY: *Loving Father, no one knows the pain of betrayal better than You, and that comforts me today. I pray that someday You will use my pain to bring comfort and healing to someone else.*

DO: Give yourself time to grieve and as you do, ask God to drain any anger, envy and weariness away through forgiveness.

When you're feeling discouraged

◄○►

READ: *Simon answered, "Master, we've worked hard all night and haven't caught anything. But because you say so, I will let down the nets."*

—LUKE 5:5 (NIV)

REFLECT: I remember all the hot Mississippi days sitting on the riverbank with my friend Jimmie, the air hanging on us thick and heavy, the mosquitoes biting, but not a nibble from a fish.

I think of those days when I read about Peter. I know how discouraging it is to fish and catch nothing. Yet Peter had faith to let down his net again because he trusted the Lord's Word.

I don't fish anymore, but there are many times I need to remember to "let down my net" in faith. Many times I don't know where the resources or the strength will come from to sustain our ministry, to sit through a child's illness, to see a friend suffer. But I have learned from Peter to say to the Lord, "Because You say so, I will do it."

—DOLPHUS WEARY

PRAY: *I'm fishing in a sea of uncertainty right now, Lord Jesus. Give me faith like Peter's to put my net down in prayer, knowing You will provide.*

DO: Read the story of Peter in Luke 5 to get a boost of faith from God's Word.

When you're feeling disorganized

READ: *I particularly urge you to pray. . . .*

—HEBREWS 13:19 (NIV)

REFLECT: Most of us have at least one special place in our lives that we try to keep in order. That's so we can cope with the multiple places where order is beyond our control. For me, it is my books. For my son Luke, it is his baseball cards. For you, it may be your workshop or kitchen. When those places are neat and shipshape, we can deal with the chaos impinging on our lives.

There's one other area, an even more important one for me, that helps to order my world: my devotional life. Each day, as I read the Scriptures, make notes in my journal and spend time with God in prayer—sometimes only a few minutes —the rest of the twenty-four hours becomes manageable.

—SCOTT WALKER

PRAY: *Father, would You help me organize my devotional life? Help me stay focused when I'm reading Your Word. When I pray, corral my scattered thoughts and fill my mind with Your peace.*

DO: Promise yourself you'll spend thirty minutes organizing the most cluttered space in your life today.

When you're feeling down

READ: *Arise, eat food, and let your heart be cheerful. . . .*

—1 KINGS 21:7

REFLECT: My new friend Anne invited me to a get-together in her home. My husband was away on an extended business trip. Feeling down, I didn't want to go out. But Anne insisted.

It was a wonderful party! Someone played the piano and we sang. Everyone seemed friendly and I began to feel better. Anne's warmth toward all of us had permeated the house.

Later, as we were getting our coats to leave, I noticed on a table a photograph of a beautiful little blonde-haired girl.

"That's Anne's child who was killed in an auto accident almost twenty years ago," said one of the women next to me. "Anne has this annual get-together on the anniversary of her daughter's death to cheer up others and to forget about her own loss."

Suddenly, I felt small. My "problem" had made me want to withdraw. Anne, in her loss, was reaching out to others.

—MARION BOND WEST

PRAY: *I praise and celebrate You today, Lord, in spite of my aching heart.*

DO: Turn a day of sadness into a celebration that will bless others.

When you're feeling empty

◄O►

READ: *My soul yearns for you in the night; in the morning my spirit longs for you.*

—ISAIAH 26:9 (NIV)

REFLECT: Rory was a student in my freshman English class. By the age of nineteen he had tried smoking, drinking, sex and drugs and had finally decided that life was nothing but emptiness. Now here he was, standing in my doorway with joy written all over his face. When I asked him why, Rory replied, "Well, I discovered an amazing thing. God had put that emptiness inside of me! He did it in order to draw me to Him. But I kept on trying to fill it with temporary external things—until I realized that the only high that lasts is Jesus."

Sometimes I get an empty feeling too, don't you? The next time I do, I'm going to remind myself that God put it there to draw me closer to Him. It will signal me to spend more time in prayer so that Jesus can replenish my spirit with the only lasting nourishment.

—MARILYN MORGAN KING

PRAY: *I've never thought to thank You for this empty feeling, Father, but I thank You for it now because without it, chances are I wouldn't be talking to You at this moment. Thank You for filling my emptiness with Yourself.*

DO: Copy this page and send it to a searching friend who has tried it all and come up empty.

When you're feeling faith-fatigue

READED

READ: *Do no put out the Spirit's fire. . . .*

—1 THESSALONIANS: 5:19 (NIV)

REFLECT: A wise and perceptive minister once told me, "Be careful about being average, son. If a man stands with one foot on a block of ice and the other on a red-hot stove, then, on average, he should be feeling pretty good, right?"

Wrong, of course; I got the point. And I still think about that old minister every time I read what God says in Revelation 3:15–16 (NIV): "You are neither cold nor hot. I wish you were either one or the other! So, because you are lukewarm—neither hot nor cold—I am about to spit you out of my mouth."

I have learned that we can't be lukewarm Christians. We either believe in Christ and His message or we don't. We endeavor to follow Him or we don't. There is no "on the average" or wishy-washy in-betweens about it. God wants us *hot*.

—RICHARD SCHNEIDER

PRAY: *I praise You, Father, for Your intense love for Your children, a love that never grows cold.*

DO: Think back to the time when you first asked the Lord into your heart. Ask Him every day to renew that love.

When you're feeling frazzled (1)

READ: *Into Your hand I commit my spirit.* . . .

—PSALM 31:5

REFLECT: Webster says *frazzled* means "worn, weak and frayed." The word suited me perfectly when our sons were young and my husband Jim worked long hours. I'd fret and "fray" and I saw myself as a weak parent. There was neither time nor energy left for activities I'd always enjoyed.

My husband suggested I enroll in a neighborhood quilting class. As I discovered the beauty of the old patchwork patterns, I thought of hands busier than mine, long ago, sewing late into the evening. Those amazing women created intricate masterpieces with a needle, some recycled thread and hundreds of little scraps of cloth.

As I learned quilting, I realized something else: the secret of becoming "unfrazzled" is not a change of circumstances, but a change of attitude. Our little patches of time can either be tossed on the scrap heap, or be used to form a lovely masterpiece of memories, bringing warmth and happiness to those we love.

—VICKI SCHAD

PRAY: *Lord Jesus, You walked the earth with constant demands on Your time and attention, yet I can't imagine You frazzled. I need Your peace, Jesus.*

DO: Sit quietly for a new minutes and clear your mind. Then clear a thing or two off your schedule.

When you're feeling frazzled (2)

◄◦►

READ: *If there is anything praiseworthy—meditate on these things.*

—PHILIPPIANS 4:8

REFLECT: Just out of a hospital, on furlough from World War II, I took a rowboat out on a glacial lake in Switzerland. I rowed far from the shore, brought in the oars, laid myself down under the seat and just drifted for hours.

The only sight I saw was the blue, almost cloudless sky. The only sounds I heard were the gentle slappings of water against the hull and the tinkling of cowbells from the mountainsides that cradled the lake. God was giving me a tiny hint of what peace in heaven is like.

Today, when life's pace gets too frantic, I draw upon the memory of that time and that place. I use it to calm myself—to bless and heal.

You have memories like this too. Stop now. This instant. Choose one that still moves you. Relive it intensely. See, hear, smell, taste . . . remember!

—MANUEL ALMADA

PRAY: *Thank You, Father, for this great idea. I remember when _____.*

DO: After you've relived a memory for a few moments, resolve to follow the advice above in Philippians 4:8 every day: think about excellent and praiseworthy things.

When you're feeling hemmed in by "Thou shalt not's"

<o>

READ: *And walk in all the ways that I have commanded you, that it may be well with you.*

—JEREMIAH 7:23

REFLECT: One morning after our Bible reading had included the Ten Commandments, our eleven-year-old Donna seemed rebellious. "Thou shalt not! That's all the Bible ever says!" she protested.

Later that morning our family packed a picnic and explored some woods nearby. On one old tree hung a sign saying, "No Trespassing." Just beyond it a fence separated us from a sunny hill that led invitingly down to a pretty stream.

"Look at that!" Donna exploded. "That sign and fence are just two more 'thou shalt not's'!" Impetuously, she climbed over the fence.

Suddenly, from woods to our left, about fifty yearling steers burst forth, bawling and bucking. They seemed to be heading for Donna, and we all had a few nervous moments before she was able to reach the fence and roll under it, just in time.

Aren't the Ten Commandments a little like that fence, wise rules for our own protection? —LUCILLE CAMPBELL

PRAY: *I admit I've been resenting all Your thou-shalt-not's without thinking about how Your laws protect me. I choose today to embrace—and thank You for— Your rules.*

DO: Pick one commandment or rule that you're resisting. Think of three loving reasons why God gave it to us.

When you're feeling impatient (1)

READ: *But as for me, I watch in hope for the Lord, I wait for God my Savior; my God will hear me.*

—MICAH 7:7 (NIV)

REFLECT: "Don't be impatient," my Chinese friend warned when I told her the book on which I was working was not progressing as fast as I'd have liked. "You know what happened to Mencius' farmer, don't you?"

I recognized the Chinese philosopher's name, but did not know the story. She then told me the parable about a farmer who went to his fields each night and returned complaining to his wife that his seedlings were growing too slowly. Finally, he became so anxious that he walked between the rows and gave each plant a slight tug, hoping it would help them grow, but the next morning to his chagrin, all the seedlings were withered and dying.

My friend concluded the fable by adding, "Few there are among us who don't tug on seedlings."

—FRED BAUER

PRAY: *Father, I've been tugging. But today I'm leaving this thing I've been trying to make happen in Your hands. I'll do my part and then trust You to bring it to life when You see fit.*

DO: Put a plant or bud nearby to remind you to let your project bloom in God's time.

When you're feeling impatient (2)

READ: *The discretion of a man makes him slow to anger, and his glory is to overlook a transgression.*

—PROVERBS 19:11

REFLECT: "When will the well-drillers be here?"

"Toward the end of the week." Harry replied. "They're being delayed by equipment breakdowns."

"That's the same thing they've told us for the last three weeks," I complained.

"Look," Harry said, "this is going to get the best of us. What do you think God might want to teach us here?"

It didn't take long to see this as an opportunity for us to practice patience. I could continue to complain, or I could accept the situation and ask God to "grow" patience in me.

The well-drillers finally did come, and we were grateful to find good water at a reasonable depth. Now into the serious house-building stage, I can almost see our heavenly Father saying with a smile, "Just look at all these opportunities I'll be giving you to practice that patience thing: delays in the building permit process, awaiting the plumber or the electrician. . . ."

—MARY JANE CLARK

PRAY: *I praise and thank You, Father, for Your patience with me. And thank You for opportunities to demonstrate Your patience to others.*

DO: The next time you're feeling impatient, ask God for a piece of fruit—patience, the fruit of the Holy Spirit.

When you're feeling insecure

---◄○►---

READ: *For the Lord your God moves about in your camp to protect you. . . .*

—DEUTERONOMY 23:14 (NIV)

REFLECT: "The white rhino's young is kept in front of the mother," our guide said. "That way, when a hungry predator appears, her immense presence discourages any attack. And she never leaves it."

Watching the baby white rhino, I was impressed by how secure it was, placidly munching the tender shoots of grass. It sensed its mother behind it. And I thought of those times when I felt as secure as the baby rhino. When I was struggling through medical school, the pressures were eased by knowing of God's constant Presence. Ask Him to stand behind you too. He will.
                                          —SCOTT HARRISON

PRAY: *Thank You, Father, that I don't have to fear for my safety, physically or spiritually. I praise You for Your awesome power to protect.*

DO: Find a picture of a baby and mother animal. Keep it handy to remind you of God's constant presence.

When you're feeling insignificant

◄◌►

READ: *"The kingdom of heaven is like a mustard seed, which indeed is the least of all the seeds; but when it is grown it is greater than the herbs and becomes a tree...."*

—MATTHEW 13:31–32

REFLECT: "For want of a nail the shoe was lost; for want of a shoe the horse was lost; and for want of a horse the rider was lost." So wrote the philosopher-poet George Herbert, who would have commiserated with me when I lost the tiny screw from my glasses. One never gives a second thought to such little things until they come up missing.

The Bible places great stock in little things and people— a mustard seed, a lost coin, a diminutive tax collector called Zacchaeus and a brave shepherd boy named David.

When it seems we are unappreciated and insignificant, it may help to remember that God's love is constant, undying, everlasting. That truth is reported in one of the littlest, but most telling, Bible statements of all: God is love (1 John 4:8).

—FRED BAUER

PRAY: *A mustard seed, used to symbolize the greatness of faith; one lost coin, used to depict God's love for every individual; and a little shepherd boy that became a king. Maybe I should be more grateful for this feeling of insignificance I'm struggling with, Lord. Maybe it's a sign of greater things to come.*

DO: A coin, a mustard seed . . . find something to remind you to appreciate the value God places on you.

When you're feeling lonely

---◆---

READ: *Never again will they thirst. . . . For the lamb at the center of the throne will be their shepherd; he will lead them to springs of living water. . . .*

—REVELATION 7:16, 17 (NIV)

REFLECT: O Lord, I've been so lonely today. And with no apparent cause. You've given me a wonderful family, students who look up to me, and many friends. Yet, still, I'm lonely. I feel as though no one in the world can understand this emptiness. It really hurts.

Remember when I was younger, how I used to run from this feeling? I'd go to parties or watch TV marathon-style. But I'm older now. And I know those thing don't really fill the loneliness.

So instead of trying to deaden this ache, today I sat down and wrote in my journal. You know what I wrote: I've turned loneliness into a friend, someone who is trying to reacquaint me with the only One Who truly understands what I am feeling. Now I see again that I have a thirst that only You can satisfy.

So here I am, Lord.

—DANIEL SCHANTZ

PRAY: *Please, Lord, be all I need. Help me to feel satisfied with You alone.*

DO: Write this reflection down and save it for the next time you feel lonely.

When you're feeling lost (1)

READ: *Show me Your ways, O Lord; teach me Your paths.*

—PSALM 25:4

REFLECT: I took a trip by car to visit friends in several different cities. I didn't bother to buy a road map. "I have a pretty good sense of direction," I reasoned.

How did I do? On the long stretches, fine. But I became hopelessly lost in Charleston, Columbia, Statesville, Burlington and Augusta. Finally, forced to admit my inadequacies, I pulled into a gas station and bought a map. What a relief it was to at last see where I was, where I needed to go and how to get there!

And today I realize that my journey in faith is like that trip. I can get through a good bit of living by using my own understanding, my conscience, and the advice of others. But when a maze of sorrows, temptations and decisions overtake me, I need a map. God's Word is a "light" on the pathway of life. I don't travel well without it.

—PATRICIA HOUCK SPRINKLE

PRAY: *Keep me on Your path for my life, Lord.*

DO: Carry a Bible with you for those times when you feel you're on the verge of taking a wrong turn.

When you're feeling lost (2)

◄○►

READ: *It is good that one should hope and wait quietly for the salvation of the Lord.*

—LAMENTATIONS 3:26

REFLECT: When I was a girl, Mom took the family to the New York World's Fair. "Remember to stick together," she said. "But in case anybody gets separated, stand still. Don't try to find us. We'll come back for you."

Sure enough, enthralled by the exhibits, I lagged behind and found myself alone. I climbed up on a bench and scanned the crowd. The family was nowhere in sight. Terribly frightened, I was tempted to run wildly after them, but then I remembered Mom's words. For what seemed ages I stood on that bench, straining my eyes in every direction. At last I saw Mom hurrying toward me. Tears of relief rolled down my cheeks. She had found me, just as she had promised.

Since then, when feeling separated, I've been tempted to search frantically for God. But I've learned to be calm, to wait and let Him find me. —BETTY RUTH GRAHAM

PRAY: *Lord, sometimes I panic when I haven't "felt" Your presence for a while. But You are more committed to finding me than I am to being "found." Help me wait patiently.*

DO: You may not always be able to "feel" God's presence, but you can always find Him, right in the pages of your Bible.

When you're feeling off-balance

◄○►

READ: *Unto You I lift up my eyes, O You who dwell in the heavens.*

—PSALM 123:1

REFLECT: I came to love ballet at a performance of *Swan Lake* at the age of five. I was thrilled—and bewildered—by the beauty and grace of the dancers. *How do they keep from spinning right off the stage,* I wondered. One day I asked a ballet teacher how the dancers kept their balance in pirouette after pirouette.

"Easy," he replied. "They just fix their eyes on one spot and return to it with each whirl."

One balmy afternoon in New York City I was trying to make my way down Fifth Avenue. I was buffeted and shoved, and as I crossed 53rd Street, I was almost pushed into an oncoming car. Angrily I whirled around, ready to hurl harsh words. But just then my eyes were caught by the spires of St. Thomas' Church with its cross silhouetted against the sky. *Jesus . . .* I thought, *fix my eyes on Jesus. That's the way to keep my balance in our dizzying world.*

—ELEANOR SASS

PRAY: *Keep my eyes fixed on Jesus? Lord, that sounds so easy, but with the world the way it is today, I'm finding it so hard. Still, with Your help that's what I'll do—keep my eyes on Jesus.*

DO: Try to do a few pirouettes in a row, and remember when you're spiritually off-balance to keep your eyes on Jesus.

When you're feeling overcommitted

———◄○►———

READ: *Then the apostles gathered to Jesus and told Him all things, both what they had done and what they had taught. And He said to them, "Come aside by yourselves to a deserted place and rest a while."*

—MARK 6:30–31

REFLECT: I remember the captain of a great airliner explaining to me once that the mighty jet engines were used at maximum thrust only for a minute or two while the plane was taking off. Then they were set back to cruising speed, which called for only a fraction of their power. "If you ran those engines constantly at full throttle," he said, "they'd wear out in no time."

That's true of us humans, too, isn't it? Are you racing your engine frantically all day long? Are you constantly running up life's escalator? If so, you need to learn to save your maximum energies for real crises, or for getting important projects off the ground. The rest of the time wise men and women will pace themselves by operating at a comfortable cruising speed. —NORMAN VINCENT PEALE

PRAY: *I confess, Father, that I don't know how to slow down. Circumstances seem to drive me rather then me driving them. Please help me find a comfortable cruising speed, Lord.*

DO: Make a list of every commitment you have. Prioritize them and make plans to phase out the least important ones from your life.

When you're feeling overwhelmed (1)

◄○►

READ: *"Be strong and courageous, and do the work. Do not be afraid or discouraged, for the Lord God . . . is with you. . . ."*

—1 CHRONICLES 28:20 (NIV)

REFLECT: Routine chores had piled up so high I didn't even know where to start. "How am I going to get going today?" I asked myself.

An idea came to me. I listed each chore on separate slips of paper: weed garden, mail letter to insurance company, call nursing-home friend, clean out refrigerator.

And then I had a little revelation. Why not give God a slip or two? So I wrote, "How about a few minutes of prayer?" And, "Why not stop and read a bit of Scripture?"

I placed each slip of paper inside a small box. After I shook up the box, I picked out a slip and set about doing what it said.

My chore box may sound silly, but from time to time it really does bring some excitement to my day, and it lends a little magic, too, especially when I pull out a prayer or a Bible slip!

—SHIRLEY POPE WAITE

PRAY: *I have so much to do, Lord, I don't know where to start. Would You order my day? Thank You that I can relax now and know that You will.*

DO: Make your own chore box.

When you're feeling overwhelmed (2)

◄○►

READ: *"You are worried and troubled about many things. . . ."*

—LUKE 10:41

REFLECT: Do you ever wonder what Martha served in that special meal that she prepared for her beloved guest, Jesus? I'm sure that nothing was too good for this occasion! What were the "things" Scripture tells us she was so busy about? Why, dishes, of course—fish, meat, breads, vegetables, fruits!

But Jesus said to her, "Martha, Martha, you are anxious about many matters, when there is need of but one thing (dish)."

Like Martha, it is easy to work more than is needed so that we end up fretful and too tired to enjoy times with the Lord. Jesus says to me, to you: "Don't. Live simply. Then there will be plenty of time to sit at My feet. Work, yes, but not so much that you have no time for fellowship with Me." Meetings, clubs and purely social activities can never satisfy the longing heart. Only one dish is needed!

—HOPE B. FRIEDMANN

PRAY: *Lord, am I too busy? Is that why I'm feeling overwhelmed? Because I have time for everything and everybody but You? Help me, Jesus, to put You first.*

DO: If possible, cancel a social engagement and spend time with Jesus today.

When you're feeling
overwhelmed (3)

◄○►

READ: *Therefore my spirit is overwhelmed within me....*

—PSALM 143:4

REFLECT: One balmy evening my husband and I attended a performance of *The Unsinkable Molly Brown* at the San Diego Starlight Theatre. The first act had barely begun when a jet-liner roared over on its approach to nearby Lindbergh Field.

The noise of the low-flying jet was deafening—and maddening! I covered both ears, squeezed my eyes shut and silently deplored commercial air travel. Then I heard the audience applauding.

Onstage, the performers had stopped statue-still, looking like an old tintype photo. Then as soon as the noise of the plane died away they resumed their act. During the performance the actors repeated this pause whenever a plane approached.

I loved the show, but it was the pauses that made the biggest impression—and taught me something. Whenever I feel overwhelmed, instead of thrashing wildly against forces I can't control, I pause and bring them to the Lord.

—JUNE MASTERS BACHER

PRAY: *I don't often have deafening jets flying overhead, Father, but I let plenty of other things overwhelm me. Instead of thrashing wildly against forces I can't control, help me remember to stop and take them to You.*

DO: Try to make a quiet place in your home where you can pray regularly. Think of it as a place of refuge from outside forces.

When you're feeling proud of yourself

◄○►

READ: *"Behold the proud, his soul is not upright in him. . . ."*

—HABAKKUK 2:4

REFLECT: When I was in junior high school, part of gym class was jumping hurdles. As my short legs plodded down that cinder track, the huge black and white hurdles seemed to grow taller and taller. Invariably I would stumble, sending the hurdle—and myself—flying.

I've long since given up attempting track feats. But I still stumble over hurdles. Especially when my pride gets in the way. I want to give the perfect dinner party—but the Cornish hens end up charred. I want to be applauded for my PTA efforts—but no one seems to notice. I'm going to be the envy of all my friends and jog every day—until the meteorologists predict showers. I've discovered that the higher up I've puffed myself, the less I depend on God. And the harder I fall.

Now I'm not only trying to master new hurdles, but to do it with humility.

—MARY LOU CARNEY

PRAY: *Father, when I enjoy the success and forget to give You the credit for the things You help me accomplish, remind me, Lord, to give You glory.*

DO: Think of two times in your past when you forgot to thank God for something you know you couldn't have done without Him. Thank Him now for His help.

When you're feeling spiritually dry

◄◊►

READ: *The Lord my God will enlighten my darkness.*

—PSALM 18:28

REFLECT: My junior-high science teacher took the class outside one sunny day and held a magnifying glass over a pile of dry leaves until they suddenly burst into flame. "This happened," explained my teacher, "because the lens concentrated the rays of the sun into a little burning knot of heat. Of course, the leaves had to be thoroughly dry in order to ignite."

Sometimes I bask in the light of God's presence, feel His love and know His nearness. But then I go into a kind of desert. My prayers seem dull and lifeless and I can't seem to recapture that inspiring sense of God's closeness. Yet it comforts me to realize that there's a purpose to the desert. God is drying the leaves of my soul, making me ready to receive, anew, the flaming grace of His Holy Spirit, through the lens of Christ's love.

Knowing that, I can stand the drying time, can't you?

—MARILYN MORGAN KING

PRAY: *I praise You, Father, for the spiritual dark times as well as the light. However long it takes, make my soul ready to receive a new flame of Your Holy Spirit.*

DO: Keep praying and praising God simply because He is worthy of praise. When the Holy Spirit renews the light of His presence, praise some more!

When you're feeling stuck in your job (1)

————————◄○►————————

READ: *The Lord is good to those who wait for Him, to the soul who seeks Him.*

—LAMENTATIONS 3:25

REFLECT: In 1962, when I was working as an aircraft engine tester, I was working the night shift. The plant was noisy, and the work was grimy and greasy. During those hours I dreamed of being a technical writer. I took classes, studied hard, and went on a lot of interviews. After each interview, I returned to the roaring engines, the oily parts, and the night shift.

My wife Ruby sensed my disappointment and said, "Try not to worry. God may have a plan." So I worked and studied, and I prayed that God would help me handle my impatience. Finally, in June 1968, I was hired as a technical writer. After one week on the job, I knew why so much time had elapsed. I was writing about aircraft engines, and without those six years in the plant I wouldn't have known how to begin. Now I understood.

Yes, prayer—and patience—makes the difference.

—OSCAR GREENE

PRAY: *Thank You, Father, for the grace to keep doing, joyfully and patiently, what You've called me to do until You tell me to do something different. I believe You have a plan; please don't let my impatience mess it up.*

DO: Think of three positive things you're gaining by being in the job you are in for as long as you've been there.

When you're feeling
stuck in your job (2)

READ: *And do not grumble. . . .*

—1 CORINTHIANS 10:10 (NIV)

REFLECT: I was strolling through the grounds of a local convent. In contrast to the beauty around me, I was grumbling and comparing the time when I was a full-time writer, teacher and speaker and, now, when I'm an accounting clerk.

At one point in my grousing, I came upon a statue of Jesus the Carpenter holding a simple piece of wood. Surely, Jesus knew of His future ministry. Yet I couldn't imagine Him complaining to God about the insignificance of the carpenter's shop compared to the importance of the waiting ministry. I saw Jesus living in the now, striving to be the very best carpenter possible.

Monday morning found me not only refreshed, but committed to living in the now, to be the best I could be.

—BONNIE WHEELER

PRAY: *Lord, help me work as if the thing I'm meant to do at this moment is my only ministry.*

DO: Focus on your work when you're on the job, but set aside a half hour after work today to plan for your future.

When you're feeling that God has let you down

READ: *Humble yourselves before the Lord, and he will lift you up.*
—JAMES 4:10 (NIV)

REFLECT: Louis XIV saw his armies make France the most powerful country of its time. He was not without losses, however. When he received the news of his crushing defeat by the English at Blenheim, he exclaimed, "How could God do this to me, after all I've done for Him?"

When I first read that quote, I had to laugh at such arrogance. But then I remembered my own exasperation when, after asking God to help me prepare a Sunday school class lesson, I knew it fell flat. Or when, after I felt nudged by God to meet with a hurting friend, he called and canceled. How dare God do this to me?

Maybe what seems to us to be "no" answers from God are actually just what we need to make us more humble when we pray. Perhaps we need to change our expectations from "I ask, You give" to "I ask, I trust."

—SCOTT HARRISON

PRAY: *God, I'm disappointed and frustrated, even though I should be grateful that You can't be manipulated by my expectations or my tantrums. Make me grateful that You're a God Who knows when to say* yes *and when to say* no, *for all the right reasons.*

DO: Think about the wasted energy of a child's tantrum, probably caused by some wise parent's "No."

When you're feeling that you've let down a loved one

READ: *Be of good courage, and let us be strong for our people. . . .*
—1 CHRONICLES 19:13

REFLECT: It's the bottom of the third inning in one of our team's most important softball games. Bases loaded . . . two outs . . . our opponent's leading hitter at bat. I'm shortstop.

The batter hits a hot smash to my right. I field the ball cleanly and throw it to first. The ball sails high over the head of the first baseman, into the bleachers—two runs scored. I fling my glove to the ground, then kick it.

Finally out of the inning, I head for the farthest corner of the bench. Not far enough from my coach, though.

"Japinga!" He sits down next to me and puts his arm around my shoulders. "Success is never final. Failure is never fatal. It's courage that counts. Go out there next inning and hold your head high."

Whenever I face failure, that's been my prayer for strength and courage to go on my way, confident in God's forgiveness and support.

—JEFF JAPINGA

PRAY: *Father, forgive me for so easily letting failure defeat me. Help me to quickly leave failure behind to face the next challenge with You.*

DO: Think back and reflect on some word of wisdom from a parent, a teacher, a coach. If you can't think of your own, take courage—and a prayer—from this reflection.

When you're feeling threatened

◄◎►

READ: *"The Lord will fight for you; you need only to be still."*

—EXODUS 14:14 (NIV)

REFLECT: We were having a picnic. Our puppy had been roaming the area, sniffing importantly under every bush. Now, barking furiously, he chased a half-grown rabbit. The scared little bunny darted into a thick clump of grass and froze there, hoping not to be noticed. From where I stood, I could see his wild, frightened eyes and the frantic pounding of his heart. Instinct warned him not to move a muscle, though, and he didn't, not even when the dog passed close to his hiding place. Then his danger passed, for the dog did not detect him and ran to hunt elsewhere.

Sometimes, when danger threatens our family, when illness or trouble or sin strikes, I become very frightened. Then I remember God's instructions to be still. I freeze like the little rabbit and just wait, hopefully and peacefully. Every time, my Lord has taken care of my deepest needs.

—LUCILLE CAMPBELL

PRAY: *Father, I wish it was more my nature to be still when I feel threatened. Instead I feel like running around frantically. Help me to be still and trust You to protect me and those I love.*

DO: Imagine you're that rabbit hiding in the bushes from danger. Think about how you're like that rabbit—and how you're not.

When you're feeling unattractive

READ: *But we have this treasure in earthen vessels. . . .*

—2 CORINTHIANS 4:7

REFLECT: I spent two weeks in Honduras, and I wanted a special memento of my visit. "Buy this, senorita," the vendor said, shoving a brightly painted jar into my hands.

I shook my head. "I want that one," I said, pointing to a plain jug on the shelf behind him.

"No, no!" he fussed. "It is ugly! How about one with gold trim?" I shook my head. "That one," I insisted. I tucked the fragile pot in my carry-on, and hugged it close all the way home.

Now it sits in my family room, a fond reminder of my days in Honduras. But it reminds me of something else too. God's "treasure," the Spirit of His Son, is housed in me, a plain, vulnerable vessel, dependent on God's care.

I've never thought of my clay pot as ugly. And its frailty has made me cherish it even more. Perhaps that's the way God feels too.

—MARY LOU CARNEY

PRAY: *Father, when I'm focused on the outside of the jar, remind me of the beauty of Your Spirit within it.*

DO: Find your own jar to remind you that you are a vessel where the Spirit of the living God dwells.

When you're feeling unloved (1)

◄○►

READ: *And He will love you and bless you. . . .*

—DEUTERONOMY 7:13

REFLECT: I'd been feeling unloved lately. Nothing serious—just no hugs, no kisses, no "I love you's." Then I recalled the words of Elizabeth Barrett Browning: "How do I love thee? Let me count the ways." I made the following list:

1. *My husband Carl* handing me his sweater as I headed for the mailbox. "Better put this on. The wind's mighty chilly."

2. *Our son Tim* calling from Virginia to ask, "Everything okay?"

3. *Our daughter-in-law Jessica's* note: "Wish you were here. The yard's filled with bluebirds!"

4. *My friend Gayla's* phone call: "Missed you at the meeting yesterday. I didn't enjoy it without you."

5. And, above all, *God's* encompassing, unfailing love.

Are there small signs of love around you?

—ALETHA JANE LINDSTROM

PRAY: *Make me mindful of the little signs of love expressed to me each day . . . and make me mindful of little ways I can show love.*

DO: Do something loving for a coworker, an elderly neighbor, a family member who is sending signals that he/she is feeling unloved.

When you're feeling unloved (2)

READ: *When I consider Your heavens, the work of Your fingers, the moon and the stars, which You have ordained, what is man that You are mindful of him, and the son of man that You visit him?*

—PSALM 8:3–4

REFLECT: Almost anything can be rendered as a scale model, except the universe. If the earth were represented by a ball only an inch in diameter, the nearest star (Alpha Centauri) outside of our solar system would have to be placed nearly fifty thousand miles away!

It's hard for my mind to consider such boundless distance. Fifty thousand miles is more than twice around our equator.

The universe—what an awesome thing to comprehend. Even more awesome is the thought that out of the six-and-one-half billion people on the earth, God cares about me. And yet He does.

—ISABEL WOLSELEY

PRAY: *Father, awesome Creator of the universe, I'm not always mindful of Your love for me but, today, I'm awed by it. I love You, Lord.*

DO: Take your thoughts off other things and try to comprehend the incomprehensible—that the Creator of the universe and everything in it loves *you*.

When you're feeling uprooted and alone

◄○►

READ: *By your patience possess your souls.*

—LUKE 21:19

REFLECT: Weeds are the enemy of gardeners, but working in my garden, I learned something from one. Pulling it up by its roots, I tossed it between two rows of peas. A few days later, returning to the garden after a rainfall, I noticed the weed had already sent out tiny new rootlets, groping toward the rich soil, struggling to get a foothold again.

Day by day, the weed sent out more and more roots, digging ever deeper into the earth. Soon, it had pulled itself upright again, had new leaf growth, was flourishing.

At times, all of us feel uprooted. A change of jobs, a death in the family, can make a person feel cut off and alone. When that happens, the important thing is to reach out to the source of life that is available to all of us. Each and every one of us can always find the courage to grow new roots. Christ is always there.

—PAT SULLIVAN

PRAY: *Lord, I have been uprooted and it's hard, but I've learned from others that transplanted lives can take root pretty quickly. I pray that will be true in this new place.*

DO: Talk to someone who's newly "transplanted" and who seems to be the better for it. Ask how he/she survived so well.

When you're feeling useless

◄○►

READ: *But the very hairs of your head are all numbered.*

—MATTHEW 10:30

REFLECT: The concert was scheduled for the next day. The conductor raised his baton, and the final rehearsal began. After only a few bars, the leader stopped the music.

"Something is missing," he said. "I don't hear the piccolo."

A young man rushed in, muttering apologies for being late, and sat down, piccolo at his lips.

Once more, the rehearsal began, and as it progressed, the conductor nodded to the tardy young man and smiled. The sound was good now, complete with the piccolo playing.

Such a small instrument! Some might consider it insignificant, but the maestro knew its worth and stopped to look for it.

You might sometimes feel small and insignificant, but always remember the Master knows your worth, and He needs you.

—DRUE DUKE

PRAY: *God, I praise You as the great Conductor of the universe! I'm amazed that my small contribution makes a difference in the whole symphony of life.*

DO: Listen to a piece of classical music and try to identify at least one or two of the individual instruments.

When you're feeling vulnerable

—◄◊►—

READ: *May the God who gives endurance and encouragement give you a spirit of unity among yourselves as you follow Christ Jesus. . . .*

—ROMANS 15:5 (NIV)

REFLECT: Our kitten had climbed our large oak tree and was making his way toward a bird's nest. The parent birds stood screeching in front of their nest, but what impressed me was an assortment of nearly thirty other birds of various kinds that had rallied to the cause. Some chirped, some cawed, some screeched, but they all had one fierce, common intent: Turn back the enemy.

And they did. They backed him down the branch until, with great relief, he scrambled into my outstretched hands.

The birds had won! As I brought my frightened kitten into the house, I thought: *How wonderful it is when Christians band together like that, determined to defeat the enemy, Satan.* This is what churches are all about—a fellowship, standing together, doing the job, succeeding where a single individual would fail.

—MARION BOND WEST

PRAY: *I doubt that I've ever really understood the strength of believers working as one body. Thank You for helping me understand.*

DO: If you're feeling vulnerable in some area, call a friend—or two or three—to pray with you.

When you're feeling weary

◄◦►

REFLECT: Our family spent a vacation hiking on the Appalachian Trail with two Sardinian donkeys (named Pinocchio and Figaro). When they grew weary, they would fall to the ground as if shot, and no amount of prodding could get them to their feet. They knew their limits, and until refreshed they would not continue.

In this respect, donkeys and llamas may be wiser than many humans. I suggested as much not long ago to a friend who was making light of my habit of afternoon siestas. "A fifteen- or twenty-minute nap after lunch will make a new person out of you," I offered. He was not convinced. Then, from the newspaper, I got more ammunition. A sleep researcher said that adult nappers are sharper, healthier, and happier. Next to Christ's invitation, "Come unto me, all ye that labor and are heavy laden, and I will give you rest." I can't think of any better midday rejuvenator for the weary.

——FRED BAUER

PRAY: *Give me wisdom, please, Lord, when it comes to ordering my time.*

DO: Try, for a week or two, to make time in your life for a short afternoon siesta. See for yourself if it doesn't renew you—body, soul and spirit.

When you're finding it hard to go to church (1)

◄◊►

READ: *There will be more joy in heaven over one sinner who repents than over ninety-nine just persons who need no repentance.*

—LUKE 15:7

REFLECT: "Void if detached," I read on my airline ticket. I had stepped into a doorway for shelter one rainy Wednesday evening, and I was idly examining the ticket for my flight to a distant city the next day.

Suddenly, I heard singing. I was in the entrance to a small church I'd never noticed before. The door was open and something compelled me to enter. A man in one of the rear seats motioned to me and held out his hymnal to share. In that instant the words, "Void if detached," took on new meaning.

I had been a churchgoer for years. But my visits had gradually become fewer. I had separated myself from the true source of happiness and peace.

The man in the pew was still offering to share his hymnal. I stepped in beside him with an almost overpowering feeling of joy. It's never too late to *attach*—to come home again.

—WALTER HARTER

PRAY: *Dear God, I pray for all those who have stopped going to church. Renew their desire to worship You with other believers and their desire to use the gifts You've given them to serve the body of Christ. That includes me, Lord.*

DO: Invite a friend to church—especially one who was once a churchgoer but hasn't been to church in a while.

When you're finding it hard to go to church (2)

◀◦▶

READ: *Now you are the body of Christ, and members individually.*

—I CORINTHIANS 12:27

REFLECT: I was called upon all through my teenage years to go to church every time the doors were open. One day when I was really tired of church attendance, I got up courage to suggest that I didn't need to be inside a church in order to worship God. I said I could worship Him any place—especially outside, in nature, where I would have the beauty of His creation around me.

Father gently explained that my relationship to God was two-pronged: not only did it involve my relationship with Him, but also with my fellow man. He pointed to our parlor fireplace where a bed of coals lay glowing. Then, with a pair of tongs, he lifted a fiery coal from the grate and placed it on the hearth. Its glow gradually diminished and finally went out.

I never again objected to going through those church doors.

—SAM JUSTICE

PRAY: *Father, sometimes I find myself going to church for all the wrong reasons, and wanting to skip for all the wrong reasons too. Help me value the relationships with my fellow man that are nurtured there, as well as my relationship with You.*

DO: Study the Bible to discover the value God puts on church attendance—and why.

When you're fretful
about the future

———◦———

READ: *He calms the storm, so that its waves are still.*

—PSALM 107:29

REFLECT: Our two cats, the Orange Brothers, rode in the car with us on the two-day trip to our new home. During stops, we put them in their cat carrier, but other times, we let them lounge around the car.

Sweet Face, completely relaxed and worry-free in the strange surroundings, accepted the offer and napped on the seat or looked out the window.

But Wheezer, the kind of kitty who inspired the expression "nervous as a cat," refused to leave the box. During the entire trip he cringed in the back of the carrier with eyes wild and muscles tense, a nervous wreck.

Poor Wheezer! He's a dumb animal, yet how easy it is for me to identify with him, for I am the fretful type myself. The difference between this poor, dumb animal and me is that, unlike Wheezer, I know I have God.

—PATRICIA R. PATTERSON

PRAY: *God, how often I stay in the "back of the crate" cringing all the way to a new place in life. In fact, it's what I've been doing even today. Thank You for this timely reminder to relax and enjoy the journey.*

DO: Buy a fat and happy-looking stuffed cat. Name him Sweet Face and use him to remind you to relax.

When you're giving up
on a dream

---◄◦►---

READ: *He has made everything beautiful in its time.*

—ECCLESIASTES 3:11

REFLECT: I once planted a red flowering crabapple tree in our yard. But it didn't exactly thrive—in fact the leaves started dropping off!

The next spring it did a little better—it had swelled buds and leaves, but no flowers. "That does it! I'm getting rid of this *flowering* crabapple!" I sputtered. But I didn't.

The third spring came. Still no red flowers. But this time some tiny clusters of red balls nestled in among the leaves.

As I watched the little red tree become brilliant with color, it reminded me of how impatient I can be with other things in my life. Dreams, for instance. Instead of nurturing them and giving them time to grow, I get impatient and rip them out.

So I decided, no matter how small and scraggly and unpromising my dreams appear, I'll plant them lovingly, nourish them with work and prayer and give the good Lord time to help them grow.

—VICKI SCHAD

PRAY: *Forgive me, Father, for giving up on the very dreams You planted in my heart. Please don't let them die. Bring them to life, Lord, for Your glory.*

DO: Allow yourself to resurrect an old dream that has all but died. What one step can you take to help make that dream come true? Take that step today.

When you're grieving (1)

READ: *My soul follows close behind You; Your right hand upholds me.*

— PSALM 63:8

REFLECT: The last time I saw my friend Eileen was when I drove her and her husband George to the airport to catch a plane bound for the Caribbean.

The next thing I knew, Eileen was dead, the victim of a boating accident. It was so sudden, I couldn't even ask God for help because I was numb and empty inside.

"How can you bear the pain?" I finally asked George.

His eyes were tired and red from lack of sleep, and he sighed deeply. "I have my faith," he said quietly.

I had faith, too, but, somehow, calling it mine made it something to cling to. That night I was able to talk to God about my grief. I began to cry as I asked Him to take away my anger, resentment, and loneliness. And as He walked with me through the days ahead, I learned what it means to have not only faith, but *my* faith.

— PHYLLIS HOBE

PRAY: *Lord, please don't let my confusion, anger and loneliness be stronger than my faith in You. Even though I don't understand, I trust You to bring good from this terrible tragedy.*

DO: Call a friend who knew the loved one you're missing. Share your grief—and your faith—to help you both through the pain.

When you're grieving (2)

<o>

READ: *Beloved, do not think it strange concerning the fiery trial which is to try you, as though some strange thing happened to you. . . .*

—1 PETER 4:12

REFLECT: All the hardships I had faced in my life were insignificant when compared with the death of a friend whom I had loved deeply.

Then another friend, watching me sink into self-pity, brought me a passage written by a psychiatrist for people who have lost dear ones. It read: "All your trials . . . are gifts to you . . . opportunities to grow. You will not grow if you sit in a beautiful flower garden . . . but you will grow if you are sick, if you are in pain, if you experience losses . . . and if you take the pain and learn to accept it as a gift with a specific purpose."

Pain a gift? I wondered. But I realized it was true. In my grief, God was giving me new insights and new friends. And I came to know God better than ever because I needed Him to help me through my grief.   —CHARLOTTE HUTCHISON

PRAY: *I never thought I'd be thanking You for the pain of this grief, God, but . . . thank You for this pain. For the insights it has brought, for the empathy for others who are grieving, for how You're going to use it in my life, thank You so much.*

DO: Encourage a friend who has also received the gift of pain so that the pain will not be wasted.

When you're harboring resentment

◀◎▶

READ: *Then Jesus went into the temple of God and drove out all those who bought and sold in the temple, and overturned the tables of the money changers and the seats of those who sold doves.*

—MATTHEW 21:12

REFLECT: I can recall a time when I harbored a lot of ill will against a young woman named Marion. I just didn't like her. Whenever I saw Marion, resentment welled up inside me and I found it hard to be civil.

Then one day, during my prayer time, I felt God nudging me about it. *Your resentment is defiling your inner temple,* He seemed to be saying. *It is blocking your relationship with Me. It must go!* Confessing my fault and asking for His forgiveness was difficult, but I did it. And as I practiced, my admiration for her grew, until one day all the resentment I had for her was gone.

Like the quiet in the Temple after Jesus threw out the moneychangers, peace had come to my soul.

—ELEANOR SASS

PRAY: *Lord, forgive me for letting something stay in my heart that blocks my relationship with another as well as with You. I'm truly sorry, Lord.*

DO: After you pray this prayer, write down the things that are feeding your resentment and throw the paper away. During the next few days, watch for changes in your responses to this person.

When you're having a conflict with your children

---◆〇▷---

READ: *But if you do not forgive men their sins, your Father will not forgive your sins.*

—MATTHEW 6:15 (NIV)

REFLECT: My teenage daughter Julie and I just couldn't communicate. I felt she misinterpreted what I said; then she would resent me, and I in turn would feel hurt. None of my prayers for Julie seemed to help.

One day a friend said, "You can spend the rest of your life praying for someone to change, but if unforgiveness is in your heart, God cannot answer your prayers."

Hot tears rolled down my face. Our problem was *me*! In desperation I confessed my unforgiveness not only to God, but to Julie.

An indefinable gloom that I hadn't been able shake lifted. Most amazing was the immediate change in Julie. We laughed together, prayed together, even went shopping together. One evening I heard her tell a friend, "My mother and I have a really good relationship."

What a powerful gift—this thing called forgiveness.

—MARION BOND WEST

PRAY: *Father, I honestly hadn't realized how much unforgiveness I'd been holding onto from conflicts with my children. Please forgive my unforgiveness, Lord, and help us to move forward to healing and a loving relationship.*

DO: If this is true of you, share this story with your child/children and ask for their forgiveness as well as God's.

When you're having business problems

READ: *Therefore, as we have opportunity, let us do good to all, especially to those who are of the household of faith.*

—GALATIANS 6:10

REFLECT: It was a blazing hot day in 1904 at the Louisiana Purchase Exposition in St. Louis, Missouri. Charles Menches was there at his ice-cream stand. Like other ice-cream vendors, he sold his treat in dishes. But he was so busy that by midmorning all his dishes were gone. Customers were turning away and his ice cream was melting.

Nearby, Ernest Hamwi from Syria was selling a Middle Eastern delicacy called *zalabia*, a crisp, pastry-like delight eaten with syrup.

"Quick," cried Menches, "give me some zalabia!" He curled the zalabia, scooped in the ice cream and handed each to a customer. They looked startled, tasted, then smiled. The ice cream was saved and thus the ice-cream cone was born!

Problems and setbacks come to all of us. But God also gives us imagination, originality, and inventiveness. Perhaps He sometimes sends a challenging little setback just to make sure those qualities don't atrophy. —OSCAR GREENE

PRAY: *I pray that I would be able to stay cool and calm in this crisis, Father, and at the same time make quick, creative decisions.*

DO: Gather prayer support for your business—and maybe some business advice—from businessmen and women you know and trust.

When you're having doubts

◄○►

READ: *His bread will be supplied, and water will not fail him.*

—ISAIAH 33:16 (NIV)

REFLECT: I stood in the warm Mexican sunshine in Acapulco and watched the divers hurling themselves off the high, rocky point to plummet into the foaming sea far below. How daring those divers are! They hurl themselves out into the air on faith, literally on faith, for when they leave the cliff there isn't enough water below to break the dive. The wave that will bring the necessary swell of water into the cove is still out in the ocean. Those divers have to have faith that the wave will be there when they need it.

Isn't that the kind of faith I need? The feeling of assurance that God—like the wave—will be there when I hurl myself into the unknown. —BARBARA HUDSON DUDLEY

PRAY: *I wish I could say I never doubt that You'll be there to catch me, Lord, when it's time to jump, but I do doubt sometimes. Please give me faith to believe that You won't ask me to jump and then let me fall.*

DO: Find a video or a picture of the cliff divers in Acapulco. If they can trust the waves, You can trust the God Who made the waves.

When you're having marriage problems

READ: *For by one offering He has perfected forever those who are being sanctified.*

—HEBREWS 10:14

REFLECT: My heart ached in church as I prayed for friends who were separating—friends whose twenty-year marriage had seemed like one of the "perfect" ones. Suddenly, I felt vulnerable. Could this happen to Joe and me?

I twisted my wedding ring and remembered the way we bought my engagement diamond. We chose a small, flawless diamond over a larger one with a flaw that cost approximately the same. Years later, I learned from a dealer that nature does not produce a perfect stone. A "flawless" diamond is only perfect to magnification of ten.

And, yes, our marriage is flawed—as defective as the two of us. But like a diamond, our relationship has beauty too: strong love and shared commitment. Joe and I could make it shine by magnifying each other's strong points, not our imperfections. I prayed God would help our friends do the same.

—MARJORIE PARKER

PRAY: *Oh, Father, my heart is breaking right now. What You have joined together, please don't let man put asunder.*

DO: Make a list of your spouse's strong points. Give the list to him/her with words of love and encouragement.

When you're having trouble trusting

---<o>---

READ: *There is no fear in love; but perfect love casts out fear. . . .*

—1 JOHN 4:18

REFLECT: I was clearing brambles from our church cemetery when a frisky, short-haired black dog bounded over to me. He crouched down, tail wagging, and then dashed off into some brambles. By the time his master had come over, "Blacky" and I were friends.

"Wonderful dog," I said.

"Yes," the owner responded, "but he wasn't always that way. He'd been abandoned. When I brought him food, he would growl and snatch it away. It was three weeks before he stopped snarling and stayed by me to eat. Then the next week he came up to be petted, but reluctantly. But the week after that he began to wag his tail when he caught sight of me. One day he followed me home. Now he's a very loving dog."

Isn't God like the patient man who kept offering love, while too often we are like Blacky, slinking in lostness and fear, afraid to trust ourselves to Him?

—WILLIAM DEERFIELD

PRAY: *Father, I see myself in Blacky so much. I've been hurt and I'm so afraid to trust. But I know deep down that even when people hurt and disappoint me, You are worthy of my trust.*

DO: Find a Scripture about trust. Write it down and tape it to a dresser or bathroom mirror. Read it daily until you've memorized it, and then say it every time you feel yourself closing off from others or from God.

When you're hoping for something

------------◀◉▶------------

READ: *For we were saved in this hope, but hope that is seen is not hope. . . .*

—ROMANS 8:24

REFLECT: I'd just received yet another wedding invitation in my mailbox—one more reminder that my own dreams of marriage still were simply dreams.

I carried my bad mood over to the couch and turned on the TV. In minutes, I was caught up in the story of an angel father who was granted heaven's permission to visit his seriously ill son on Earth. As the two talked, the boy questioned his dad about the future: "What will happen to me? When? How?"

I was instantly alert as I recognized those familiar words, and I waited for the answers almost as anxiously as he. Finally, the angel's voice answered, "I could tell you everything, but I wouldn't be much of a father if I took away your chance at hope and faith and dreams, now would I?"

I decided then I'd take my chances . . . every chance at the hope and faith and dreams God saw fit to give.

—MELANIE BRITT

PRAY: *Father, it's out of Your goodness that You've kept my hopes and dreams alive by not revealing my future yet. Give me faith, Lord, that You'll bring them to pass in Your time and in Your way.*

DO: Even now, as you wait, you're fulfilling God's plan for your life. Try to find the joy you've been given today as you anticipate and hope for tomorrow's.

When you're ill (1)

◀◐▶

READ: *Your hands made me and formed me. . . .*

—PSALM 119:73 (NIV)

REFLECT: There was a man who suffered from a constant pain in his elbow. Doctors treated it, but the pain persisted and gradually grew worse.

One day, the man's wife brought home an appliance that she had purchased. It refused to work. Her husband, looking at the warranty, discovered a line that said, "If this appliance fails to function properly, return it to the manufacturer for prompt attention."

So he did. Then he thought. *What about this elbow of mine? The local repairmen can't seem to fix it, so I think I'll just wrap it up in a respectful prayer and return it to the Maker for His prompt attention.*

That's what he did, sending up a "respectful prayer" every day. In a short time the elbow was completely healed. The truth is, all medicine is God's medicine, whether it takes the form of a pill or a prayer. Be sure you have the right combination of both!

—NORMAN VINCENT PEALE

PRAY: *Dear God, I'm sending my _____ to You in prayer for healing. I can't seem to find a cure for it here, but if it's Your will, You could easily heal me. Thank You for doing that, Lord, in Your way and in Your time!*

DO: Pray daily for your healing. Check off each day on your calendar that you pray.

When you're ill (2)

READ: *Even today I declare that I will restore double to you.*

—ZECHARIAH 9:12

REFLECT: When our son was twelve, he had a third relapse of hepatitis. He faced weeks in bed and months of reduced activity. One day in the market I greeted another nurse, a Christian woman with whom I had worked briefly. "Just take one day at a time," she said.

I began to ask God to give us strength to make it through that day. I tried to help our son center his thoughts on that day, not to look ahead to a bleak future. Always, my prayer was answered.

A year later he was well. Two years later he was named "Most Valuable Player" of his soccer and track teams. One day he said, "You know, I was thinking about when I had hepatitis and I thought, 'How did I ever make it through that?'"

"God led you through," I said with a full heart. "One day at a time."

—DEE ANN PALMER

PRAY: *Father, I can't help but worry about tomorrow . . .*
unless You give me Your grace just for today—
every day.

DO: Call someone who's also been taken out of commission for one reason or another—an elderly neighbor, a newly retired friend, someone in the hospital. What could you do together to make today more enjoyable?

When you're in pain

◀◉▶

READ: *So He touched her hand, and the fever left her. And she arose and served them.*

—MATTHEW 8:15

REFLECT: When I was about ten years old, I was in danger of losing my left leg because of a severe infection. Finally the danger passed, but the recuperation was long and painful. The only time that the pain seemed bearable was when my great-grandmother would come into my darkened room and place her cool, work-worn hand on my forehead. She seemed to sense my relief and she would keep her hand there, sometimes for hours, until at last I fell asleep. And this is what God does for us when we are in pain. Just the touch of His loving concern brings relief beyond measure.

—PHYLLIS HOBE

PRAY: *Father, I'm hurting today and need a special touch from You. Thank You for comforting and healing me.*

DO: Get a Bible and read the passage in Mark 5 about the woman who was healed just by touching Jesus' clothes.

When you're learning a new skill

◄o►

READ: *By faith Abraham obeyed when he was called to go out to the place which he would receive as an inheritance. And he went out, not knowing where he was going.*

—HEBREWS 11:8

REFLECT: I was a timid six-year-old when Mom felt it was time I learned how to handle a boat. Every morning, when the winds were slight, she would take me out in a small dinghy and teach me to sail. I learned how to find the wind, maneuver the boat, adjust the sail and come into shore.

Then one day I stepped into the dinghy . . . and Mom pushed me out into the bay all by myself. (Little did I know she was ready to rescue me if I needed it.) I was petrified. Clinging to the tiller and mainsheet, I sailed from buoy to buoy, never venturing far from shore. Gradually, with each tack, my confidence grew. By the time I landed, I was radiant. "I can sail!" I announced to Mom.

"All by yourself," she agreed, smiling at my victory.

Faith. It's the courage God lends us to push off into unfamiliar waters! —RICK HAMLIN

PRAY: *Father, even though I often feel afraid when learning something new, I'm so grateful You don't leave me in my comfort zone, doing the same things over and over and over. Use my new skill for Your glory, Lord.*

DO: Ask a friend who needs a challenge to learn this new skill with you.

When you're looking for love

READ: *His banner over me was love.*

—SONG OF SOLOMON 2:4

REFLECT: As a child, *love* was smelling spicy cookies baking; the damp, musty smell of laundry hanging in the house on a rainy day; waking in terror from a nightmare to feel loving arms soothing, rocking. I could hear love in my father's voice as he read fairy tales and spun dreams while holding me on his lap. And love was the way my mother would put her arms around me in generous, tender hugs.

I remember holding tightly to my father's hand as he pointed out wonderful things along the byways of our neighborhood. I felt love as my mother vigorously brushed my long brown hair. Love was being cared for, protected, wanted. It was being a child in a secure and happy home.

Now, love has become a sunset, the purring of my kitten, the presence of my God. Through His promise I know that the greatest of love's experiences is still to come.

—DORIS HAASE

PRAY: *Loving Father, I wish I'd known as a child what I know now—that I could find nurturing love in You, God. I still need it, Father, not only for myself, but also to pass on to others.*

DO: The love you're seeking, God has in abundance. Find a quiet place and spend a few minutes basking in His love.

198

When you're losing a beloved pet

◄○►

READ: *Surely He has borne our griefs and carried our sorrows....*
—ISAIAH 53:4

REFLECT: Time had run out for Bridget, our Border collie. My mind accepted that she was suffering, that putting her to sleep was a kindness, but my heart agonized at letting go. I sat beside her on the kitchen floor, glancing anxiously at the clock. How could I possibly go through with it?

Very quietly a Voice inside me said, "You can't. Give your grief to Me."

There, crying into Bridget's graying muzzle, I offered my sorrow to Jesus. As I did, I felt Him enter my suffering and absorb it until it became His pain. I no longer carried this heavy sadness alone. Straightening up, I spoke gently, "Come on, old girl. It's time to go."

Try letting Jesus into your hurt. He will share it with you and make it bearable.
—CAROL KNAPP

PRAY: *Jesus, I invite You into my hurt. Help me do the loving thing for my beloved _____. Please help carry my sadness in this loss.*

DO: Invite a close friend to come be with you, one who can also carry some of your sadness.

When you're losing a loved one

READ: *"I have heard your prayer and seen your tears. . . ."*

—ISAIAH 38:5 (NIV)

REFLECT: When my mother was dying of emphysema, she became a hospice patient, and this sensitive, gentle group of people helped us learn how to care for her so she could spend her last few days in her own bed. They taught us how to make her comfortable and, perhaps more importantly, how to cope with the emotional task of facing her impending death.

One nugget of their advice vividly sticks in my mind even today, because it not only guided my time with her but continues to help me with the priority of being open and honest in all relationships. "Take care of all unfinished business with the people you love," a hospice nurse urged me one morning near the end. "Say what you want to say. Do what you want to do. Today. Don't wait until tomorrow."

When she died, I was comforted in my grief. There was no unfinished business.

—CAROL KUYKENDALL

PRAY: *Father, praise You for the people who help the rest of us prepare for the death of loved ones. Bless them all and the families they are serving today.*

DO: Consider a donation to hospice as a token of your gratitude.

When you're losing hope

◄○►

READ: *We trust in the living God. . . .*

— 1 TIMOTHY 4:10

REFLECT: Nine-year-old Tasha was our guest. "You know," she remarked during dinner, "our family is so lucky!"

"In what way?" I asked. Since her father's death five years earlier, it seemed to me that the family had experienced nothing but trouble.

Tasha began listing her blessings. "Rob nearly lost his leg when the water tank fell on him, but now he's able to walk. Most of our baby pigs died, but the ones that lived are so cute! Sybil's horse spooked and ran, but another horse stepped in front of it and slowed it down just long enough for Sybil to jump off." She turned her sunny smile on me. "See? God really takes care of us."

I did see! Tasha's family had faced nearly every problem imaginable. Yet Tasha was never without hope.

Hope's essence—and the secret of victorious living—lies in seeing the good in every situation God permits to come into our lives.

—PENNEY SCHWAB

PRAY: *Lord, I must confess that with every recent development that's come in the front door, a little hope has flown out the back. Father, help me get my eyes off the circumstances and back on You, the source of my hope.*

DO: Do a Bible study on *hope* to renew yours.

When you're making room for a new person in your life

───────────◄○►───────────

READ: *And above all things have fervent love for one another, for "love will cover a multitude of sins."*

— 1 PETER 4:8

REFLECT: My boyfriend handed the phone to me. "My father wants to talk to you," he whispered.

A second later, I was saying "Hello" to a man I had never met. John's dad joked for a few minutes, capping with the instructions, "Make sure my son treats you right!" I laughed, but I had a backer!

Then John's mom got on the phone. We chatted a bit, and she closed with, "Well, honey, we love you already!" I had never imagined such openness.

John's parents had prayed for each of their children's spouses-to-be before their children were even born! Occasionally a friend will ask, "How do you get along with your in-laws?" My answer is simple:

"Great! They loved me before they met me."

Is a new person coming into your life? A new in-law, a new pastor, a new neighbor? Will you give this person the gift of predetermined love?

—STEPHANIE LINDSELL

PRAY: *Only by Your Spirit, Lord, can I love someone I've just met or have yet to meet. But I do ask You to open my heart the way I would like hearts to be open to me.*

DO: Express your love and acceptance to the new person coming into your life, even if it is a choice of the will and not an emotion.

When you're newly retired and don't know what to do with yourself

READ: *They shall still bear fruit in old age; they shall be fresh and flourishing. . . .*

—PSALM 92:14

REFLECT: Over the years I have known many elderly people who seemed to be just as busy at their work, their hobbies and their personal interests as they ever were. I have asked several of them how they managed it. Time and again I have been told, "There is so much that I can do for others now that I have the time for it. I may be old but I am not dead!"

Ralph Waldo Emerson once said, "We do not count a man's years until he has nothing else to count."

I suspect that the decrepitude of old age is not a matter of years but a matter of simply quitting. When we give up as individuals, we also give up as children of God, dismissing the gifts He has given us.

—GLENN KITTLER

PRAY: *Lord, my biggest fear in retirement is that I will waste time, and waste away in mind, body and spirit. With Your help, God, I'll never dismiss the gifts You've given me. In fact, I'll look forward to new ones I've yet to discover.*

DO: After a season of rest in your new retirement, ask a retired friend you admire for his/her secret.

When you're nursing feelings of rejection

READ: *If you have anything against anyone, forgive him, that your Father in heaven may also forgive you your trespasses.*

—MARK 11:25

REFLECT: When I was in college, I fell head over heels in love with a young lady who didn't return my affections. Finally, she began to shower attention upon a young man I felt unworthy of her. I was crushed.

The rejection left an ache in my heart, shattering my confidence.

Later I taught school in the Midwest. One day a colleague confronted me. "It seems like you turn away when anyone tries to be your friend. Why?"

I was perplexed. But after some reflection it became clear to me: I had been using that early rejection as a shield against others because I hadn't found it in my heart to forgive the young lady. The rejection was not the problem—it was the way I had reacted to it. Our Savior asked forgiveness for those taking His very life. On a far lesser scale, couldn't I do the same?

—OSCAR GREENE

PRAY: *Father, I can see how my unforgiveness is causing me to keep people at a distance today. I choose to forgive, Lord, and let the hurt go. Remind me when others keep me at a distance that there could be some hurt in their heart too.*

DO: Rewind your memory to the moment you closed your heart. Rewrite the script to include forgiveness and a heart open to others.

When you're overextended (1)

READ: *My heart took delight in all my work. . . .*

—ECCLESIASTES 2:10 (NIV)

REFLECT: The heavy rains that started in the spring of '93 and never let up discouraged me from having my usual large garden behind the college where I teach. Instead, I just set out a few things around the house: four tomato plants, a dozen okra plants, a few flowers and some asparagus.

This little planting gave me more pleasure than my large garden, and plenty of produce. The reason? The small garden was more manageable. The bigger garden was always ahead of me with weeds and bugs and the need for cultivation. But four tomato plants? I could weed, water and fertilize them, stake them, and check them for worms in only a few minutes a week. And those four plants produced more tomatoes than fifteen plants the year before, and I had enough okra to feed the neighbors too.

Overextending is an easy mistake to make. Next time I'm tempted to do too much, I'll remember my garden.

—DANIEL SCHANTZ

PRAY: *Father, You'll have to convince me that it's okay to have some down time in life, not to be rushing from one thing to the next. That's just standard operating procedure in our society. If you could do that, Lord, I'd be so grateful.*

DO: Make a list of your commitments and choose two you can cut back.

When you're overextended (2)

◄○►

READ: *Therefore we also pray always for you that our God would count you worthy of this calling, and fulfill . . . the work of faith with power. . . .*

—2 THESSALONIANS 1:11

REFLECT: Every day had been filled with "worthy" causes. Monday, the United Way; Tuesday, a school meeting; Wednesday, a church report. . . . I wrestled with the question: *Have I overextended myself?* And believing that to be the case, I prayed that God would take some of my responsibilities away from me.

Not long after that I came across a quotation from the American clergyman Phillips Brooks. He said, "Do not pray for easy lives. Pray to be stronger men! Do not pray for tasks equal to your powers. Pray for powers equal to your tasks."

I was praying all wrong. To be sure, there are times when I need to say "no" and not crowd my life unnecessarily. But when the problem is not one of too much to do, but of attitude (or lack thereof), then instead of asking God for a smaller crop, why not ask Him to help me carry a bigger basket?

—TERRY HELWIG

PRAY: *I honestly don't know if I have too much to do, Lord, or just need a bigger basket. Could You somehow make that clear to me?*

DO: It's okay to use your own wisdom in making your decision. Decide to drop something—maybe the thing you've been doing the longest or the commitment lowest on your list of things you value. If that decision brings you more joy and energy than the thought of continuing it, let it go. God is capable of letting you know if you're making a mistake.

When you're praying for a friend

READ: *Clearly you are an epistle of Christ, ministered by us, written not with ink but by the Spirit of the living God. . . .*

—2 CORINTHIANS 3:3

REFLECT: I've started something new recently: I write prayer letters. Here's an example:

Dear God, You sure gave me a solid-gold friend when You brought Cathy and me together. I am praying right now that You will refresh her and brighten her day with the light of Your presence, Lord. Thank You for all of Cathy's work with her church's teens, and for her generously giving spirit. Bring her thoughtful ways back to her in a swirl of blessings.

Is there someone who needs a word of comfort or cheer? Perhaps you have a friend or family member whom you want to bring nearer to God? Write a prayer letter to Him about them and your feelings for them. These letters can stay private between you and God, or you can send your prayer-letter friend a copy to lift his or her spirits and let your friend know he or she is cared for. Let your prayer letter pray blessings into another's day.

—CAROL KNAPP

PRAY: *Father, I pray a blessing on _____ today. May Your Spirit rise up within him/her to give him/her peace and joy and every provision he/she will need for today. Thank You for bringing him/her into my life.*

DO: Write out your prayer for the friend prayed for today and send it to him/her.

When you're
procrastinating (1)

 ◄◊►

READ: *This is the day the Lord has made. . . .*

—PSALM 118:24

REFLECT: In a friend's house I noticed a framed sampler on the kitchen wall that read:

> BLESS OUR HOME, FATHER,
>
> THAT WE MAY CHERISH THE BREAD BEFORE THERE IS NONE,
>
> DISCOVER EACH OTHER BEFORE WE LEAVE,
>
> AND ENJOY EACH OTHER FOR WHAT WE ARE WHILE WE HAVE TIME.

While we have time! I once had an easygoing cousin whose favorite phrase was "one of these days." One of these days, he would take that back-pack trip in the Rockies with the youngsters; one of these days, he would learn to play the guitar; one of these days, he would take his wife on the church retreat for married couples. Then, on one of those days, he had a sudden heart attack—and there were no more days.

"This is the day," the Psalmist sang. Not tomorrow, or the day after, or the day after that. *This* is the day for us to rejoice and be glad in it.

—ARTHUR GORDON

PRAY: *Father, please don't let me keep putting things off until tomorrow until there are no more tomorrows.*

DO: Forget the things you didn't get done yesterday. Decide what you most need to get done today. Commit to doing it, or at least starting it, today. Ask a friend to hold you accountable. And promise yourself a reward when you get it done.

When you're procrastinating (2)

◄◦►

READ: *In Your hand it is to make great and to give strength to all.*
—1 CHRONICLES 29:12

REFLECT: I promised myself that when I came home from work, I'd get to the important letter I'd put off writing. But after dinner I flopped down in front of the television and before I knew it, I was too tired to turn the thing off. *Well,* I told myself, *I'll do the letter tomorrow.*

On came an educational program about plant life. Amazingly, the strength exerted by a seedling as it pushes its stem above the ground's surface is roughly 450 pounds per square inch. A time-lapse film sequence showed a cluster of shoots pushing through clods of earth, nodding and quivering as they straightened their stems and unfolded their leaves.

I was awed by the power God has placed in even the tiniest of His creations. I thought: *If He has given a tiny organism such strength, how much must I have inside me, untapped?*

I snapped off the television and sat down to write.

—CHRISTINE CONTI

PRAY: *Father, You know how little strength I have on my own to break the procrastination habit. Show me the root of it, please, Lord, and whether it's lack of energy, motivation, love for others, or too great a commitment to my own comfort, please get me moving.*

DO: Maybe procrastination is a symptom of some other root issue in your life. Maybe not. But ask God so you'll know what you're actually battling.

When you're ready to quit

———◄○►———

REFLECT: Should I? Shouldn't I? Should I? Shouldn't I? Like picking petals from a daisy, I'd debated for weeks about whether to continue on the leadership team of the women's ministry at my little country church.

I had been feeling burdened with obligations—homeschooling my daughter, freelance editorial work and daily family and household demands. *The women's ministry should probably go,* I thought.

Then I received a magazine in the mail. One article was about the apostle Paul and his friendships, which, at first glance, had nothing to do with leading a women's ministry. But one sentence in the article had everything to do with it: Paul "was gripped by a powerful vision of friendship as a catalyst for spiritual growth."

I'm no Paul, but the women at Garden Valley Bible Church were dear friends. Suddenly my decision wasn't about an obligation; it was about loving and helping friends grow. Now *that* I have time for.

—LUCILE ALLEN

PRAY: *Father, let me know whether to quit or stay . . . and help me to do it for the right reasons.*

DO: Pray about your options. Check your motives for wanting to quit, and resolve not to make a move until you're convinced you're doing the right thing.

When you're regretting the past

◄◦►

READ: *For it is the God who commanded light to shine out of darkness, who has shone in our hearts. . . .*

—2 CORINTHIANS 4:6

REFLECT: My four-year-old granddaughter Cassie came to spend the day with me. I planned all her favorite treats, the highlight being to rent her beloved video, *Cinderella*. But when we were settled in front of the TV, Cassie confessed that the mean stepmother always frightened her. Concerned, I said, "Maybe we should have rented something else."

"Oh no, Grandma," she said, patting my hand reassuringly. "I just fast-forward past the scary parts." And so she did, zipping past each scary part and looking up at me with a serene smile.

I couldn't help speculating on how blissful it would have been to fast-forward past certain parts of my life, until I got to the good parts. Things like my brain surgery for an aneurysm when I was thirty-two. But no, not that part. That's when I learned that instead of praying frantically when I'm afraid, sometimes I need to be still so I can hear His reassurance.

The next time you run into a scary part, remember it's just a rough spot that eventually leads you to the good part: a clearer perspective and a wiser point of view.

—BONNIE LUKES

PRAY: *I have regretted some of my past, Father, but I can also see the light You brought out of my bad choices. Thank You, Lord, that You'll do that for the mistakes I have yet to make.*

DO: Think of some of your finer qualities and see how they're connected to the things you regret.

When you're reluctant to reach out

READ: *Live in harmony with one another. . . .*

—1 PETER 3:8 (NIV)

REFLECT: The woman had experienced a drinking problem for years, and we were careful to avoid her. Then one day my wise friend Angie invited her to join our prayer group.

"Will you come?" Angie asked her.

"I can't come to a God-meeting smelling like bourbon. What would the other ladies think?"

Angie smiled and replied, "Oh, we all smell of something. One of us has a problem with gossip. And another with unforgiveness. God knows how we all 'smell,' but He still loves us. Won't you come?"

The stunned woman began to laugh and cry. "Yes, I'll come. Thank you."

True, we were uncomfortable at first. But the more we opened ourselves to our new member, the more we came to love her. Oh, she still has some tough problems to overcome. I guess she's a lot like the rest of us.

—MARION BOND WEST

PRAY: *Father, forgive me for judging others. I pray they will feel loved and welcome in my heart, my home, my church.*

DO: The next time you're in church, make it a point to speak words of welcome to a visitor.

When you're sad (1)

◄○►

READ: *Those who sow in tears shall reap in joy.*

—PSALM 126:5

REFLECT: I once spent a few weeks with my Aunt Therese and Uncle Fernand in southern France. During the first night of my visit, there was an extraordinary storm. The rain was heavy. Thunder and lightning shot through the air. It was one of the scariest nights I've ever had to sleep through.

In the morning, I woke up and heard—singing! Curious, I followed the joyous sound up toward the attic. There, I saw my aunt laughing and singing as she cleaned up the huge mess of water and mud the strong winds had blown into the attic. I stood there speechless.

"But, Christopher," she said, "I spent many years in a prison camp during the war. It was horrible. No work for me today is unpleasant."

My aunt's songs of joy came out of terrible years of tears. And that morning she gave me a gift: the joy of every waking miracle moment.

—CHRISTOPHER DE VINCK

PRAY: *Dear Father, I don't know firsthand the pain and suffering in a prison camp, and pray I never do, but I have suffered the sorrows of an unredeemed human heart. Let me find joy now in every moment of my redeemed life.*

DO: Think of someone you've met or heard about who managed to find joy in the midst of hardships. Write down three things that strike you about that person's attitude to life.

When you're sad (2)

<o>

READ: *He who is of a merry heart has a continual feast.*

—PROVERBS 15:15

REFLECT: I remember the night before my mother-in-law's funeral. The family decided to go out for pie and coffee. As we solemnly waited for the orders, someone broke the silence. "Remember when Mom tangled with that old gander?" Then my husband spoke up, "Remember Mom's charge onto the high school football field when I banged up my knee?" The group relaxed as each family member recalled a funny incident from Mom's life. Within minutes, tears of laughter rolled down our cheeks. The waitress thought we were crazy, but that evening's mirth made it much easier to say our final good-byes the following day.

When you're dealing with sorrow, illness or tension on the job or home front, recall humorous things. Browse through a joke book, funny cards in the card shop or watch your favorite TV comedy. Let something tickle your funny bone!

—SHIRLEY POPE WAITE

PRAY: *Father, let some laughter into my heart.*

DO: Think of someone you know who needs cheering up and ask God for the right time to ease his/her heart with humor.

When you're searching for the perfect gift for a loved one

---◄◦►---

READ: *But earnestly desire the best gifts.*

—1 CORINTHIANS 12:31

REFLECT: When I was four, my family gathered for a reunion on St. Simons Island off the coast of Georgia. When it came time to leave, no one seemed to realize my misery at not being able to stay at the ocean. I felt so happy there.

But I discovered that someone did realize. As Mother, Dad, John and I headed for our car to drive the two hundred miles inland to Macon, Rosa took me aside. Rosa, the large, quiet, smiling cook, handed me a bag, saying, "Here, missy, this is for you."

It was full of beautiful shells—memories to take home with me. Somehow I knew her act of kindness to be much more important than anything I'd yet received.

Rosa was perceptive and willing to go out of her way to make someone else happy. I realized, as I gazed at the shells throughout my childhood, those were the essentials for gift-giving.   —SAMANTHA MCGARRITY

PRAY: *That's the kind of gift I want for my friend, Father, a gift that will stay with him/her for life.*

DO: First ask God for the perfect gift idea for your loved one and listen carefully for clues. If nothing comes, ask others, keeping in mind that what sounds like a bad idea from our limited perspectives, could turn out to be the perfect thing.

When you're seeking direction

◄◦►

READ: *"Look at me and do likewise. . . ."*

—JUDGES 7:17

REFLECT: It had been a white-knuckle day. Three back-to-back classes, two papers to type and hand in by 5:00 PM, interviews to discuss career possibilities, putting in hours at my part-time job. I felt as though I were living in a popcorn popper.

"God, what am I going to do with my life?" I asked out loud to the gray and barren sky. (Graduate students sometimes get this way.)

I stopped by my mailbox on the way to my room. Inside was a "letter" from a four-year-old pen pal. A dot-to-dot picture of a giraffe. I smiled, but then the letter gave me pause. The little boy had created the picture by moving his pencil from dot to dot, one by one. Couldn't I do the same? God knows the plan; He holds my picture. I need only strive to connect, dot by dot.

—LAUREN V. LAMAY

PRAY: *Oh, Lord, I don't need to know where You're taking me; I just need to know what to do next—and then the next thing after that. Let me enjoy each moment with You, not be looking ahead to a final destination.*

DO: Find a child's connect-the-dot book. Every time your mind begins to question God for direction, work one or two of the pictures to remind you to enjoy Him in the moment and to seek just the next step.

When you're self-absorbed

◄○►

READ: *He who finds his life will lose it, and he who loses his life for My sake will find it.*

—MATTHEW 10:39

REFLECT: Mary had led a dissolute life. In her twenties she married, bore three children and calmed down somewhat. Still, she was short of being an exemplary wife and mother. In her thirties, just when it seemed as though her marriage might end, Mary came to know Jesus.

After that she became a virtuous and hard-working wife and mother, giving an inordinate amount of time to her church and to helping others. So radical was her change that her family feared for her sanity and maneuvered her into a hospital for psychiatric testing.

The doctors reported that Mary was in fine mental health. Anyone, they said, who freely ministered to others as she did, was in no danger of losing her sanity. Illness, they added, occurs when a person's sense of self becomes the center of his or her universe.

Mary's story reveals not a mere secret of sanity, but the secret of happiness: not self, but others.   —VAN VARNER

PRAY: *Father, thank You for showing me the way to true happiness. Give me the energy, the interest, and the strength to help You meet someone's need today.*

DO: Find someone who needs a helping hand. Cook a meal for a sick friend, read to a shut-in, or offer to baby-sit for friends who could use an evening out.

When you're shy about sharing your faith

◄○►

READ: *It is like a mustard seed, which a man took and put in his garden; and it grew and became a large tree. . . .*
—LUKE 13:19

REFLECT: At the Chula Vista Nature Center near San Diego, the guide told us how the Franciscan friars, who set up the chain of missions along the West Coast, scattered trails of mustard seeds to find their way in rugged areas. The seeds began to sprout, and within a few years had created a prodigious growth of these sturdy shrubs all over the state.

I began to wonder: Do I scatter any mustard seeds of faith as I walk my daily route?

When my neighbor asked me where we went to church, I answered matter-of-factly and said no more. I could have invited her to join us one Sunday. Or when the young grocery clerk complimented me on the cross I wear, I said only, "Thanks." I easily could have added something meaningful about Jesus.

Such small acts may seem insignificant, but everyone knows that the tiny mustard seeds can grow into enormous bushes!
—GINA BRIDGEMAN

PRAY: *Father, I'm so grateful someone sowed a seed of faith in my direction, and that it took root and grew. Show me someone today who would be good spiritual soil where I can sow seeds of faith too.*

DO: Invite a neighbor or coworker to church with you.

When you're struggling to reach a goal

―◁◦▷―

READ: *Your word is a lamp to my feet and a light to my path.*

—PSALM 119:105

REFLECT: On vacation in Central America, a friend took us into a rain forest. We drove for hours to a dirt road. From there we had to walk every step. Soon we could not see the sky, as the trees grew so thick and tall. Just when I felt that I could not take another step, we entered a huge clearing.

A beautiful waterfall cascaded into a pool, tropical flowers gave off a sweet scent and brightly colored birds flew through the mist. Never had I been so aware of the way God lavishes His beauty on the world.

But soon our friend led us away. After just a few minutes of walking we reached our car.

"That beautiful waterfall was so close to the road. Why did you take us the long way around?"

Our friend answered with a grin and a wink, "Old Spanish proverb says that nothing in life is appreciated so much as the thing you must struggle for." —PAT SULLIVAN

PRAY: *Dear God, please make me more like Jesus, Who kept His eye on the goal of eternity with You, instead of the day-to-day journey of getting there.*

DO: Picture in your mind the finished product or the end result of the thing you're working toward. Let that vision renew your energy to complete the task.

When you're struggling with a job offer

◄◦►

READ: *I have set before you life and death, blessings and curses. Now choose life, so that you and your children may live. . . .*

—DEUTERONOMY 30:19 (NIV)

REFLECT: A job offer came that seemed above and beyond my capabilities, but with good income potential. No matter how I weighed the facts, I couldn't get the courage to say either "yes" or "no."

I went to the mountains and sat by a rushing stream. At my feet was a small, deep pool. A stick came floating by and was drawn into the eddy where the continual centripetal pull of the water started it going around and around.

I began to think, *That is how I am, just going 'round and 'round in the same old rut.* 1 began counting the revolutions. When I got to 495, I knew that stick would never get out on its own. I jumped up, grabbed the stick from the whirlpool and tossed it into the onrushing current.

At once I knew I had to say "yes" to new opportunities to learn and grow . . . "yes" to life active instead of life passive.

—PHYLLIS WALK

PRAY: *Whether or not this job is the right one, Father, life active always beats life passive. I trust You to make it clear when the right job offer does come along.*

DO: Ask a friend to talk over your decision with you.

When you're struggling with a problem

◄○►

READ: *Trust in the Lord with all your heart, and lean not on your own understanding. . . .*

—PROVERBS 3:5

REFLECT: Years ago I was struggling with a particularly stubborn problem. I'd prayed about it feverishly for several weeks, begging, pleading, but without any results. Then one evening I walked outside to get the paper and found my son Paul, who was a toddler then, trying to pull open the petals on a tightly closed rosebud. He looked up at me wide-eyed and said, "Paul make pretty flower bloom."

As I heard myself explaining to him that you can't make a flower bloom by pulling on it, something clicked inside of me. I had been handling my problem the way Paul had handled the rose! By begging, pleading, trying to force an answer, I had been trying to manipulate God. I needed to take my hands off, wait patiently, and trust in the creative power of God to open up a right answer for me. When the answer did come, it was not what I had expected. It was better.

—MARILYN MORGAN KING

PRAY: *Father, forgive me for trying to help You answer my prayers, and thank You for answering them better than I could have imagined.*

DO: Picture the best possible result you can imagine for the problem with which you've been struggling. Write it down. Now, make a choice to let it go and trust God with it. When His answer comes, write it down and compare your answer with His.

When you're struggling with doubts

◄◦►

READ: *The fear of man brings a snare, but whoever trusts in the Lord shall be safe.*

—PROVERBS 29:25

REFLECT: At 2:00 PM, Hurricane Bob roared into Kennebunk Beach, Maine, where my wife Ruby and I were guests. Rains pelted and winds lashed. Skies blackened and thunder rumbled. Then our hostess said, "Come here. Look!"

At one corner of the window, a triangular spider web clung to the window and an outside shutter. In the teeth of the gusting gale, the web swayed gently as if saying, "Be calm, dear friends, and trust." Waves continued to crash over the sea wall hurling stones onto the lawn, and we wondered if both the web and our courage would hold.

At dusk, the storm subsided and we peeked at the spider. This fragile, delicate miracle had survived Hurricane Bob, and so had we.

Sometimes I feel fragile and delicate when it comes to courage, faith and trust. But now, with God's help, I try to trust the future, knowing the storms of doubt will subside.

—OSCAR GREENE

PRAY: *Dear God, I want to be like the spider that never wonders if its web is secure enough to hold it. Help me to ride out this storm—calmly, securely in Your arms.*

DO: Find an unoccupied spider web, test its strength, and marvel at its resiliency—just like the human spirit.

When you're stuck in a project

<o>

READ: *So Jesus stood still and called them, and said, "What do you want Me to do for you?" They said to Him, "Lord, that our eyes may be opened."*

—MATTHEW 20:32–33

REFLECT: I once had to move our household while my husband was traveling elsewhere. I rented a large moving van to drive cross-country myself.

On the day of the big move, I was feeling as confident as a veteran trucker. That is, until I heard the horrible screech as the van wedged itself under the door of our apartment's underground garage, and I burst into tears.

Then a white-haired man appeared through a side door. I wiped my eyes and said, "I'm so sorry for blocking the doorway."

The man said, "Why don't you just let some air out of the tires?" Now, I could have run around the truck for hours and that solution never would have occurred to me.

Now, whenever I'm feeling "stuck," I ask the Lord to open my eyes to new ideas and solutions—especially the simple, obvious ones.

—SUSAN WILLIAMS

PRAY: *I'm stuck, Lord. Open my eyes to new ideas and solutions, especially the obvious ones I haven't thought of yet—or bring someone by with ideas to help me.*

DO: Call a friend with expertise in your area of need. See if he/she has a simple (brilliant) idea you haven't thought of yet.

When you're stuck in the darkness

◄◉►

READ: *God is light and in Him is no darkness at all.*

—1 JOHN 1:5

REFLECT: Whenever I take up a task that is going to require my best effort for success, I remember a story about the famous lace shops in Bruges, Belgium. Certain rooms are reserved for making the finest, most delicate designs. Each room is dark except for a beam of light from a tiny overhead window that falls directly onto the pattern of lace being spun. The choicest lace is wrought when the worker himself is in the dark and only his pattern is in the light.

Being merely human, I often struggle in confusion when I try to accomplish difficult tasks by myself. But if I expose them to God's power by asking His help and blessing every step of the way, success often comes. Perhaps I'm a little like those lace-spinners in Bruges—spinning in darkness, but capable of my best work in the radiance of God's perfect light.

—NORMAN VINCENT PEALE

PRAY: *Lord, allow me to see darkness as the good thing it can be. Let me stay in the darkness if it means a more beautiful result for Your glory.*

DO: Think of some other beautiful things accomplished in the dark: a seed in the ground, a baby in the womb, the Cross.

When you're stuck on "What if?"

◄○►

READ: *Therefore do not worry about tomorrow, for tomorrow will worry about its own things.*

—MATTHEW 6:34

REFLECT: Some children drive their parents crazy asking, "Why?" My precocious son Geoffrey was a worrier who asked a more potent question: "What if?" Here's a typical conversation with him:

"It's snowing outside," I observe.

"What happens if the road freezes up?" he asks.

"The snowplow will dig us out."

"What if it breaks down?"

"The city will use the sand trucks."

"What if they run out of sand?"

"Then they'll use salt."

"What if the salt doesn't melt the ice?"

I tell him not to worry, and he believes me, not so much because of what I say, but because of the authority I have and the love I show.

When the question "What if?" races pell-mell through my mind, I turn to the best Authority of all to dispel my fear about tomorrow. —LINDA CHING SLEDGE

PRAY: *Father, what if I get stuck on "What if?" and never move on to trusting You? What a waste of time that would be! Please give me peace about tomorrow and all the tomorrows You have in store for me.*

DO: Memorize Matthew 6:34. And just for a moment ask yourself what life will be like if you never stop asking God "What if?"

When you're suffering from a chronic condition

◄◦►

READ: *Heal me, O Lord, and I shall be healed; save me, and I shall be saved, for You are my praise.*

—JEREMIAH 17:14

REFLECT: Years ago I developed a severe case of asthma. We finally had to get an electric-pressured inhalator, which forced medicated air into my lungs. I tired very easily. Even taking a walk became almost impossible.

One day I knelt beside my bed. "All right, Lord," I said. "I've done all I can. If I must have asthma, okay. But please give me a sweet and cheerful disposition to go with it."

Hard to know when it happened, but I needed the breathing machine less and less. By that summer, I could swim several widths of a pool again, and my doctor found no wheezing on subsequent check-ups.

Looking back, I suspect Jesus has a sense of humor. Faced with the request of granting a sweet disposition or healing an illness, He, in my case, found the latter an easier task.

Seriously, when friends ask what became of my breathing problem, I answer, "I gave it to Jesus."

—MAY SHERIDAN GOLD

PRAY: *Lord, I give this illness to You and ask You to heal it or give me the grace to endure it cheerfully.*

DO: Ask someone you know who has been healed of a chronic illness to pray for your healing.

When you're tackling a difficult project (1)

◄◦►

READ: *"'Not by might nor by power, but by My Spirit,' says the Lord of hosts."*

—ZECHARIAH 4:6

REFLECT: At a boys' ranch, we ran about fifty head of white-faced cows and one Angus bull. One year our herd contracted pink eye and we had to treat all of the animals.

Things went smoothly until we got to the bull. His neck was like a sequoia tree trunk. I walked up cautiously and put my arms around his neck. As another man reached for the bull's eyelid, the big Angus flicked its head and sent me sprawling. After a few more tries, I asked the Lord to help us. It was no casual prayer. I really meant it.

Then I put a rope around the bull's neck and tied him to a support post. Another man reached for his eyelid. Amazingly, the bull stood rock steady while the ointment was put under both eyelids.

I've done a lot of praying for some of the "bulls" I've faced in life. I've learned that the power of God can calm the most volatile situation. —BRIAN MILLER

PRAY: *Lord Jesus, You came to earth to show us how to handle the "bullish" situations we will encounter. It wasn't by human might or power, but by the Holy Spirit that You were victorious.*

DO: Are you tackling your project in your own power—your physical strength? Your wit? Your resources? Invite the Holy Spirit into the process however many times it takes to remind you it's by His power that you will be victorious.

When you're tackling a difficult project (2)

◄○►

READ: *With God all things are possible.*

—MARK 10:27

REFLECT: Our newspaper carried a picture story about an oriole trying to drink from a hummingbird feeder. The bird fluttered wildly and tried to hover in the air, but its wings couldn't keep it aloft. Then it sat on the spout and tried to drink from above, but it couldn't reach into the opening. Finally, it gripped the spout from underneath and, hanging upside down, was able to enjoy the drink.

Once as I was going through my files, I came across an article that had been rejected by several publishers—and finally even by myself. Curious, I read it over and, like the oriole, decided to try again. After asking God's blessing on the rewritten version, I resubmitted it to a publisher. The article was accepted.

Many times projects seem impossible only because we give up. But when we ask for God's help and keep on trying, we can usually find a "perch that works."

—DORIS HAASE

PRAY: *Father, I'm so glad that You don't give up on me when I disappoint You. Thank You for sticking with me until I become the person You created me to be.*

DO: Resurrect an old project, something you've set aside that you once had vision and energy for. Set a deadline for starting—and completing—that project.

When you're taking life too seriously

◄◦►

READ: *"God has made me laugh, and all who hear will laugh with me."*

—GENESIS 21:6

REFLECT: I had completed a form to do some volunteer work and now I sat facing a woman for my lengthy interview. One question caught me off guard. She asked, "What do you do for fun, Mrs. West?"

I stared at the woman for a few moments. Nothing came to mind. Finally we went on to another topic, but her question hung over me. I knew I was too serious, too judgmental —of others and of myself. Thanks to the woman's question, I would try to change.

I went out back and tossed a Frisbee with my collie. Soon we were running together, and I was laughing. I hadn't been to the movies in over a year, but I invited my daughter and her little girl to see one with me. We went out for dinner, then pigged out on popcorn. Sitting there in the dark, I realized I was smiling, enjoying the film. Why, I was actually having fun!

—MARION BOND WEST

PRAY: *Father, there's no doubt about it—my life lacks fun. I enjoy having fun occasionally, but I've lost the fun in my heart. Would You help me get it back, God?*

DO: What's the last thing you remember that gave you a good laugh? Pass it on to a friend, and ask him/her to share his/her last good laugh with you.

When you're tempted to be preachy

READ: *My little children, let us not love in word or in tongue, but in deed and in truth.*

—1 JOHN 3:18

REFLECT: Once a zealous young man went to St. Francis of Assisi and implored the saint to teach him how to preach.

"Gladly," said Francis. "Come with me."

All afternoon the young man followed Francis about. They stopped in a field crowded with reapers, and Francis helped the laborers load the hay onto a cart. Next they went to the town square, where Francis lifted a bucket of water from the well for an old woman and carried it home for her.

Finally they went into the church—but Francis only knelt silently to pray.

At last, they returned to the place from whence they had started. "But when," the perplexed young man asked, "are you going to teach me how to preach?"

Francis smiled. "I just did."

—PATRICIA HOUCK SPRINKLE

PRAY: *Lord, God, thank You for this reminder that our actions are more powerful than our words. Let my actions speak of Your love and goodness.*

DO: Think of someone who needs the Lord—and preach to him/her with your actions today.

When you're tempted to get even

—◄◦►—

READ: *Those who plow iniquity and sow trouble reap the same.*

—JOB 4:8

REFLECT: The tale is told of a child who lived high in the Smokey Mountains. One day when she was being naughty, her mother disciplined her.

The little girl ran to the edge of a precipice and shouted at her mother, "I hate you! I hate you!" And an echo came back from out of the valley, "I hate you! I hate you!"

Frightened, the child ran to her mother, sobbing.

But her wise mother led her back to the rim of the ravine and said, "Now call, 'I love you! I love you!'"

The child did so, and a clear, sweet voice came back— "I love you! I love you!"

Taking the little girl in her arms the mother said, "My dear, always remember that in life we get what we give."

—ZONA B. DAVIS

PRAY: *I don't feel like giving love right now, Lord. I feel like getting even. But I'm going to pray for _____ anyway. Take the anger from my heart and replace it with Your Spirit.*

DO: After you've prayed for the person who hurt you, pray for others he/she has hurt who may also be wanting to get revenge.

When you're thinking negative thoughts about someone

————————◀◉▶————————

READ: *Therefore be merciful, just as your Father also is merciful.*

—LUKE 6:36

REFLECT: Through the years, I've struggled with a critical attitude. I confessed this to a close friend who admitted she faces the same struggle but has found a helpful solution. "I turn every criticism into a prayer of intercession for the other person. That not only helps me stop when I start being critical, it turns a negative thought into a positive action."

"Prayer enlarges the heart until it is capable of containing God's gift of Himself," I once heard Mother Teresa say. I'm learning that "God's gift of Himself" squeezes most of the contempt and criticism out of my heart.

—CAROL KUYKENDALL

PRAY: *Lord, forgive my critical attitude toward _____ and help me to see the positive qualities You've put within him/her.*

DO: Put that person at the top of your prayer list for the month.

When you're too busy

◄○►

READ: *"This is the rest with which You may cause the weary to rest"*. . . .
                                            —ISAIAH 28:12

REFLECT: As I was sweeping the sidewalk and mentally enumerating the chores to be done before dark, from his sandbox next door my two-year-old neighbor Tyler came running.

After his usual, "Whatcha doing?" he said, "Let's swing in your swing."

"I'm too busy today," I told him.

Disappointment spread over his face. I glanced toward the swing; it *did* look inviting.

"All right," I told him. "Just for a few minutes."

He raced up the front steps and I lifted him into the swing beside me. He didn't talk, just snuggled against me. A butterfly fluttered past my face. Two bees hummed among the flowers and a slight breeze stroked my tired body. Tension and anxiety began to slip away. Soon I was humming softly. I became aware of the flowers, the brilliance of the day, the wonder of the small boy beside me, all creations of a loving God.

                                            —DRUE DUKE

PRAY: *Father, unfortunately I don't have a porch swing or a two-year-old within reach, but the thought is so inviting. Instead I'll come to You, Who is always within reach, for the rest You promise in Your Word.*

DO: Relax and read your Bible and let the breeze of the Spirit refresh you.

When you're trying to diet (1)

◄◦►

READ: *And do not lead us into temptation. . . .*

—MATTHEW 6:13

REFLECT: "Have a piece of cake," Martha insisted. It was party time again in my office, my third party—and fifth extra pound—that week.

"If only they would stop tempting me," I had recently fussed to my son.

"Mom," Neil interrupted. "They can't *make* you eat. Listen. I read in a Christian diet book that whenever you're tempted, imagine God saying, 'Feast, instead, on Me.' Then read a verse or two in your Bible. It's supposed to really work."

Feeling a little strange, I imagined God's voice.

Feast, instead, on Me.

All at once that cake didn't sound quite so irresistible.

"Not just now," I answered Martha, smiling.

—DORIS HAASE

PRAY: *Father, Your Word says one fruit of the Holy Spirit is self-control. Now there's something I can feast on, Lord. Pass the self-control, please!*

DO: Every time you're tempted to eat something you know it's best not to eat, ask a friend to pray with you to help you focus on God instead of what you shouldn't have.

When you're trying to diet (2)

◄◦►

READ: *I can do all things through Christ who strengthens me.*

—PHILIPPIANS 4:13

REFLECT: "You have to lose weight," the doctor told Aunt Lucy. "It isn't healthy to be so heavy."

Lucy was sulky. Food was one of the great pleasures of her life.

That night, she sat up in bed reading her Bible. Then she went downstairs to the kitchen for a glass of milk and some cookies. *I simply can't diet*, she muttered to herself.

Lucy was about to take a cookie when a Bible verse she had just read came to her: "I can do all things through Christ who strengthens me."

All things, whispered Lucy. The cookie was returned to the cookie jar and the milk would wait until breakfast.

Lucy did lose weight—and as she did, she gained in faith. "I had a lot of help," she says, "once I realized that I couldn't do it by myself."

—PHYLLIS HOBE

PRAY: *Lord God, You know better than I do how powerless I am without Your help to stay on this diet. Please increase my desire to lose weight until it's stronger than my desire to eat.*

DO: Tape Scriptures in strategic places—on your fridge, on your mirror, in your car—to remind you to rely on God's Word and not only your own strength as you diet.

When you're waiting for guidance

◄○►

READ: *But those who wait on the Lord shall renew their strength; they shall mount up with wings like eagles. . . .*

—ISAIAH 40:31

REFLECT: Bald eagles are our national emblem. They aren't really bald, but get their appearance of baldness from the white feathers on their heads. They have wingspreads of as much as eight feet, and when they soar through the skies, nothing could be more regal.

But flying isn't as easy for them as it looks. They have a problem getting themselves launched. The secret of becoming airborne is that they perch on the edges of high cliffs and wait for the right wind to come along. When it does, they let go and mount up, soaring with the current, rising higher and higher as they bank. Their uncanny understanding of air currents enables them to get maximum mileage from the wind.

Just as eagles are borne aloft by waiting for the right wind current, we must wait to catch the direction of God's Spirit, and then let go and soar according to His will.

—SAM JUSTICE

PRAY: *Lord, I've been praying for new direction for a long time so I can sure relate to the eagle who has trouble getting himself launched. And like the eagle, I'll keep waiting for the right current no matter how long it takes.*

DO: Buy a small picture or refrigerator magnet of an eagle to remind you, when you get impatient, to wait for God's direction.

When you're wondering if God cares

━━━━━━━━━━━━━━━◄○►━━━━━━━━━━━━━━━

READ: *You are familiar with all my ways.*

—PSALM 139:3 (NIV)

REFLECT: When I was young and my sister Diane was younger, our minister, Dr. Cropp, visited our Sunday school class. He talked about God and how God cared about us and was interested in everything we did. Then Diane raised her hand. Dr. Cropp looked at her quizzically. "Yes?" he said.

"We had cornflakes for breakfast!" she beamed.

Mom apologized to Dr. Cropp when she later heard about Diane's remark. "She must not have been listening."

"On the contrary," he said. "I think she understood very well. I was explaining how God cares about everything we do. I couldn't have picked a better example if I tried!" His eyes crinkled with pleasure. "Yes, sir—God cares about what we eat for breakfast, as much, I'd say, as who we are at breakfast—or at any time!"

—RICK HAMLIN

PRAY: *God, so many little things—and some big things— are cluttering my mind right now. Thank You for this reminder that You're a God who cares about every detail of my life and thank You for the comfort that brings.*

DO: Make a list of all the things on your mind that you can't seem to give to God. Tuck the list into your Bible to symbolize God carrying those things for you.

When you're wondering if God hears you

READ: *"I have looked upon My people, because their cry has come to Me."*

—1 SAMUEL 9:16

REFLECT: One day when I was a child, I watched Betsy, our cocker spaniel, push her puppies off the dock into the lake. You should have seen the startled looks on those little faces as they discovered—to their amazement—that the water was capable of holding them up.

I felt a little like that last week when I faced a big disappointment. I seldom cry anymore. I'm much more likely to repress my feelings, bury my sorrow and hide my hurts. But this time all my defenses just went, and I ran into the bedroom and cried. For the first time in a long time, I didn't hold back. I just let myself fall into the depths and then gradually there arose a strong, solid, sustaining Presence that bore me up. Today I realize that part of the preciousness of my God lies in the fact that there are depths and that out of those depths I may cry, and that my cry will be heard.

—MARILYN MORGAN KING

PRAY: *Father, if the cry of Your people in biblical times reached You—and You say right there in I Samuel 9:16 that it did—then I know my cry reaches You too. Thank You, Lord, for that reassurance from Your Word.*

DO: Look up *cry* in a concordance and see what else God says about crying out to Him.

When you're worried (1)

◄○►

READ: *"Lord, I believe; help my unbelief!"*

—MARK 9:24

REFLECT: Once, my husband left on a trip to Japan only days after a tragic plane crash had shocked the world and other terrorist threats of more plane bombings had been looming. As the monitor in the airport lounge flashed "Departed" next to his flight number, my stomach began to tighten. It would be fourteen hours before he would be on the ground again, and I was in for a real worry marathon.

Then a prayer came to me: "Lord, I believe; help thou mine unbelief." I kept repeating these words to myself, until the din of fearful "what-ifs" was replaced by feelings of calmness and confidence in the Lord. My husband returned safely, of course, but more than that, my faith was steady once again. That's not to say that faith insulates us from life's sorrows or tragedies. But always, we can believe in Him Who carries us through anything.

—STEPHANIE ODA

PRAY: *I do want to trust You more, Lord. Please help me overcome my unbelief.*

DO: Play the "what-if" game, but this time, replace all the bad things with good ones.

When you're worried (2)

◄○►

READ: *Give thanks in all circumstances, for this is God's will for you in Christ Jesus.*

—1 THESSALONIANS 5:18 (NIV)

REFLECT: I sank into the chair in the hospital waiting room. Poor Mother! First, Dad's death, and now this. If she survived this broken hip, how could she get along, living alone? The more I thought about Mother's future, the more bleak it seemed. Then I noticed a plaque on the wall with this quotation: "One act of thanksgiving made when things go wrong is worth a thousand when things go well."

All of my prayers for my mother during the long days that followed were thanksgivings, and I came to know that, no matter what happened, God was in control.

Mother did recover and was able to live in her own home for her remaining years. And that quotation has rescued me from negative thinking many times since. If there's something wrong in your life today, remember the formula of 1=1,000.

—MARILYN MORGAN KING

PRAY: *Thank You, Father, for the way You're going to work out my problem for my good and for Your glory.*

DO: List all the positive things you can think of that could come out of the situation you're most worried about.

When you're worried (3)

◄○►

READ: *Therefore take up the whole armor of God, that you may be able to withstand in the evil day, and having done all, to stand.*

—EPHESIANS 6:13

REFLECT: As a young man, I once went to my father with a set of problems that troubled me. Father listened with interest, but also with increasing exasperation—for nothing seemed to ease my worries. Finally, he said, "Son, go read Ephesians!"

"Ephesians?" I was astonished. "What for?"

"Because there," he said, "you'll find the greatest antidote in the world for worry. It's where St. Paul advises the Ephesians, once they've done everything they can, to just stand.

"You're in danger of becoming a chronic worrier," my father went on. "There's nothing wrong with *some* worry if it impels you to take action against your difficulties. But when you've taken that action, it's just plain senseless to go on worrying. How much better to stand quietly, as St. Paul says. In other words, *relax.*

"If you have a problem, do the best you can with it. Then leave it in God's hands."

—ARTHUR GORDON

PRAY: *Father, I confess that I worry about problems before they even become problems . . . and solve very little that way. Now I'll try to do what I can and after that, I'll just stand.*

DO: Write Ephesians 6:13 on a card. Keep it in a visible place to remind you to do what you can and then just stand.

When you're worried about aging parents

◄○►

READ: *For when I am weak, then I am strong.*

—2 CORINTHIANS 12:10

REFLECT: I was having lunch in a coffee shop, worrying again about my mother in a nursing home in Michigan, hundreds of miles away from rainy Manhattan.

Then Bob walked in. I was grateful to have him join me. Sometimes I slip up and say that my friend Bob beat a terrible drug and alcohol addiction. After all these years I should know better. "I didn't beat anything," Bob is quick to correct me. "It beat me. All I did was surrender."

I've learned a great deal from his sobriety, watching him rebuild his life into something far richer than he could have ever imagined. Bob is a great success story, and he sees a spiritual solution to nearly every problem in life. He is always "letting go and letting God."

The subject of my mother never came up during lunch with Bob, but afterward I felt a whole lot better. I was ready to surrender.

—EDWARD GRINNAN

PRAY: *Father, I've been worrying about my aging parents. Today, I surrender them to You; I trust to You to have Your way, which is always the best way, in their lives.*

DO: Tell your parent(s) you've been worried, but that, emotionally and spiritually, you've surrendered their well-being to God. Your trust in Him can only encourage their trust in Him.

When you're worried about finances

<o>

READ: *"He who gathered much had nothing left over, and he who gathered little had no lack."*

—2 CORINTHIANS 8:15

REFLECT: My wife Sharon showed me our savings balance and I got a queasy feeling in my stomach. My mind began to spin. What will we do in our old age? Will we have all the material comforts we need? Will we have enough to pay our bills and still enjoy life?

Sometimes I feel guilty because I don't have every day of my life "covered" in advance, as some of my friends do. They have elaborate insurance and savings programs. One of them even has his tombstone engraved and sitting on a prepaid lot!

"The Bible doesn't promise God's blessings in advance," Sharon reminds me, and I know she is right. If God guaranteed our security, why would we have to trust Him?

"Let's increase our savings," Sharon says, "a little bit at a time."

"And to that, add an increase in our trust, too," I say sheepishly.

—DANIEL SCHANTZ

PRAY: *Lord, if I could and should be doing more to provide for our future, please show me what that would be. And help me to trust You to provide for our future as well.*

DO: Talk to a financial planner about how to better prepare for your family's future.

When you're worried about your children (1)

◄○►

READ: *"For as the heavens are higher than the earth, so are My ways higher than your ways, and My thoughts than your thoughts."*

—ISAIAH 55:9

REFLECT: I sadly drove home from Portland's airport after watching my sons' respective planes disappear. The older boy was heading for a missionary flight-training school; the younger to a Bible college near Chicago.

I was scared. *Small planes are dangerous,* I thought. *There's so much crime in big cities, Lord. I feel utterly helpless. What can I do when they're so far away?*

At the stoplight I idly watched a Greyhound bus pull alongside. Then I saw its slogan on the side: "Leave the driving to us." *Leave the driving to us.* That was the Lord's answer to my heavy-hearted question!

God had made my sons. Christ had died for them. The Holy Spirit had promised to guide them in His ways. Three Holy Caretakers!

We'd taught the boys this. We all believed it. Yet it took that Greyhound's slogan to soothe the sense of loss that I was feeling.

—ISABEL WOLSELEY

PRAY: *Lord, help me not to worry about something over which I have absolutely no control. Instead give me peace of mind and trust in Your faithfulness.*

DO: Make a sign: LEAVE THE DRIVING TO ME. LOVE, GOD. Put it in strategic places until you can do exactly that.

When you're worried about your children (2)

◄◦►

READ: *The Lord is your keeper. . . .*

—PSALM 121:5

REFLECT: I was sweeping the kitchen as I worried about the troubles of a newly married son and his wife. I decided I hadn't prayed hard enough.

Pausing a moment, I looked toward the mountains that loomed beyond the window. The very sight of them was calming. And now five words came into my mind: *They, too, have their angels.* I blinked my eyes. *How odd.* That was no thought of mine.

I saw how presumptuous I had been to think that nothing but my own insistent prayers could keep my dear ones from foundering on the rocks of life. God might possibly remember them even if I weren't around to prompt Him.

In time the young folks' problems worked out better than we had dared hope. I still pray for my children, but I find it much easier to "let go and let God" when remembering that they have their angels too.

—GERTRUDE NAUGLER

PRAY: *I confess that I've been praying as if my children's future depended upon my prayers and not on You, God. Thank You for showing me that sometimes the best thing I can do is not pray more, but let go.*

DO: Pray for your children *and* let them go.

When you're worried about your children (3)

◄◌►

READ: *For in Him we live and move and have our being. . . .*

—ACTS 17:28

REFLECT: I worried relentlessly about my children—their late hours, their friends, their lack of church attendance. Although I tried to trust them to God, I couldn't help but feel that He could use my assistance.

But things fell apart. When my eldest son was having problems and I thought he could benefit from my counsel, he rejected my sage advice, getting himself into scrape after scrape. Finally, he got tired of me and took off for Florida.

That really upset me, and I told God about it. His answer was: You love him and trust Me. Well, God did much better with my son than I did. After he finished college and went to work, I paid him a visit. I was amazed to see that he had accomplished so much. He must have read my mind because he looked me in the eye and said, "Thanks, Dad, for giving me up, but not giving up on me."

—SAM JUSTICE

PRAY: *Father above all fathers, You loved me enough to let me go my own way and brought me back to You. I can trust You enough to do that for my children— starting today.*

DO: If your child or children are agreeable, schedule time alone with each one. Read this reflection and pray with them. Entrust them to Him, and leave them with your prayers and blessing.

When you've been asked to serve (1)

◄◦►

READ: *There are differences of ministries, but the same Lord.*

—1 CORINTHIANS 12:5

REFLECT: In our church, there are thousands of opportunities for service—everything from scrambling eggs at the Saturday soup kitchen to reading the lesson on Sunday morning. I wish I could do it all. But I can't. It puts me in a terrible dilemma; how do you say no to church?

The choices I've learned to make have to do with gifts. For instance, I'd love to participate in a church work session, but I'm terrible with a hammer. I'm happy to wash dishes for a church supper, but don't ask me to prepare the main course. On the other hand, when I march up to the choir loft and take my seat with our tenor section, I'm right where I belong.

It's never necessary to say no to church. There's a place for each of us. Our biggest yes comes when we share our special gifts.

—RICK HAMLIN

PRAY: *Lord, help me to say no to opportunities to serve that I should pass up. And give me opportunities to use my gifts in Your service.*

DO: Think about what you love to do because you're good at it. Volunteer to put that skill to use at your church, at your office, or in your community. (And don't feel bad about saying no to the things you don't do so well.)

When you've been asked to serve (2)

<hr>

READ: *"As soon as you have entered it you will find a colt tied, on which no one has sat."*

—MARK 11:2

REFLECT: I've seen enough Western movies and read enough books on animals to know that breaking a horse can be a tedious job. The animal who has never been ridden will buck and pitch and make every effort to throw a person from its back. Yet this unbroken colt Jesus chose was submissive and accepted the Master with no struggle when the Lord had need of him.

How wildly I struggle sometimes when my Lord has need of me! *Too busy,* I argue when asked to serve on a committee at church. *I have no talent for that,* when needed to take charge of a program. Or *I don't know how to do it* is always a good out. Or—

On and on I go like the stubborn animals that refuse to be broken. Why can't I humbly submit to Him and let Him use me as He needs?

—DRUE DUKE

PRAY: *I want to be like the colt, Lord, content with what You have me doing and ready for change when You give the word.*

DO: Follow your heart when deciding to accept this commitment, but be willing for a less-than-perfect fit if it is something you sense that God is asking you to do.

When you've been disappointed

READ: *The foolishness of God is wiser than men, and the weakness of God is stronger than men.*

—1 CORINTHIANS 1:25

REFLECT: I stood in the gymnasium with a bunch of my friends, staring in disbelief at the bulletin board. The basketball coach had just posted the list of those who had made the team, and my name wasn't on it.

Later, in the lunchroom, our athletic director found me, hunched over a bologna sandwich and feeling plenty sorry for myself. "This may not be the best time to ask," he said, "but we need a public-address announcer for the basketball games. Would you be interested?"

Figuring that it would be better than sitting in the bleachers, I took the job.

To my surprise, I began having more fun than I ever had playing. And my announcing opened up new opportunities for me: sportswriting, state competitions in radio broadcasting, a scholarship.

It always amazes me how God works, especially in those times when He seems so far away. —JEFF JAPINGA

PRAY: *By now, Father, I should know You well enough to trust that when You close a door that I think would be perfect for me, You're going to open one that really is. Help me remember that next time.*

DO: Give yourself time to get over this disappointment and then watch for God's perfect opportunity.

When you've been humbled

READ: *Clothe yourselves with humility toward one another. . . .*

—1 PETER 5:5 (NIV)

REFLECT: When he was eight, Jonathan and I were gliding across a lake in our canoe. Without preamble he asked, "Dad, how did you ever get such a beautiful lady like Mommy to marry you?" He was so serious I couldn't laugh.

Then Jon found his own answer: "I guess she just felt sorry for you, Dad!"

It was a great lesson in humility. To Jon, I was just some dud who got lucky enough to marry that most glorious of all creatures, his mother. Humility is not a bad garment to wear sometimes. Although we might wish to appear more wonderful, the real view is the one that others can accept and love. How do I know? Later that night Jon snuggled next to me in his sleeping bag and said, "I had a great day being with just you, Dad."

"Me too," I replied.

"Good night. Dad—I love you."

—ERIC FELLMAN

PRAY: *Thank You, Father, for the honesty of children. Make us all as they are.*

DO: Schedule some one-on-one time with a child—your own, a relative's, a friend's or, even better, a child who lives without the love and support of parents.

When you've been hurt (1)

◀○▶

READ: *The Father himself loves you. . . .*

—JOHN 16:27

REFLECT: When I was cleaning the family room I found a piece of paper on which my small daughter had written her name, her age and several facts about herself and the family. The last item stated, "My brother is mean to me sometimes."

My husband evidently had found the scrap of paper earlier, for in his handwriting the list continued, "But my father loves me."

Isn't there a message here for all of us who think the world is treating us badly? Just write father with a capital *F.*

—RUTH DINKINS ROWAN

PRAY: *Father, I felt that someone I love was mean to me today and it hurt. Thank You for Your love and kindness that helps the hurt go away.*

DO: Do something nice for the person who hurt you today.

When you've been hurt (2)

READ: *If your brother sins against you, rebuke him; and if he repents, forgive him.*

—LUKE 17:3

REFLECT: We were student teachers, new to the methods of education.

"What do I do," someone asked the instructor, "if an experienced teacher puts me in a bad light in front of the pupils?"

"There are times," she replied, "when you must love others enough to confront them with the truth. If a person embarrasses you, say so. But gently."

It has always been far easier for me to ignore a wrong than to let the offender know—even in a gentle way—that my feelings have been hurt. The problem, of course, is that I have not really ignored the hurt—I've just pushed it way to the back of my mind. Then one day it's likely to surface, blown all out of proportion. And, even worse, I've been harboring resentment.

Yes, it's best to talk over a hurt, as my instructor of long ago prescribed.

—JUNE MASTERS BACHER

PRAY: *Jesus, when Your best friends' actions hurt You, You gently confronted them with the words, "Could you not watch with me one hour?" Thank You for Your example then that gives me strength today to do the hard but loving thing.*

DO: Explain to the one who hurt you a gentler way to handle the situation.

When you've been hurt (3)

READ: *I will lift up my eyes to the hills—from whence comes my help?*

—PSALM 121:1

REFLECT: Our younger daughter came home from school in tears. Another child, Sally, had been mean to her and she was heartbroken. "Why?" she asked.

I sent up a little prayer and the answer came almost instantly.

"Elizabeth," I said. "You know how unhappy Sally is at home. Her parents were divorced and her new father is very unkind. Perhaps something happened this morning and when she got to school her reaction was to hurt somebody, and you were the first person she met.

"Go to school tomorrow and love Sally, absorb her hurts, do something kind and generous. Make her love you." She did and the two girls became lifelong friends.

—RUTH STAFFORD PEALE

PRAY: *Heavenly Father, wounds from the wounded are no less painful, but they are more easily forgiven. Make me a kind and generous person who can absorb the hurts of others for the sake of lifelong friendships.*

DO: Do something kind for a person who hurt you, expecting nothing in return. If you gain a lifelong friend, give thanks to God.

When you've been rejected

READ: *Your love to me was wonderful. . . .*

—2 SAMUEL 1:26

REFLECT: I'd like to tell you about a friendship. Actually it's a broken friendship that began years ago. We had much in common then: the same business interests; children of similar age. We were able to work together, play golf together, even vacation together. But suddenly all that ended.

I'm still not sure what happened. I wondered if he had taken offense at something I had said. But when I tried to find out, he refused to see me. Asking friends to intercede didn't work. I have never been so hurt. I finally had to admit that we would never again be friends.

Being rejected by a person for whom you've cared deeply isn't easy. But when you've done everything you humanly can, it's time for divine intervention. Thank God for your friend and the love once shared and the laughter experienced. Put him or her into God's safekeeping, then move on, committing to love even more. —SCOTT HARRISON

PRAY: *Lord Jesus, who knows the deep pain of rejection better than You? Somehow we think because You're God it must not hurt so much, but if that were true, You wouldn't be able to comfort us in our rejection. Thank You so much that You can and do. It really helps ease the pain, Lord.*

DO: Be grateful for the time shared with the one who rejected you and even more so for the many loved ones who haven't rejected you. Then pray for the ones you've rejected.

When you've been
the victim of gossip

READ: *For Your lovingkindness is before my eyes, and I have walked in Your truth.*

—PSALM 26:3

REFLECT: A woman wrote to me, "I need your prayers. I have been labeled something I am not because of vicious gossip. Pray that I can find a way to combat this untruth."

Abraham Lincoln came under heavy attack while he was President and was reviled by many leaders of the day. In response to all the things he was called, Lincoln posed this question: "How many legs does a lamb have if you call its tail a leg?" His answer was "Four, because calling a tail a leg doesn't make it one."

When you are maligned—and everyone is at one time or another—your best defense is the life you live. If you are honest, fair, just, those who know you will speak on your behalf. What others say won't matter. Ask for God's grace to strengthen you and go forward with your head held high.

—FRED BAUER

PRAY: *Like Psalm 26 says, Lord, please help me to walk in truth—which is not what's been said about me. But if I can walk in truth and live the truth, then I pray that, eventually, others will speak the truth.*

DO: Ask for God's grace to strengthen you and go forward— in truth—with your head held high.

When you've disappointed yourself

READ: *You have granted me life and favor, and Your care has preserved my spirit.*

—JOB 10:12

REFLECT: "You numbskull," I muttered. I had just muffed a presentation to a client, and was talking to myself in the mirror in the ladies' room at work. A coworker had walked in and looked around, shocked. "Who are you talking to?"

"Just myself," I admitted sheepishly.

My friend was aghast. "Would you dream of talking to somebody else that way?" When I shook my head, she reminded me, "Remember, it says in the Bible, 'Love your neighbor as yourself.' Never treat yourself any worse than you would treat another human being."

Turning back to the mirror, I said firmly, "You did the best you could. There's always a next time." My shoulders got a little straighter, and I resolved to give all my comments the "Would you say that to a friend?" test.

—LINDA NEUKRUG

PRAY: *What great advice, Father. Forgive me for treating a child of Yours—myself—so unkindly. I promise I'll try to be nicer to myself—and Your other children when they mess up or disappoint me.*

DO: Encourage yourself today with kindness. Become your own best friend by believing in yourself and changing the way you talk to yourself when you feel you've messed up in whatever way.

When you've had a
falling-out with a friend

READ: *If you bring your gift to the altar, and there remember that your brother has something against you. . . . First be reconciled to your brother. . . .*

—MATTHEW 5:23–24

REFLECT: When they decided to build a bridge across the river at Niagara Falls, they had a problem. They needed to get one rope across the river to start the suspension bridge. But the river was impossible to cross.

Finally they came up with an ingenious idea. They flew a kite across the river. Once it had been caught on the other side, a cord was tied to its string. The cord was used to pull the rope across the river.

There are times when I've had a falling-out with someone and a gulf has widened that I felt couldn't be bridged. But I've found that if I pray about it, there is always a way to make amends. A telephone call or any tiny gesture can be the start of my bridge of reconciliation.   —LOIS E. WOODS

PRAY: *Lord, I miss my friend _____. Help me be willing to take the first step toward reconciliation and help me know what that step should be.*

DO: As soon as a good idea comes to you about how to reach out to your friend, do it at the first opportunity.

When you've had a setback (1)

◄◦►

READ: *This I recall to my mind, therefore I have hope.
Through the Lord's mercies we are not consumed,
because His compassions fail not.*

—LAMENTATIONS 3:21–22

REFLECT: The slopes of the Rocky Mountains offer fragile footholds to trees. Storms, drought and bitter cold warp their growth. But the trees live on.

I stood before one twisted ponderosa pine, marveling at the disasters it had survived. Ice had broken its limbs, fierce winds bent its trunk almost level. Yet the tree was not only alive, it thrived—thrusting the new year's growth toward the sun.

Studying that gnarled outline, I saw in fact that this was the secret of the tree's survival. After each assault, its branches once more sought the sun, reaching skyward from wherever the latest setback had left them, sustaining the overall pattern of upward growth.

Scientists call this persistence in plants *heliotropism*, "turning toward the sun." There's a word for the same quality in human life, the ever-repeated turning to God, no matter what traumas come our way. The word, of course, is *hope*.

—ELIZABETH SHERRILL

PRAY: *Father, I'm feeling a lot like that ponderosa pine—
beat to the ground by yet another setback. I turn now
to You, the Light, for new growth and renewed hope
as You shape my heart, not in spite of these setbacks,
but through them.*

DO: Imagine or draw a picture of a damaged tree, thriving in spite of the traumas it has survived.

When you've had a setback (2)

READ: *"He reached down from on high and took hold of me; he drew me out of deep waters."*

—2 SAMUEL 22:17 (NIV)

REFLECT: Only a writer could fully appreciate the despair Thomas Carlyle felt when his friend John Stuart Mill told him that his maid had used the only copy of a Carlyle book manuscript to start the morning fire. The writer was understandably inconsolable for days. But then he recalls that he looked out his window one morning and saw some bricklayers at work. "It came to me," he wrote, "that as they lay brick on brick, so could I still lay word on word, sentence on sentence." Thus it was that he began to rewrite *The French Revolution*, a classic that would be absent from literature were it not for Carlyle's ability to rebound from misfortune.

—FRED BAUER

PRAY: *God, if You'll help me get over the discouragement of this setback, I'll try again—with Your help.*

DO: Try to resist the urge to place blame for your setback. Get back on track as soon as you can—How about tomorrow?

When you've had a setback (3)

<o>

READ: *Watch, stand fast in the faith, be brave, be strong.*

—1 CORINTHIANS 16:13

REFLECT: My friend Jack loves athletics as much as I do. Given the chance, I think he'd play ball twenty-four hours a day. But chance is one thing Jack hasn't always had.

In high school he was injured while playing football and unable to finish the season. Then in his freshman year at college a concussion ended his football season again—and after that he spent most of the basketball season on crutches. And next he developed a rare form of arthritis and had to drop out of school.

To play the game—the game of life—is to risk the pain and disappointment that come with injury or defeat. But through faith, Jack continues to seek joy in life . . . and it's from him that I've learned how faith strengthens us to endure life's hardships.

He reminds me of the apostle Paul's words: "I have fought a good fight . . . I have kept the faith."

—JEFF JAPINGA

PRAY: *Thank You, God, for friends who inspire me. Remind me about Jack when yet another obstacle pops up in my path, keeping me from my goal.*

DO: Write a note to a friend who has inspired your faith. Let him/her know what a positive example he/she has been to you and thank him/her for staying strong in faith.

When you've hurt someone

◄○►

READ: *Does a spring send forth fresh water and bitter from the same opening?*

—JAMES 3:11

REFLECT: I'm a real neatness nut. When JoAnn and I were first married, her cluttered style of housekeeping bothered me. I even went so far as to "apologize" for her in front of guests. JoAnn became upset and told me, "I don't understand how you can say 'I love you' one minute and cut me down the next."

I never realized how much words could hurt someone. The third chapter of James says the tongue can be like a fire —and that the person who is wise should let his actions reflect it.

I decided that my tongue would not "cut down" anymore but would stick to "I love you." I learned to talk over problems with JoAnn—in private—and to compliment instead of criticize. I learned that a neatness nut can be just as irritating to live with as a clutter nut. And if any mess starts to bother me too much, I can clean it up myself!

—WALLY METTS

PRAY: *Father, I'm sure my thoughtlessness and insensitivity have wounded more than one heart. Guard my tongue with a sensitive spirit and let only "fresh water" flow from my mouth.*

DO: Apologize to someone you've hurt with your words or actions and vow to try to become an encourager and not a criticizer.

When you've listened to gossip

<o>

READ: *A gossip separates close friends.*

REFLECT: Before I moved to a new city, a friend (whom I'll call Pam) wrote about the people I would meet. Somehow her descriptions always included something negative. "Sue is a lot of fun, but her child is a brat." "Lottie is a lovely person, but she dates a terrible bore."

So I was wary. I avoided visiting Sue at home and arranged to meet Lottie alone. I seemed unable to make new friends and decided the move was a mistake.

One day Sue insisted I come for coffee. I became so enthralled with little Timmy that I sat on the floor and helped him scatter toys around us.

Later Sue commented, "You're not at all as Pam described you." My dismay must have shown for Sue added quickly, "It's okay. No one pays attention to the gossip Pam spreads."

But I had, and caused myself a great deal of grief. I resolved right then to start over. —RUTH DINKINS ROWAN

PRAY: *God, gossip is so easy to come by and so hard to get away from. Help me to look for the good in others so I'll be ready to counteract gossip with positive comments.*

DO: The next time you hear something negative about someone else, neutralize that negative with a positive.

When you've lost
a loved one (1)

◄◌►

READ: *I give them eternal life, and they shall never perish. . . .*

—JOHN 10:28

REFLECT: When I began teaching a class of eight-year-olds at church, I asked them to go around the circle telling about their families and where they lived. As the first child started, I realized my mistake. Sitting in the circle was Susan. Her only sister had just died.

Despairingly, I waited. When it was Susan's turn, she said in a quiet, steady voice, "I'm Susan Clark. I live on Stone Mountain. I have one sister."

Oh, Lord, I thought. *The child is afraid to admit her sister is dead.*

"My sister doesn't live with us anymore," Susan continued. "She lives with Jesus now in Heaven. And because I know Him, too, I'll be able to see her again one day. Her name is Carol."

—MARION BOND WEST

PRAY: *Father, I praise You for the truth in this little girl's prayer. My loved one is still alive, is living with Jesus, and I will see him/her again. Help me to believe it in my saddest moments.*

DO: Pass this on to a friend or relative who is also grieving the loss of a loved one.

When you've lost a loved one (2)

READ: *I will abide in Your tabernacle forever; I will trust in the shelter of Your wings.*

—PSALM 61:4

REFLECT: A young, recently ordained rabbi officiated at my grandmother's funeral. She had come to America from Poland in the 1880s, and her struggle to give her large family the best had lasted three loving generations.

I felt disappointment at how young and unfamiliar this rabbi was. I was only half-listening until I heard the words, "I feel honored to be permitted to share with you this day of rejoicing for Rifka Strizik.

"When a ship sets forth with precious cargo onto a turbulent sea, we worry that it may founder in a storm. When it puts into port unscathed after its perilous adventure, we rejoice. Therefore, we should expend our tears least of all after ninety years of overcoming life's travails. And so I ask you to rejoice with me; Rifka is home safely at last."

—NAOMI LAWRENCE

PRAY: *Father, my loved one is gone. I'll celebrate for him/her, trusting he/she is with You. But I come to You to grieve.*

DO: Allow yourself time to grieve—and to celebrate.

When you've lost the joy of living

◄◦►

READ: *You shine as lights in the world, holding fast the word of life. . . .*

—PHILIPPIANS 2:15–16

REFLECT: One day someone told me the story of a little boy who was asked in Sunday school to define a saint. The boy thought hard, then remembered the stained-glass windows in the church sanctuary, the ones depicting various saints. "A saint," he answered, "is a person the light shines through!"

That definition can be true of each one of us. We can let God's light shine through us. Today, perhaps you can take the time to talk with the stranger in the checkout line, the one who reveals that she and her husband have just moved to town. Or perhaps you'll find a way to be patient when a child asks, "Why?" for the umpteenth time. I'm going to find a way to let my faith shine, and I know you will too.

—TAMMY RIDER

PRAY: *Father, is anything blocking Your light from shining through me today?*

DO: Ask God to help you remove one of the things that He's brought to mind, whether it's by making up for a wrong you've done, forgiving someone who's hurt you or opening your heart to someone you don't particularly like.

When you've made a mistake

◄○►

READ: *Who can understand his errors? Cleanse me from secret faults.*

—PSALM 19:12

REFLECT: Hawaiian Kuulei Pavao learned the art of *lauhala* weaving from her mother, who learned from her mother's mother. Long before, Polynesians had perfected the craft of making ornaments from the slender leaves of the *halo* or "walking tree."

The traditional patterns are passed from one generation to another. The bracelet Kuulei had just completed, though, was like no other I'd seen, an intricate sequence of diagonals, complex and beautiful.

"What an unusual design! Is it a family secret?"

Kuulei laughed and shook her head. "Sometimes," she explained, "my mind is far away when I weave. I make a mistake! But I do not throw the work away. I look to see how I can fit the mistake into the whole. In the end I have a pattern no one has made before."

I'm so grateful my Father weaves my very failures into His unique design for my life.

—ELIZABETH SHERRILL

PRAY: *Father, I'm so looking forward to seeing which "mistakes," the outcomes that didn't look like I expected, were part of Your design for my life from the beginning.*

DO: Talk to an artist to learn how he/she handles mistakes in the creation of a painting.

When you've missed your morning quiet time

READ: *Arise, shine; for your light has come! And the glory of the Lord is risen upon you.*

—ISAIAH 60:1

REFLECT: The bus I take every morning to work in New York seems, at first glance, to be an unfriendly place. Most riders stick to themselves, staring out the window, or reading. You have a sense that people are preparing themselves for the day, that their minds are on the problems ahead of them.

What took me by surprise one morning was noticing how many of my fellow travelers were reading small Bibles or devotional books. The Hispanic woman thumbing through her *Santa Biblia*; a businessman reading a favorite Bible passage taped inside his briefcase; the woman staring so pointedly out the window has a prayer book in her lap. Over a third of the passengers on that bus seem to be practicing a morning devotion of some kind. They use their trip to work as part of their spiritual journey.

What better way to prepare for the day?

—RICK HAMLIN

PRAY: *Lord, I thank You that You aren't in just one place at just one time, and if I miss it, I've missed You. Thank You for going with me everywhere I go.*

DO: Even if it isn't first thing in the morning, commit your day to the Lord right now. Ask Him to be with you the rest of the day.

When you've quarreled with a loved one

READ: *And be kind to one another, tenderhearted, forgiving one another, even as God in Christ forgave you.*

—EPHESIANS 4:32

REFLECT: I had just hung up the phone on my cousin Diane. I felt bad, but, after all, Diane was at fault and she should be the one to apologize. A month went by. Neither of us attempted to get in touch. Then one evening, at the office, the cleaning woman asked me to type this poem for her:

What makes life worth the living

Is our giving and forgiving;

Giving tiny bits of kindness

That will leave a joy behind us.

For the little things are bigger

Than we often stop to figure.

—Thomas Grant Springer

I made a copy of the poem for myself, then wrote a note of apology to Diane. Soon after, she called. How good it was to be unburdened from bitterness.

—SAMANTHA MCGARRITY

PRAY: *Father, my conflict with _____ has gone on too long. Let my love and commitment to the relationship be greater than the need to place blame.*

DO: Go ahead . . . make the first move toward reconciliation in whatever way is easiest for you—a note, a phone call, a surprise delivery of flowers.

When you've quarreled with someone

READ: *"Love your enemies, do good to those who hate you".* . . .

—LUKE 6:27

REFLECT: I had thought of every excuse to fire Toby, my assistant in a large department store advertising office. He was talented, but we were constantly at odds, and colleagues said he had tried to undermine me with my boss. Finally, to my relief, he resigned.

Later, the president of another department store asked if I knew of a good man to head his advertising department. Toby's name came to mind. But after what we'd been through . . . I debated: *Could he do the job? Yes, he's a natural. Well?*

Soon he accepted the job, a very choice one. When Toby invited me to dinner, I realized fully that I had done the right thing. He confessed his former enmity and asked my forgiveness. As we shook hands, he said, "Friends are better than enemies, aren't they?"

That's when the truth of "love your enemies" came surging through. When you love them, they vanish and return as friends.

—CHARLES M. DAVIS

PRAY: *Lord Jesus, most of us don't have real enemies in the sense that you did and still do. But there is this conflict, Lord. I don't care for this person any more than he/she cares for me. Could we actually be friends? If that's Your goal, Lord, it's mine too.*

DO: Begin to imagine this person as a friend. Pray and be willing to let the imagined become reality.

When you've received a kindness

READ: *I will bless you . . . and you shall be a blessing.*

—GENESIS 12:2

REFLECT: One morning on business, I took a shortcut between two desert towns. Before I realized that I'd taken a wrong turn, I had gone miles off-course. At two in the afternoon, with desert heat at 112 degrees, I ran out of gas on a sparsely traveled road. And my thermos of water was diminishing rapidly. Of course, I prayed.

Imagine my relief when a car soon came by carrying both extra gasoline and water for just such an emergency.

When I tried to pay the motorist for the gas, he refused, saying, "No, just pass it on. You see, that's what *I'm* doing—ever since a man once gave me gas when I ran out."

Each time I give gas and water to a stranded motorist, I feel again the blessing experienced that day.

Sometimes we get so involved enjoying God's abundance that we selfishly forget to pass any of it on to others.

—JEANNE HILL

PRAY: *Thank You, Father, for the blessing I've received through _____. I pray for those who are in need of a blessing today. Bring a kind soul to share Your goodness with them.*

DO: Think of someone around you who could use a blessing today and pass on the blessing you've received.

When you've taken your blessings for granted

◄○►

READ: *But just as you excel in everything—in faith, in speech, in knowledge, in complete earnestness and in your love for us—see that you also excel in this grace of giving.*

—2 CORINTHIANS 8:7 (NIV)

REFLECT: I answered a knock to find a neighbor standing at the door. He held an orange-soda bottle I had put in the trash barrel the evening before.

"Pardon for this disturbance," he began in the formal school-learned English of Uganda, "but as I passed your house my eyes beheld this." He held up the empty bottle. "Is it that you have no further plan for it?" he stammered. "I am not a thief..."

I now stammered for words. "Of course... take it."

He headed up the road—running, leaping, all but dancing in the exhilaration of sudden wealth.

Ours has been called the throwaway society—stripping the forests, polluting the seas, despoiling the earth. If we made do with less, I've been asking myself, might we, too, dance with the joy of gratitude? —ELIZABETH SHERRILL

PRAY: *Forgive us, Father, for the way we're spoiling Your creation—and ourselves—by taking it for granted. Make us grateful for the smallest of blessings.*

DO: Look around and find five blessings you've taken for granted. Thank God for them.

When your child is facing a challenge

<hr>

READ: *Remember now your Creator in the days of your youth. . . .*

     —ECCLESIASTES 12:1

REFLECT: Tim was almost thirteen, awkward and shy. So when he left for Boy Scout camp, my heart ached for my gentle son. Everything at camp was intensely physical and competitive.

Then his first letter arrived. "Yesterday, I had to swim one hundred meters using four different strokes. I sat on the porch of the lifeguard's hut to wait my turn. I still didn't know if I'd try but then I saw something on the wall. A photo of a race and this verse: 'I can do all things through Christ which strengtheneth me' (Philippians 4:13, KJV).

"I decided then to go ahead with it, and when it came to my turn, I repeated the verse inside my head as I swam. It was hard, but I PASSED! I PASSED!"

He had gone away that summer to face some new challenges alone. He'd returned a little grown-up, with new self-confidence—and a renewed faith in God.

     —LINDA CHING SLEDGE

PRAY: *Father, thank You for letting Your children struggle and for strengthening our faith through those struggles.*

DO: Plan a family celebration in honor of your child's accomplishment.

<hr>

When your child's heart is burdened

◄○►

READ: *Close the door and pray to your Father, who is unseen.*

—MATTHEW 6:6 (NIV)

REFLECT: Tim, who is home for college break, is in his room with the door shut playing his guitar; he is upset at—who knows what?—a girl, perhaps, or college, or maybe even me. As he sings, his voice cracks with youthful emotion.

I want so much to walk through the door in order to soften whatever pain has driven him to such sad music. I touch the doorknob. His fingers strike a chord . . . and my hand drops away.

What right do I have to interrupt his solitary song? I myself have sat behind a similarly closed door, overwhelmed temporarily by some burden. With my loved ones waiting on the other side, I would read, rest and pray until strength and understanding returned and I could open the door to them again. My heart aching, I turn to go downstairs, and grant him what he needs and desires: a time-out with God.

—LINDA CHING SLEDGE

PRAY: *Lord, I pray that You would replace the sad song in my child's heart today with a song of joy.*

DO: Play some joyful music and praise God for the growth that happens in our children during the heavy times.

When your children and grandchildren have moved out on their own

———————————— ‹o› ————————————

READ: *Behold, children are a heritage from the Lord, the fruit of the womb is a reward.*

—PSALM 127:3

REFLECT: As a youngster I always attended church with my parents. When I went to a church-sponsored junior college, I continued to attend every Sunday—primarily because it was required. Then I went to a state university and found myself getting up for church every Sunday, even though it wasn't required, and my roommates weren't churchgoers.

One year, my mother confided to me that she had been praying for me daily, not only that I would continue my church attendance, but that I would put God first in my everyday life. Her devotion inspired me and I never forgot it.

As my five children grew up, I prayed for them and now I also pray for their children. I've decided there's nothing like a mother's or a father's prayers to help open the channels between a living Heavenly Father and His children. It takes so very little to do, but its effect can last a lifetime.

—SAM JUSTICE

PRAY: *I pray today, Father, for my children and grandchildren. Draw them to Yourself, and to a church where they can grow and serve and find the joys of being part of the body of Christ.*

DO: Call, write or e-mail your kids and grandkids today to keep the connection open between you.

When your children are acting up

READ: *Let your saints rejoice in goodness.*

—2 CHRONICLES 6:41

REFLECT: One day my son and daughter were upstairs having an earsplitting, uproarious squabble. When my nerves could take no more, I stormed up the steps, raging, "Can't you kids ever get along peacefully?"

I'll never forget my daughter staring quizzically at me, lifting her eyebrows high. "Of course we can," she said. "But you never notice us when we do."

And it was true. I was guilty of taking my children's good behavior for granted.

Too often, I realize, I take God's good efforts for granted too. Sunshine, flowers, family, friends, love—I'm apt to expect and accept them all without a thought or praiseful prayer for God.

—ROSALYN HART FINCH

PRAY: *God, would You get my attention when my kids are enjoying each other so that I can tell them how much it pleases me? And, Lord, I praise You for all Your wonderful blessings that I so easily overlook.*

DO: Reward your kids with a special treat the next time you notice their kindness to each other.

When your children are getting on your nerves

◄◦►

READ: *A feast is made for laughter. . . .*

—ECCLESIASTES 10:19

REFLECT: It was a hot afternoon, and my eight-year-old son Zeb ran off to play with Mike and Devin. A couple hours later he walked into the kitchen—covered with mud. When I found my voice, I asked, "What did you do?"

"Oh, we were just playing in some mud," Zeb answered with classic understatement.

I wasn't sure if I should lecture him or laugh. So I drew him a bath. As the tub was filling, Zeb said, "Mike was in big trouble when his mom saw him."

"What did she say?" I asked, feeling a kinship with Mike's mom.

"'You get in here *right now!*'"

I stifled a laugh.

Devin was being cared for by his grandma that day and I asked how she had responded to the awful sight.

"She said, 'Wow! You're a *masterpiece!*'"

And suddenly it was my heart's prayer that I'll be able to respond to my son's childhood as lightly as Devin's grandma.

—ELLYN BAUMANN

PRAY: *Father, I can imagine You responding like Devin's grandma to some of my messes. Make me able to do that not just for my children, but for everyone.*

DO: Let your little ones play in the mud the next time it rains. In fact, why don't you join them?

When your children are getting ready to leave the nest

◄◉►

READ: *To everything there is a season, a time for every purpose under heaven. . . .*

—ECCLESIASTES 3:1

REFLECT: After delivering our two older kids to college, my husband and I started our trek home. Our youngest daughter had stayed home to begin her junior year in high school. Before we knew it, she would be away in college too. The more I thought about it, the deeper I sank into sadness.

Then we pulled into a fruit stand on the western slope of the Colorado Rockies. "The peaches are still great," said a jovial lady as she handed us each a fat, juicy piece. "You should enjoy them while you can." We purchased a whole bushel.

As we headed home, I thought about opportunities to enjoy Kendall's last two years of high school—like saying "yes" when she asks me to go shopping with her, helping her study Spanish at 10:00 PM, and spontaneously going to see a Saturday afternoon movie.

All the way home, the smell of those fresh peaches kept reminding me, "Enjoy them while you can."

—CAROL KUYKENDALL

PRAY: *Thank You, Lord, for the reminder to enjoy my children while they're still "in the nest."*

DO: Do something extra special with your kids today—something *they* choose.

When your children are growing more independent

────────────◄O►────────────

READ: *Unless the Lord builds the house, they labor in vain who build it. . . .*

—PSALM 127:1

REFLECT: "Mother," said our teenage daughter, "I don't want to ride the bus to school anymore! I'm too old for that. I want to take the subway to school, the way my friends do!"

I had qualms about New York City subways, and I said so. But Elizabeth begged and pleaded. "All right," I said finally, "you can go with a group of friends. But remember: My prayers are going with you every day, every step of the way."

And I did pray, placing Elizabeth in God's hands every morning and thanking Him for bringing her home safely every afternoon. Elizabeth knew this; she felt protected and loved. Once she did tell me that two men got into a noisy altercation not far from her group. "But we just got off at the next stop," she said, "and waited for another train." I was sure that the Lord, watching over her, put this simple and sensible idea into her head.

—RUTH STAFFORD PEALE

PRAY: *Lord, help me neither cling too tightly to my fledgling children nor let them go too easily. Let the knowledge that they are covered in prayer give them courage to walk fearlessly through every door You open before them.*

DO: Write your prayers for your children in a journal.

278

When your children delight you

◄◦►

READ: *Mercy and truth belong to those who devise good.*

—PROVERBS 14:22

REFLECT: The branch scrapes against the window and bids me to look out upon the cold, gray day. I am depressed. Even the steaming cup of tea and a warm slice of banana bread do little to lift my spirits.

My daughter Mandy passes through the kitchen sipping juice through a straw. She lifts her hand and gives me "the sign"—her thumb, forefinger and little finger raised in the air. I smile and do the same. Without words we have just said "I love you" in sign language.

I feel as if a ray of sunlight has just streamed through the kitchen. Mandy has brightened my morning and given me an idea. Why don't I use some sign language of my own to say "I love you"?

I called my sick aunt and sent a card to a friend who had moved away.

What sign language can you use today that says "I love you"?

—TERRY HELWIG

PRAY: *Thank You, Father, for my child, whose presence can change a dark, gloomy day into a delightful one.*

DO: Tell your child how much you delight in who God made him/her to be.

When your children need attention (1)

READ: *Stand still and consider the wondrous works of God.*

—JOB 37:14

REFLECT: "Hey, Mom! Let's go cross-country skiing today," my twenty-year-old son Derek suggested as I sat facing a pile of projects. It was just days before he was to go back to college, and I faced a choice: *Do I drop everything and seize the moment, or stick to my planned agenda?* Something nudged me in the direction of Derek.

Within an hour, we found ourselves on a high mountain trail. Around noon, we came upon a picnic table where we ate sandwiches and talked. Derek had accumulated some tough questions. "How do you *know* what God wants you to do?" he asked me. "Does God *really* see us as righteous as Jesus?"

By the time we arrived back at the car, I felt bone-tired but exhilarated.

"Thanks, Mom," Derek said as he put away our skis. "Our talk gave me a lot to think about."

No doubt about it, I had made the right decision.

—CAROL KUYKENDALL

PRAY: *Father, I'm amazed that it delights Your heart when Your children come to You "just to talk." Make me grateful, rather than irritated, for the times when my children need my attention.*

DO: Take your children on an outing for the sheer pleasure of their company.

When your children need attention (2)

◄○►

READ: *When my father and my mother forsake me, then the Lord will take care of me.*

—PSALM 27:10

REFLECT: "What is the worst thing that can happen to anybody?" That question was posed to my psychology class, and the students came up with a variety of answers: terminal illness; the death of a loved one, child abuse.

But the answer of a famous psychologist was very different than ours. "I was walking through our clinic one day," John Gardner wrote, "and overheard the conversation of three boys. 'My mom yells at me,' the first boy said. 'My dad hits me,' the second said. The third, the most forlorn-looking of the three, slowly raised his eyes. 'My dad doesn't even hit me,' he said. Oh, the worst thing that can ever happen to a human being is to be isolated and ignored."

Immediately, I thought of the last promise that Jesus made to us before He ascended—that no matter the circumstances, He will never abandon us. What a Friend we have in Jesus!

—JEFF JAPINGA

PRAY: *Thank You so much, Lord, for this gentle nudge to tune in to my children. Thanks for reminding me how hurtful it is for kids to be brushed aside and help me to never do that to my children no matter how busy or tired I may be.*

DO: Look at your calendar and block out some time today for one-on-ones with your children.

When your children rebel

READ: *Position yourselves, stand still and see the salvation of the Lord. . . .*

—2 CHRONICLES 20:17

REFLECT: The summer after my senior year was a fun time. I didn't have a care in the world. I knew I didn't want to go to college, and neither of my parents pressured me at first. But the weekend before fall semester arrived, Mom came into my room, tears in her eyes. "I love you," she said, "and it tears me apart inside to make you do something you hate so much, but sometimes change is necessary. We're taking you up to enroll in college."

I don't think I said three words the entire two-hour trip to the university. They helped me enroll, unpacked my belongings in my room, and left me.

College was wonderful. It gave my life direction and helped me grow. I'll never forget the courageous love my parents showed me by their firmness. It makes me wonder: If God doesn't give me what I want, isn't it possible He's giving me what I need?

—JOHN COEN

PRAY: *Father, You are the Parent of all parents. Give me wisdom in raising my children and make me strong enough to do what's best for them.*

DO: Try to remember the disagreements you had with your parents. Tell your child about one or two of them.

When your conscience is bothering you

———◄◊►———

READ: . . . *Holding on to faith and a good conscience.*

—1 TIMOTHY 1:19 (NIV)

REFLECT: One day my eight-year-old granddaughter Sherri came in from school looking downcast, and her mother immediately knew something was wrong. "What's the matter, honey? Bad day at school?"

Sherri confessed to copying a word from another student's spelling test. "I wrote it down and it looked funny. Then I saw her answer and knew it was right, so I changed mine." A guilty conscience was bothering Sherri.

The next day brought a surprising turnaround. Sherri ran in the door after school. "You know what, Mother?" she said. "We didn't finish our spelling test yesterday and our teacher gave our papers back today." A smile spread across her face as she concluded, "I changed that word to the way I spelled it the first time!" The relief of a clear conscience outweighed a higher grade.

My granddaughter reminded me that we can always pray for God's forgiveness, and, with His blessing, start anew.

—VIRGINIA POEHLEIN

PRAY: *Thank You so much, Lord, that we can start each day afresh. Forgive me for _____, and help me to forget it as quickly as You do.*

DO: Admit your fault, however slight it may seem to others. Ask God for forgiveness and then move on with a forgiven, happy heart.

When your creative juices seem to have dried up

◄◉►

READ: *The works of the Lord are great, studied by all who have pleasure in them.*

—PSALM 111:2

REFLECT: I'm a writer so you'd think my mind would be teeming with stories, plots and characters demanding to be put to paper. Unfortunately, that's not the case. The writing process from beginning to "The End," while enjoyable in many ways, can be quite excruciating.

Once, while laboring over a writing project, I decided my time might be better spent laboring in prayer first. That's when it came to me that God was a little amused with my writer's block. Gently, He reminded me that *He* is the Word and the creator of all words. His mind is the most brilliant . . . His thoughts the deepest . . . His creativity the most original. And, most amazingly, by His Holy Spirit, He delights to share it all with me.

I don't know that I wrote my most dazzling piece that day, but what really matters is that I finished it with a heart full of renewed awe for the ultimate Creator. —LUCILE ALLEN

PRAY: *Thank You, God, Author of all creativity, for new ideas. I need a few now, please.*

DO: When you ask God for a fresh approach to a creative project, wait for it. It *will* come.

When your dreams have yet to blossom

———————◀◦▶———————

READ: *There is a proper time and procedure for every matter. . . .*

—ECCLESIASTES 8:6 (NIV)

REFLECT: Carol and I wandered along, enjoying the beauties of the desert. After we stopped now and then to examine closely a cougar track, a cactus bud, I bent over a straggly weed, attracted by the dainty blue flowers it bore. About a quarter of an inch across, each had five oval petals and a minute yellow center.

"I don't remember seeing these before," I exclaimed.

"Well," Carol said, "the paper says that some plants are up that have been lying dormant for twenty-five years."

"Twenty-five years!" I could picture a tiny seed, hidden under hard earth, waiting twenty-five years for exactly the right conditions so it could grow. I'm impatient because I don't know what the Lord is going to do with me next month!

What of the seed within my own deepest desire? I don't know what its flower will look like. But if I wait. . .

—MARILYN J. NORQUIST

PRAY: *. . . if I wait, Lord, You'll cause it to bloom not just in good time, but in Your perfect time.*

DO: Plant a small seed. Wait and watch as it blooms, just as you're waiting for your dreams to bloom.

When your faith doesn't seem to make sense

<hr/>

READ: *God presented him as a sacrifice of atonement, through faith in his blood.*

—ROMANS 3:25 (NIV)

REFLECT: We were drifting down the Zambezi river. Our guide pointed to a large leopard walking at the water's edge. He looked back and then suddenly leaped up the bank and was gone.

I remembered another leopard that terrorized this same Zambezi valley many years before by killing and mauling local children. In desperation the tribesmen went to their missionary Oria Blair for help. The missionary had struggled for years to get them to understand the story of Christ's sacrifice. Now, although opposed to hunting, he took his rifle, selected a sheep from the tribe's herd and tied it to a tree. When the leopard struck, it was over in an instant.

The missionary carried the dead leopard and lamb back to the village. "You have saved us," they shouted.

"No," he replied, "the lamb did." Now they understood and believed.

—SCOTT HARRISON

PRAY: *Thank You, Jesus, for dying for me. Help me to understand—really understand—what that means for me today and for all eternity.*

DO: Copy this page and send it to a missionary friend.

When your hurts won't heal (1)

◄◦►

READ: *The Lord is near to those who have a broken heart, and saves such as have a contrite spirit.*

—PSALM 34:18

REFLECT: Mary X confessed to me, "I've been praying for ten years that my husband will come back to me. He divorced me when our children were teenagers. Why won't God answer my prayer?"

Mary and I prayed about her problem intensively and, gradually, we began to see the problem. She wrongly believed that only her ex-husband could end the pain she felt, and by believing this she was keeping God from carrying out His plans for her.

Finally, Mary was able to pray: "Father, at this moment I let go, freeing both Joe and me into Your care, opening a place for Your perfect wisdom."

Mary taught me a great lesson—a hurt not given up to God is a hurt that might never heal.

—MARILYN MORGAN KING

PRAY: *Father, could this be my problem? Could this be why all my prayers about this haven't brought healing? Right now, at this moment, I let go, Lord. I trust You to have Your way in my life.*

DO: Call a trusted friend—someone who will pray for your continued healing—and explain your choice to let go.

When your hurts won't heal (2)

◄○►

READ: . . . *That we may be able to comfort those who are in any trouble, with the comfort with which we ourselves are comforted by God.*

—2 CORINTHIANS 1:4

REFLECT: Much has been written about the healing of memories, but it seems there is something to be said for unhealed ones. For instance, a friend was deeply humiliated as a child by never having proper clothes, and her wounds are still there. But out of this has come great compassion for every child she sees in rags.

So, she opened the Perris Closet in three rent-free civic rooms, and contacted local churches for good, used clothing. They responded. Thanks to the desire of my friend to spare children the heartache she suffered—and still suffers through unhealed memories—thousands of these youngsters were outfitted in new jeans and sneakers and shirts and dresses.

So if you have painful memories, believe now that your wounds have served their purpose in making you a more caring person. Your memories will remain, but you'll have in your heart the peace that Jesus promised.

—LAVERNE RILEY

PRAY: *Father, use these painful memories for others' good and for Your glory.*

DO: Think of two of your most positive qualities. Can you see any connection between those qualities and your past hurts? Thank God for them.

When your life is changing

◄○►

READ: *The Lord is my strength and my shield; my heart trusted in Him, and I am helped; therefore my heart greatly rejoices, and with my song I will praise Him.*

—PSALM 28:7

REFLECT: We'd prayed for direction before deciding to move, and everything had seemed so right. But now, when it was time to pack and say good-bye to the loved and the familiar for a strange, friendless place, it all seemed wrong.

As I stood at the kitchen window scanning the backyard, Obie, our flop-eared dog, came running, carrying a bone bleached white from the sun.

That awful bone, I thought as I stepped to the refrigerator to get the meaty ham bone I'd kept for him. *Wait till he sees this!*

I called him to me and held out my succulent treat. But he drew back, loyally guarding his old white bone. He didn't even look to see what I had. He didn't trust me enough to trade the familiar for the unknown.

I left the bone on the grass for Obie to accept when he was ready.

—PATRICIA R. PATTERSON

PRAY: *Lord, help me see Your goodness in this change and give me Your guidance, too, as I adjust to it.*

DO: Copy this page and send it to a friend who has recently faced a major change.

When your life is in turmoil

READ: *Every branch in Me that does not bear fruit He takes away; and every branch that bears fruit He prunes, that it may bear more fruit.*

—JOHN 15:2

REFLECT: When my brother and I were very young, we spent our summers with our grandparents in the little town of Lynchburg, Ohio. I will never forget one wild night when a tremendous storm came crashing around the house. In the flashes of lightning I could see the great maple tree in the front yard writhing and thrashing about. I pulled the covers over my head, convinced that the whole house was blowing away.

By morning all was serene. The sun shone. The big maple still stood, the ground around it littered with fallen branches. I asked my grandfather if the tree had been hurt by losing all those branches.

"No, son," he replied, "those are just dead branches, useless limbs that the tree didn't need anymore. The wind is simply God's way of pruning a tree, making it healthier and stronger than ever, that's all." —NORMAN VINCENT PEALE

PRAY: *Gracious God, when will I ever learn to be grateful for the pruning You do in my life? Even though this turmoil is unsettling and I don't love the process, I love You for loving me enough to strengthen me through it.*

DO: Trust God with the timing and order of your life as you prayerfully make the necessary decisions to the best of your ability.

When your life seems to be going nowhere

◄○►

READ: *To this end I labor, struggling with all His energy, which so powerfully works in me.*

—COLOSSIANS 1:29 (NIV)

REFLECT: The great inventor Thomas Alva Edison used to take special pleasure in showing his guests around the grounds of his New Jersey home. On the way back to the house, there was a fence with a narrow opening and a turnstile that his visitors had to pass through, one at a time.

"Why the turnstile?" people often asked.

"Each time you pass through," Edison would explain, "you pump eight gallons of water into a tank. We use that water for bathing and drinking."

Edison was a towering genius. How like him not to overlook the natural energy that God has stored up in every human being, energy too often untapped.

Whenever I think of Edison now I am reminded of the divine potential within myself. The ideas in a corner of my mind I have yet to explore. The unlimited power of love that lies unused within my heart.

—MANUEL ALMADA

PRAY: *Sometimes I feel like there's got to be more than this, Lord. Would You unearth the deposit of ideas, gifts, talents—the divine potential—lying dormant within Your children and renew our energy to explore and use them?*

DO: Search the recesses of your memory for some ember of interest or potential that's been allowed to die out. Reignite the flame; it could lead to your next passion.

When your plans
have been thwarted

◄○►

READ: *In all your ways acknowledge Him, and He shall direct your paths.*

—PROVERBS 3:6

REFLECT: I was taking my dog for a late walk along a quiet country road. It was getting dark, and I wanted to go to the library before it closed.

Finally, I decided we had gone far enough. "Let's go home," I said, turning around. But Suzy kept facing in the other direction, looking back at me, concern in her eyes.

From the fields around us, I heard a high-pitched sound. The grasses parted, and a scruffy, black and white kitten stumbled toward us, crying pitifully. I carried it home, where it was only too happy to eat and fall asleep curled up next to Suzy. It grew into a handsome cat named Dennis, who gave our family lots of joy.

I was disappointed that I didn't get to the library. But God had something more important He wanted me to do— and I've always been thankful that He helped me to stop and listen to His plan.

—PHYLLIS HOBE

PRAY: *Father, I never enjoy having my will thwarted . . . but I love knowing You have a purpose for the change in plans.*

DO: Try to remember the last two or three times you were frustrated by a change in plans. Now try to remember how that change turned out for the better.

When your spirit needs a lift

◀◉▶

READ: *Oh, give thanks to the Lord of lords! . . . to Him who alone does great wonders. . . .*

—PSALM 136:3–4

REFLECT: Has your life seemed lacking in miracles lately? Nothing to lift your heart? Nothing to make you glad you're alive?

When I feel that way, I think of my favorite poetry book title, *Who Tells the Crocuses It's Spring?* Then for ten minutes I list similar questions, beginning with "Who?"

Who makes the trees turn all those beautiful colors in the autumn?

Who splashes silver rain in shining puddles?

Who makes the stars shimmer in the night?

Who gives me sight so I can delight in a cardinal's brilliant crimson against the sparkling snow?

Who puts the love in my beloved collie's soft brown eyes?

God does. That's who. And I bet you, too, can find the Who in your life that makes it all worthwhile.

—ALETHA JANE LINDSTROM

PRAY: *Praise You, Lord of lords, who alone does great wonders! I'm so grateful for the beauty of creation all around me and, especially, to know the One who created it.*

DO: Make your own *Who?* list today and put it where you can see it daily.

When your struggles seem too much to bear

—◈—

READ: *In this you greatly rejoice, though now for a little while, if need be, you have been grieved by various trials. . . .*

—1 PETER 1:6

REFLECT: An old violinmaker was once seen struggling up a mountainside.

"Where are you going?" a friend asked.

"To the timberline," he answered. "I need some wood for a violin."

"But you have fine trees all around you. Why must you go so far to get wood?"

"Ah," said the violinmaker, "because the wood up there is the most resonant of all. The trees on the timberline have struggled all their lives, fighting a never-ending battle with the winds. As a result, they are of rare quality, strong and full of character. Violins made of their wood produce the most beautiful music in the world."

When you face some difficult task, ask God for strength to meet the test. Out of wind-whipped souls comes some of the most beautiful music in the world.

—FRED BAUER

PRAY: *Father, give me strength to meet the tests that come my way so that my life can be music to other wind-whipped souls.*

DO: Find a picture of a tree, a violin, a musical note—some symbol to remind you that God will use the struggles in your life for good.

When your teenager is feeling misunderstood

READ: *For the Lord searches all hearts and understands all the intent of the thoughts.*

—1 CHRONICLES 28:9

REFLECT: It wasn't a major infraction, or even a major punishment. He'd just "hung out" with the guys long enough past curfew to be grounded for two days. He stormed off to his room, muttering, "You just don't understand!"

But I did. Suddenly, I was a teenager again, standing on a quiet street corner with my best friend. It was a pleasantly warm summer's evening. We were safe, staying out of trouble, and we had important things to discuss.

Suddenly, a car I knew only too well pulled up and my father, furious at being sent out at midnight, ordered us in. As I stomped to my room, I muttered, "You just don't understand!" Of course, he really did.

Even now, especially when I'm feeling guilty, I'm often tempted to mutter to God, "You just don't understand!" But being a parent, I know He does, and the guilt I'm feeling is His gentle way of grounding me.

—TONI SORTOR

PRAY: *Help me remember the intensity of emotion my teen is feeling right now, Lord. Give me the love and wisdom to discipline fairly and give him/her the grace to receive it . . . and some day even appreciate it.*

DO: Read in Scripture how God disciplined those dearest to His heart—Moses and David, for example—and be encouraged.

Authors and Subjects Index

◆◇◆

"Abba," 97
Absorbing the hurts of
    others, 253
Abundance
    sharing our, 125
Acceptance
    of mysteries, 84
    of others, 7
    sincere gestures of, 47
Accepting help, 100
Actions
    power of, 230
Addiction
    battling, 124
Allen, Frances Fowler, 10
Allen, Lucile, 35, 124,
    210, 284
Almada, Manuel, 153,
    291
Always try, 68
Anger
    letting go of, 122
    put to death, 121
    stop, look, and listen
        to, 120
    that overrules
        concern, 119
Angus, Fay, 60
Appreciation
    expressing, 32
    for God's blessings,
        52
    of what we must
        struggle for, 219
    reminders of, 91
Asking for help, 99, 117,
    118, 128
Attitude
    adjusting one's, 45,
        67, 137
    change in, 152

Bacher, June Masters,
    19, 39, 166, 252
Balance

keeping one's, 162
Bauer, Fred, 72, 98, 131,
    155, 158, 180, 255,
    259, 294
Baumann, Ellyn, 276
Being a doer, 15
Being prepared, 94
Being there, 12
Believing that prayers
    will be answered,
    130
Best, the
    bringing out, in
        children, 134
Betrayal, 146
Bible, the
    as our map, 160
    battling temptation
        with, 145
    expressing our feel-
        ings with, 58
    our comfort in, 49
    reading, to prepare
        for the day, 267
    refreshing ourselves
        in, 233
    relevance of, in daily
        life, 54
    self-improvement
        through, 103
    turning to, when we
        are in need, 87
    turning to, when
        you're dieting, 234,
        235
Blessings
    gratitude for the
        smallest, 271
    passing on, 270
Boredom, 126, 127
Bramblett, John, 140
Bridgeman, Gina, 15,
    74, 218
Brinckerhoff, Kathryn,
    97

Brisbine, Thelma, 76
Britt, Melanie, 193
Brown, Mary, 20, 50
Business problems, 189

Calming ourselves, 153
Campbell, Lucille, 26,
    100, 133, 154, 173
Carney, Mary Lou, 36,
    90, 109, 130, 167,
    174
Carrying each other's
    burdens, 6, 21
Celebrating the lives of
    loved ones, 264
Chafin, Barbara, 102,
    108
Challenges
    facing, with courage,
        141
    giving thanks for, 142
Change
    adjusting to, 289
    facing, willingly, 140
    in plans, 292
Cheney, Annamae, 145
Children
    being firm with, 282
    dealing with difficult,
        134
    disciplining our, 295
    encouraging inde-
        pendence of, 278
    enjoying our, while
        we can, 277
    facing challenges, 272
    forgiveness and our,
        188
    God's wonders
        through their eyes,
        53
    honesty of, 250
    letting go of our, 245
    making time for our,
        43

not giving up on, 246
our delight in, 279
praising good behavior of, 275
prayer for, 274
responding to lightly, 276
seizing the moment with, 280
their need for time-outs with God, 273
trusting our, to God, 56, 244
tuning into our, 281
Choosing contentment, 76
Church community
creating a, 31
fellowship in, 179
Churchgoing
going home to, 181
value of fellowship in, 182
Clark, Mary Jane, 125, 156
Coen, John, 282
Commitments
cutting back, 205, 206
prioritizing our, 163
Compassion
for one's enemies, 144
Compliments
instead of criticisms, 261
Conflict, 129
Confronting others with the truth, 252
Confusion, 131-33
Connor, B. J., 8, 82
Constructive criticism, 24
Conti, Christine, 209
Controlling our impatience, 61
Courage
and faith, 197
in the face of failure, 172
to grow roots, 177
to try new things, 123
Creativity
praying for, 284

Davis, Charles M., 269
Davis, Zona B., 22, 31, 231
De Vinck, Christopher, 213
Death
comfort of eternal life in the face of, 263
preparing for, 22, 200
Deerfield, William, 192
Depression, 5, 45, 91, 135, 149
Devotional life
organizing one's, 148
Dexter, Pat Egan, 6, 46
Dieting, 234, 235
Disappointment, 3, 4, 13, 37, 238, 249, 256
Disciplining our children, 295
Discouragement, 136, 147
Disorganization, 148
Distracting ourselves when we're depressed, 135
"Don't look back!," 123
Doubts, 30, 190, 222
Drawing closer to God, 150
Dreams
fulfilling our, 77
nurturing our, 184
taking our chances with, 193
waiting patiently for our, 285
Dudley, Barbara Hudson, 190
Duke, Drue, 78, 95, 178, 233, 248

Edlen, Lorena Pepper, 14, 116
Ellis, Kristen, 64
Emptiness, 150
Encouragement
in the face of disappointment, 13
of others, 261
of yourself, 256
power of, 23

Enthusiasm
performing routine tasks with, 127
Eternal life
our reunion with loved ones in, 263

Failure, 70-73, 172
Faith
Christ's sacrifice and, 286
honest questioning of, 30
intense, 151
keeping the, 260
"letting down your net" in, 147
our courage as, 197
overcoming addiction through, 124
sharing one's, 14, 218
strengthened through struggles, 272
walking in, 98
when we have doubts, 190
when we're grieving, 185
Fear
and standing fast in God's comfort, 115
cast out by God's love, 111
faced by thinking, evaluating, and praying, 113
giving over to God, 112
letting go of, 114
of the unknown, 116
overcome with patience, 17
"Feel Good File," 91
Fellman, Eric, 21, 53, 112, 250
Fellowship
our strength in, 179
Filling ourselves up with God, 159
Finch, Rosalyn Hart, 275
Finishing tasks, 57
Focusing on what one has, 67

Forgiveness
  and letting hurts go,
    204
  and our children, 188
  freeing ourselves
    through, 107
  practicing, 4
  through God's grace,
    108
Friedmann, Hope B.,
  165
Friends are better than
  enemies, 269
Friendship
  carrying each other's
    burdens in, 6
Fun
  value of, 229
Future, the, 183

Getting what we give,
  231
Gift(s)
  expressed apprecia-
    tion as a, 32
  kindness as a, 215
  pain as a, 186
  predetermined love
    as a, 202
  sharing our, 247
  using our, 72, 291
Giving
  and receiving, 118
  as well as getting, 40
  comfort, 12
  fear over to God, 112
  yourself permission to
    rest, 93
Giving thanks
  as the antidote to
    worry, 20
  for challenges, 142
  for God's help, 167
  for "no" answers to
    prayer, 27
  for our blessings, 271
  for our children's
    good behavior, 275
  for our failures, 70
  for ourselves, 60
  when things go
    wrong, 240
Goals

keeping one's eye on,
  219
setting high, 85
God
  as our father, 97
  in our daily life, 237
God's abundance
  passing on, 270
God's beauty
  opening our eyes to,
    126
God's blessings
  appreciation for, 52
God's closeness
  recognizing, 34
God's comfort
  when we are in pain,
    196
God's creation
  our delight in, 293
God's forgiveness
  praying for, 283
God's grace
  forgiveness through,
    108
God's guidance
  in times of change,
    289
  waiting for, 236
God's hands
  leaving our problems
    in, 241
God's healing
  seeking, 9
God's help
  perfect timing of, 96
  when we want to
    change, 116
God's knowledge
  of our worth, 178
God's laws
  our protection in,
    154
God's light
  seeking, 5
  shining through us,
    78, 265
  when we're stuck in
    darkness, 224
God's love
  constancy of, 62, 158
  despite our faults, 75
  freely given, 106

healing through, 74,
  146
intensity of, 151
our assurance of, 11
our awe at, 176
our security in, 198
that casts out fear, 111
that helps the hurt go
  away, 251
unconditional, 63, 92
God's loving care, 104
God's plan
  being open to, 48
  finding our way in,
    216
  following patiently,
    169
  our faith in, 193
  our mistakes woven
    into, 266
  stopping and listen-
    ing to, 292
God's power
  our victory through,
    227
God's presence
  constancy of, 36, 157
  everywhere we go,
    267
  in our time of need,
    19
  light of, renewed, 168
  listening in, 64
  making time to sit in,
    42
  that bears us up, 238
  waiting patiently to
    feel, 161
  when we feel lost, 132
God's redemption
  of our disappoint-
    ments, 37
God's spirit
  housed in us, 174
God's stillness
  immersing ourselves
    in, 143
God's voice
  in silence, 35
  our comfort in, 115
God's wonders
  through a child's
    eyes, 53

Gold, May Sheridan, 69, 226
Good, the
  looking for, 44
  seeing, in every situation, 201
Goode, Robin White, 68, 114
Gordon, Arthur, 40, 123, 141, 208, 241
Gossip, 255, 262
Graham, Betty Ruth, 106, 128, 161
Greene, Oscar, 99, 169, 189, 204, 222
Grief, 18, 185, 186
Grinnan, Edward, 242
Growth
  our, through serving, 248

Haase, Doris, 38, 198, 228, 234
Hamlin, Rick, 63, 110, 197, 237, 247, 267
Hansen, Janice L., 62
Happiness
  our, in helping others, 217
Harrah, Madge, 12, 41, 135
Harrison, Scott, 157, 171, 254, 286
Harter, Walter, 181
Healing
  by giving one's illness to Jesus, 226
  grief as the process of, 18
  one day at a time, 195
  our hurts, 287
  through prayer, 194
  through tears, 88, 139
Heaney, Ruth, 75
Helping
  by doing, 15
  others cry, 16
Helwig, Terry, 16, 144, 206, 279
Hill, Jeanne, 57, 270
Hobe, Phyllis, 34, 104, 105, 137, 185, 196, 235, 292

Holmes, Marjorie, 44, 70
Hope
  as seeing the good, 201
  renewed, 258
Humility
  wearing, 250
Humor
  value of, 33, 214
Hutchison, Charlotte, 186

"If onlys," 76
Illness, 19–21, 139, 194–95, 226
Impatience, 155-56
Insecurity, 157
Insignificance, 158

Japinga, Jeff, 61, 132, 172, 249, 260, 281
Joy
  in the midst of hardship, 213
  of finishing tasks, 57
Judgment
  avoiding, 7
  outreach instead of, 212
Justice, Sam, 54, 55, 67, 182, 236, 246, 274

Kania, Kathie, 11, 91
Kidd, Pam, 65
Kindness
  as a gift, 215
  in return for a hurt, 253
  responding to, 47
King, Marilyn Morgan, 7, 150, 168, 221, 238, 240, 287
Kittler, Glenn, 73, 203
Knapp, Carol, 66, 111, 199, 207
Knowing our limits, 180
Komp, Diane, 118
Kuykendall, Carol, 52, 101, 120, 200, 232, 277, 280

Lamay, Lauren V., 216
Laughter
  as medicine, 90

sharing, 109
value of, 33, 214, 229
Lawrence, Naomi, 264
Laying up treasures in heaven, 22
Let go and let God, 66, 242, 245, 287
Letting go
  of fear, 114
  of hurts, 74
  of the old, 81
Life active
  saying "yes" to, 220
Lightening up, 276
Lindsell, Stephanie, 202
Lindstrom, Aletha Jane, 103, 126, 134, 175, 293
Living in the now, 170
Living simply, 165
Loneliness, 159
Looking for the good, 44
Lorenz, Patricia, 25
Love
  courageous, 282
  expressing, 39, 106, 279
  for a new person coming into your life, 202
  for one's enemies, 269
  power of, 23
  simple acts of, 122
  small signs of, 175
  surrounding others with, 8
  that preserves the dignity of a friend, 119
"Love is a decision," 82
Lukes, Bonnie, 136, 211

Making amends, 257
Making way for the new, 81
Marriage
  commitment in, 191
McDermott, James, 84, 85
McGarrity, Samantha, 23, 59, 142, 215, 268

Memories
  meditating on, 153
  that make us more
    caring, 288
Metts, Wally, 261
Meyer, Mary Jane, 146
Miller, Brian, 80, 227
Mills, Joan Rae, 5
Ministering to others,
  217
Mistakes, 266
Mysteries, 84

Naugler, Gertrude, 49,
  245
Neukrug, Linda, 17, 33,
  37, 79, 107, 256
Norquist, Marilyn J., 285
Nurturing our dreams,
  184

Oda, Stephanie, 139, 239
Old age
  using our gifts in, 203
One day at a time, 195
Opportunities
  believing in new, 3
  in challenges, 189
  in disappointment,
    249
  in failure, 71
  saying "yes" to new,
    220
  to practice patience,
    156
Ordering one's day, 164,
  180
Overextending, 205, 206

Pain
  as a gift, 186
  God's comfort and,
    196
Palmer, Dee Ann, 119,
  195
Panic, 64
Parker, Marjorie, 191
Past, the
  learning from, 211
Patience
  in prayer, 25, 28
  moving ahead with,
    169

overcoming fear with,
  17
practicing, 156
value of, 155
waiting for our
  dreams with,
  285
working on, 101
Patterson, Patricia R.,
  183, 289
Peale, Norman Vincent,
  30, 47, 163, 194,
  224, 290
Peale, Ruth Stafford, 56,
  129, 253, 278
Perseverance, 68, 69,
  228
Poehlein, Virginia, 283
Positive, the
  focusing on, 240
  neutralizing negatives
    with, 262
  practicing, 79
Potential
  recognizing one's,
    291
Prayer
  answers to, "in
    progress," 130
  creative, 25
  for a struggling
    friend, 51
  for co-workers, 78
  for creativity, 284
  for healing, 194
  for one's enemies, 59,
    231
  for our children, 274,
    278
  for strength, 294
  for those in pain, 9
  gratitude for "no"
    answers to, 27
  heeding promptings
    to, 65
  importance of daily,
    83
  instead of criticism,
    232
  our need for, 38
  patience and faith in,
    28
  stillness and, 110

unexpected answers
  to, 26
waiting patiently in
  our, 221
when you can't sleep,
  55
with others, 31
Prayer letters, 207
Preparedness, 94
Present, the
  enjoying our children
    in, 277
  living in, 170, 208
  seizing, 209
Pride, 167
Priorities
  setting one's, 131, 163
Procrastinating, 208, 209

Quitting
  vs. continuing, 210

Reaching out
  instead of judging,
    212
  to others, 149
Realizing our dreams,
  77
Rebounding from
  misfortune, 259
Reconciliation, 257, 268
Refuge
  ours, in God, 95, 166
Rejection, 204, 254
Rejoicing in the lives of
  loved ones, 264
"Relax and go with it,"
  41
Renewal, 86
Resentment
  rooting out, 187
Resolving conflict, 129
Responding with
  sweetness, 46
Rest
  value of, 137
Resting, 93
Retirement
  using our gifts in, 203
Rider, Tammy, 93, 265
Riley, Laverne, 288
Rowan, Ruth Dinkins,
  94, 251, 262

Sanchez, Georgiana, 42
Sass, Eleanor, 58, 143, 162, 187
Saying thank you to pivotal people in our lives, 29
Schad, Vicki, 117, 152, 184
Schantz, Daniel, 77, 92, 159, 205, 243
Schneider, Richard, 151
Schwab, Penney, 24, 201
Secrest, Ellen, 18
Seeking direction, 216
Seizing the moment, 280
Self-absorption, 217
Self-doubt, 63
Serving
    using our gifts in, 247
    willingly, 248
Setbacks, 258-60
Setting a good example, 230
Setting one's sights higher, 85
Sharing
    each other's pain, 105
    joy of, 99
    laughter, 109
    one's faith, 14, 218
    our abundance, 125
    our burdens, 128
    the burden of sorrow, 199
Sherrill, Elizabeth, 28, 96, 258, 266, 271
Sledge, Gary, 43
Sledge, Linda Ching, 13, 86, 225, 272, 273
Solutions
    opening ourselves to new, 223
Sorrow
    made bearable by sharing, 199

Sortor, Toni, 29, 295
Spending time wisely, 138
Sprinkle, Patricia Houck, 4, 48, 83, 121, 127, 160, 230
St. Johns, Elaine, 27, 81, 113
Starting each day fresh, 283
Stillness
    finding clarity in, 143
    in the face of danger, 173
    prayer and, 110
Sullivan, Pat, 51, 177, 219
Support
    expressing, 16
    for others, 8, 50
Surrendering, 242

Taking care of unfinished business, 200
Taking failure in stride, 73
Taking responsibility, 80
Taking time apart, 102
Talking over a hurt, 252
Tears
    as markers of the meaningful, 89
    healing through, 88, 139
Temptation, 145
Tengbom, Mildred, 3
"Thou shalt not's," 154
Time-out with God
    when hearts are burdened, 273
Tragedy, 48, 49
Transplanted lives, 177
Trust in God
    complete, 136
    despite His "no" answers, 171

for answers to our prayers, 221
for our children's welfare, 56, 244, 246
for the future, 183, 243
in the midst of turmoil, 290
to overcome our unbelief, 239
when we are confused, 133
when we are hurt and fearful, 192
when we can't see our way, 98
when we doubt, 222
when we're stuck on "What if?," 225
Turmoil
    that strengthens us, 290

Varner, Van, 217
Visiting the sick, 10
Vulnerability, 179

"W-A-I-T," 101
Waite, Shirley Pope, 164, 214
Walk, Phyllis, 220
Walker, Scott, 32, 45, 89, 138, 148
Walking in truth, 255
Weariness, 180
Weary, Dolphus, 147
West, Marion Bond, 71, 87, 115, 149, 179, 188, 212, 229, 263
"What if?," 225, 239
Wheeler, Bonnie, 170
Wilbee, Brenda, 88
Williams, Susan, 9, 223
Wolseley, Isabel, 122, 176, 244
Woods, Lois E., 257
Worry, 239-46

Scripture Index

Acts
  17:28, 246

Chronicles 1
  16:34, 67
  19:13, 172
  28:9, 295
  28:20, 164
  29:12, 209
  29:18, 131
Chronicles 2
  6:41, 275
  20:17, 282
  30:8, 41
Colossians
  1:11, 68
  1:29, 291
  3:5, 8, 121
Corinthians 1
  1:25, 249
  7:7, 72
  10:10, 170
  12:5, 247
  12:27, 182
  12:28, 100
  12:31, 215
  13:4, 47
  13:4–5, 82, 122
  13:8, 23
  15:42–43, 77
  16:9, 3
  16:13, 260
Corinthians 2
  1:4, 288
  3:3, 207
  3:18, 110
  4:6, 211
  4:7, 174
  4:8, 45
  4:16, 45
  5:7, 98
  6:18, 19
  8:7, 271

  8:15, 243
  9:11, 125
  12:10, 242
  12:19, 210

Deuteronomy
  7:13, 175
  23:14, 157
  30:19, 220

Ecclesiastes
  2:10, 205
  3:1, 277
  3:3, 88
  3:11, 184
  3:17, 70
  4:8, 37
  7:9, 46, 120
  8:6, 285
  10:19, 276
  12:1, 272
Ephesians
  1:3, 52
  4:26, 121
  4:32, 268
  6:13, 241
Exodus
  14:13, 114
  14:14, 173
  15:26, 104
Ezekiel
  36:26, 74

Galatians
  2:6, 140
  6:2, 6
  6:7, 103
  6:10, 189
Genesis
  2:2, 93
  12:2, 270
  12:4, 116
  19:17, 123

  21:6, 229
  50:17, 108

Habakkuk
  2:4, 167
Hebrews
  1:3, 54
  3:13, 32
  10:14, 191
  10:23, 115
  10:36, 101
  11:1, 136
  11:8, 197
  12:11, 141
  13:19, 148

Isaiah
  26:9, 150
  28:12, 233
  33:16, 190
  38:1, 94
  38:5, 200
  40:8, 58
  40:31, 236
  53:4, 199
  55:9, 244
  60:1, 267

James
  1:3, 30
  1:22, 15
  3:11, 261
  4:10, 171
Jeremiah
  7:23, 154
  17:14, 226
  31:3, 92
  31:34, 107
  48:32, 16
Job
  4:8, 231
  6:14, 51
  8:21, 33, 109

Job, continued
  10:12, 256
  29:21, 35
  33:26, 38
  37:14, 280
John
  3:8, 84
  7:24, 113
  8:36, 124
  10:17, 62
  10:28, 263
  11:41, 28
  14:1, 49
  14:4, 132
  15:2, 290
  16:24, 99
  16:27, 251
John 1
  1:5, 224
  3:18, 230
  4:8, 158
  4:18, 192
Jonah
  3:8, 87
Joshua
  24:15, 138
Judges
  6:12, 12
  7:17, 216

Kings 1
  19:12, 64
  21:7, 149
  22:5, 103

Lamentations
  3:21–22, 258
  3:25, 169
  3:26, 161
  3:40, 73
Luke
  5:5, 147
  6:12, 83
  6:27, 269
  6:36, 232
  6:38, 40
  10:41, 165
  13:19, 218
  15:7, 181

  17:3, 252
  21:19, 177

Malachi
  3:6, 18
Mark
  2:21, 81
  4:41, 36
  6:30–31, 163
  9:24, 239
  9:37, 43
  10:27, 228
  11:2, 248
  11:25, 204
Matthew
  4:10–11, 145
  5:23–24, 257
  5:44, 59
  5:45, 44
  6:6, 273
  6:7, 25
  6:13, 234
  6:15, 188
  6:20, 22
  6:34, 225
  7:7, 128
  7:11, 27
  8:15, 196
  10:30, 178
  10:39, 217
  10:42, 144
  13:31–32, 158
  19:19, 103
  20:32–33, 223
  21:12, 187
  24:44, 127
  25:36, 10
  28:20, 39
Micah
  7:7, 155

Numbers
  11:17, 8, 21

Peter 1
  1:3, 86
  1:6, 294
  3:8, 212
  3:8, 9, 78

  4:8, 202
  4:12, 186
  5:5, 250
  5:10, 69
Philippians
  1:3, 29, 58
  2:3, 14
  2:13, 135
  2:15–16, 265
  4:6, 20
  4:8, 153
  4:11, 76
  4:13, 235, 272
Proverbs
  2:8, 133
  3:5, 221
  3:6, 292
  3:12, 24
  3:17, 79
  14:22, 279
  15:2, 129
  15:13, 90
  15:15, 214
  16:18, 117
  16:28, 262
  17:17, 119
  17:22, 91
  19:11, 156
  23:7, 103
  24:32, 80
  25:15, 17
  29:25, 222
Psalms
  8:3–4, 176
  9:9, 143
  10:17, 63
  18:2, 11
  18:28, 168
  19:12, 266
  23:3, 102
  25:4, 160
  26:3, 255
  27:1, 111, 142
  27:3, 65
  27:10, 281
  27:14, 25
  28:7, 289
  30:5, 139
  31:5, 152

34:18, 50, 287
37:7, 96
46:1, 95
51:15, 134
55:14, 105
56:8, 89
61:4, 264
63:8, 185
68:32–33, 130
77:1, 9
77:14, 53
90:14, 106
92:14, 203
102:1, 56
103:5, 112
103:8, 4
107:29, 183
111:2, 284
118:24, 208
119:73, 194
119:105, 219
121:1, 253
121:5, 245
123:1, 162
124:8, 71
126:5, 213
127:1, 278
127:2, 180

127:3, 274
131:2, 42
136:3–4, 293
139:3, 237
139:14, 60
139:23, 34
143:4, 166
147:3, 13

Revelation
3:15–16, 151
7:16, 17, 159
Romans
3:25, 286
5:5, 61
8:15–16, 97
8:24, 193
8:26, 85
8:28, 48
8:31, 66
10:12, 146
12:5, 31
14:13, 7
15:5, 179

Samuel 1
9:16, 238
10:6, 26

Samuel 2
1:26, 254
22:17, 259
22:29, 5
Song of Solomon
2:4, 198
2:12, 126

Thessalonians 1
5:14, 118
5:18, 240
5:19, 151
Thessalonians 2
1:11, 206
Timothy 1
1:2, 137
1:14, 75
1:19, 283
2:1, 55
4:10, 201
Timothy 2
1:7, 111
4:7, 57

Zechariah
4:6, 227
9:12, 195

305

A Note from the Editors

This original book was created by the Books and Inspirational Media Division of Guideposts, the world's leading inspirational publisher. Founded in 1945 by Dr. Norman Vincent Peale and his wife Ruth Stafford Peale, Guideposts helps people from all walks of life achieve their maximum personal and spiritual potential. Guideposts is committed to communicating positive, faith-filled principles for people everywhere to use in successful daily living.

Our publications include award-winning magazines like *Guideposts, Angels on Earth* and *Positive Thinking*, best-selling books, and outreach services that demonstrate what can happen when faith and positive thinking are applied in day-to-day life.

For more information, visit us at www.guideposts.org, call (800) 431-2344 or write Guideposts, 39 Seminary Hill Road, Carmel, New York 10512.